Darkness Visible

Darkness Visible

The Cinema of Jonathan Glazer

John Bleasdale

Sticking Place Books
New York

ISBN 979-8-89976-019-8

CONTENTS

To Lidia

…yet from those flames
No light, but rather darkness visible
Served only to discover sights of woe,
Regions of sorrow, doleful shades, where peace
And rest can never dwell, hope never comes
That comes to all; but torture without end
Still urges, and a fiery deluge, fed
With ever-burning sulfur unconsumed.

Paradise Lost
John Milton

INTRODUCTION

> I have the stringent criteria of a painter. It's an immersion. It's like thinking your way through to a feeling. I read that Francis Bacon once spent six months mixing black. That makes perfect sense to me.
>
> Jonathan Glazer*

Darkness Rising
"What rubbish is all this stuff about light and dark. And how I have luxuriated in it."

So speaks Samuel Beckett's narrator in *The Unnameable* (1953), the final novel in his tragicomic trilogy. He could have been talking about the cinema, a medium which, especially in its earlier flickering stages of the twentieth century, employed intervals of darkness as a condition of its modus operandi. It was black and white, film noir, silver nitrate, cigarette smoke and shadows, frost, night and rain. The plush seats and velvet darkness suggested the allure of the Land of Nod. Alan Watts—one of the most engaging and effective popularisers of Buddhism in the West (his ASMR-worthy voice lives on across YouTube and he was played by Brian Cox in Spike Jonze's 2013 film *Her*)—once noted that when we

---

* Selena Schleh, "Jonathan Glazer on Shades of Black and Pursuing Perfection," *Shots*, 18 July 2018.

sit in a cinema, we're actually sitting in darkness for half the time, during that fleeting interval when one frame advances through the projector gate while the shutter is closed. Eyes wide shuttered. The next frame in place, the shutter opens, light once again hits the screen, and an illusion of motion is created.

Darkness comes and goes. In the pioneering days of film, the concern was having adequate and constant light in order to be able to capture anything on the celluloid. The result of this was that the film industry established its base in Southern California, where blue skies and sunlight prevailed. Silent films were shot on sets in which even the interiors were exteriors: roofless three wall set-ups, lit by the sun. In some of those Chaplin shorts, you can catch the breeze lifting a newspaper on the table or stirring the hair of characters meant to be indoors.

But as soon as light was secured, darkness returned. The history of cinematography would become a journey toward filming in ever deeper shadows. Advances in film stock sensitivity made it possible to shoot in low light and to maintain control over every detail. Filmmakers moved onto vast indoor stages where wind couldn't stir a curtain and stray dogs wouldn't wander into frame.

The influence of German Expressionist cinema ushered in a wave of wild imaginings and brooding pessimism. As the 1930s drew to a close, W. H. Auden wrote: "Waves of anger and fear/Circulate over the bright/And darkened lands of the earth." That line lingers in the mind as the Earth slowly turns in the Universal Studios logo. Film noir of the 1930s and 1940s answered this new pessimism. The world was fixed. Shadowy figures moved through unknowable spaces and anti-heroes succumbed to the inevitable doom of fate. John Huston directed *The Maltese Falcon* (1941), in which both detective Sam Spade, played by Humphrey Bogart, and criminal Brigid O'Shaughnessy (Mary Astor), descend in the final shot—

one by stairs, the other by elevator. They are both going to Hell, but one will get there quicker.

Darkness was also cheap. If the audience can't see the set, filmmakers don't need to build the set. Or they can use the same set, lit in startlingly interesting and different ways. Dimly lit hotel rooms and deserted nighttime streets were relatively inexpensive. The only special effect was a cigarette lighter and the muzzle flash of the occasional gunshot.

The Western was escapist and sunny, with even the nights shining a bright cerulean blue, cast by a prairie moon. "Day for Night," they called it. For the noir, we had alleyways and rain-wet streets. As cameras got lighter and stock improved, filmmakers stepped outside. With the post-war boom and Eisenhower optimism at its peak, the noir declined, even as Billy Wilder gave it one of its thematically darkest and visually brightest entries in 1951, with *Ace in the Hole*. Darkness at noon, indeed. Technicolor brightened the prospect. This extended through the psychedelia of the Sixties, the disco of the Seventies, the brash energy and New Romanticism of the Eighties.

These are sweeping statements which don't deserve to be taken too seriously. And yet: let me double down. That Fifties optimism, followed by young John F. Kennedy, wasn't blotted out by Vietnam and Nixon. Even the Zapruder film, a home movie of an assassination, was in colour. So was the napalm that exploded across Vietnam and TV sets, named after its own warm colour: Agent Orange. Has there ever been a more photogenic form of explosive? Francis Ford Coppola would make full use of its aesthetic qualities in *Apocalypse Now* (1979), a movie that wants to be anti-war but is consumed and seduced by the sounds and colours and sensations of the war it wishes it could condemn. "You smell that, son? Nothing in the world smells like that. Smells like cinema," Colonel Kilgore almost says. John Milius, the film's co-writer, was a celebrator of the warrior ethos and a gun enthusiast who loved owning the libs before it was even a concept. As Samuel Fuller said of *Full Metal Jacket* (1987), it was "another goddamned recruitment film."

And yet the New Hollywood of the Seventies had its own darkness. *Apocalypse Now* charts a descent from the blinding Saigon sun and the blaze of napalm into the heart of darkness—where shadows conceal Marlon Brando's bulk and make it difficult for him to read the T. S. Eliot poems he held so dear. In Coppola's Mafia diptych—*The Godfather* (1972) and *The Godfather: Part II* (1974)—deals were struck in the warm, golden-brown glow of private studies, complete with kittens, high-backed armchairs, and polished mahogany. The darkest elements in the mise-en-scène were the shadows cast by Marlon Brando's heavy brows and the shark-black of Al Pacino's eyes. When the film was first screened for Paramount executives, they assumed there had been a lab error—the image seemed far too dark. Pacino himself, watching the dailies, was bewildered: not only could he not tell if his performance was landing, under Gordon Willis' single-light cinematography, he could barely see it at all.

But there is light. In fact, in *The Godfather* films, violence happens during the day: in airports, bars, at a toll booth at midday, in a car stopped by the roadside. A severed horse's head is discovered early one morning. Michael Cimino and Terrence Malick photograph their tales of murder and exploitation in beautiful sunlight, the latter glorying in his magic hour cinematography even as his stories bend with elegiac sadness towards violent tragedy. Influenced by the sunny footage from Southeast Asia and Dallas in late November, New Hollywood shows violence bursting out in broad daylight. The assassinations of *Bonnie and Clyde* (1967), *Easy Rider* (1969) and *Nashville* (1975), the massacres and mass shootings of *The Wild Bunch* (1969), all happen in broad daylight. The noirish throwback *Taxi Driver* (1976) feels like the exception that proves the rule, but even Travis Bickle scopes out a possible assassination attempt during the day.

Meanwhile, a rough beast slouched towards Hollywood Bethlehem to be born. Bethlehem in this case was the holiday resort town of Amity, and with *Jaws* (1975), the blockbuster was born. Existential dread was gone from popular entertainment. We just didn't want to be eaten on the Fourth of July. Amity, along with the desert planet of Tatooine and the jungles and deserts of Indiana Jones, proved a fittingly sunny setting for the rise of Ronald Reagan's Morning in America.

"You want it darker?"—Leonard Cohen
An early indicator of the darkness rising once more came at the end of the 1980s. Tim Burton's *Batman* (1989) turned out to be revolutionary. No comic book fan, Burton, a former Disney employee, was drawn to the idea of making the film as a result of reading Alan Moore's reimagining of the DC character: *The Killing Joke* (1988). The most successful comic book adaptation to date had been the Christopher Reeve-starring *Superman* series (1978-1987). These films had been largely family entertainments, in the primary blue and red colours of the hero, action comedies which petered out with diminishing returns, especially when Superman sought to address real-world issues like nuclear proliferation.

Against Superman's bright cheerful colours, Batman was to be dark. He put the goth back in Gotham. The campness of the TV series that starred Adam West was dialled down and consigned largely to the scenery-munching antics of Jack Nicholson's Joker. The slight Michael Keaton was a melancholy presence in immediate contra-distinction to the muscle-bound superstars of the day: Arnold Schwarzenegger and Sylvester Stallone. Burton's sequel, *Batman Returns* (1992), was, if anything, even darker. Too dark, apparently, as producers changed tack and produced ever-sillier entries in the franchise. Schwarzenegger would be recruited as a pun-spouting heavy.

The struggle between light and darkness took on new form—now played out between DC and Marvel. For a time, Sam Raimi's *Spider-Man* films reclaimed the bright primary colours of Superman, making Spidey the only superhero in town.

But something was changing. The trailer for Raimi's first *Spider-Man* film had to be withdrawn soon after it was released. The teaser showed a helicopter trapped in a web suspended between the twin towers of the World Trade Center. Now those buildings no longer existed, and the world had changed. Following 11 September 2001, waves of anger and fear circulated once more over the dark and bright lands of the earth, so when Christopher Nolan rebooted Batman in *Batman Begins* (2005), his film began a process of reimagining with a hand on the dimmer switch. It was gothic architecture, witty but bitter, ironic but without a trace of camp. There's something thrilling about just how dark Nolan is willing to go. See, for instance, that moment when Liam Neeson as Bruce Wayne's mentor absolves him of guilt for his mother's death, only to lay the blame squarely with Bruce's beloved but, let's face it, wimpy father. This is nightmarish tough love, irresistible and borderline abusive, the kind of stuff the incel legions will lap up decades later from Jordan Peterson.

Nolan was to become the key Hollywood filmmaker of the epoch, an anti-Spielberg whose crystalline insights replaced Spielberg's messy awe and wonder with despair and anxiety, emotion with intellectual engagement. Even when he's having fun (*Inception* [2010] and *Tenet* [2020]), his heroes and often his audiences are lost and confused, and nothing is ever fully resolved. The sound design offers a kind of aural murk as well, resembling the sort of mix Harry Caul in *The Conversation* (1974) would spend an absorbing hour fiddling with to discern one line of dialogue. Nolan's spectacle gains its apotheosis in an atomic explosion. The ultimate darkness manifested in a flash of blinding light. His uncertainty is quantum.

As cinema entered the digital era, technology moved forward, but in some ways, aesthetics moved backward. Colour timing, or colour correction, had been a laborious process that took place in the labs to make film shot in different lighting conditions (especially exterior shots) consistent. But when Roger Deakins wanted a dustbowl sepia tone for the Coen Brothers' comedy *O Brother, Where Art Thou?* (2000), he was able to digitally manipulate the colour and give it a golden sheen which the actual footage, shot in a lush green Mississippi summer, didn't have. The film is actually chromatically black and white but shot in colour. The Wachowskis' *The Matrix* (1999) had done the same, but reaches back to a noir aesthetic, which never really went away.* In the digital era, whole films could have their colour palettes aligned and rendered consistent, so that even though films weren't necessarily black and white, they were teal and orange, red and green, yellow and purple.

The move to darkness at this point seemed irreversible, triumphant. Even the family entertainment of Peter Jackson's sexless and child-friendly *Lord of the Rings* (2001–03) headed for Mordor. HBO's *Game of Thrones* went further, taking J. R. R. Tolkien's fantasy-

---

* See Sheri Chinen Biesen, *Through a Noir Lens: Adapting Film Noir Visual Style* (Columbia, 2024).

scape, misspelling some names (Joffrey?), and adding rape and random horrifically gory deaths of beloved characters to the mix. It was in keeping with a new Golden Age of television which was perhaps more burnt amber than gold. *The Sopranos* (1999–2007) and *Breaking Bad* (2008–13) tore into the myth of the middle class American nuclear family with the wild abandon of murderers. Cartoons of talking animals—usually a safe bet for some cheery nonsense—dealt with alcoholism and suicide (see *BoJack Horseman* [2024–24]). Even light entertainment was named after dystopian concepts (*Big Brother* [1997] and *Survivor* [2000]), and it soon became apparent that the surveillance-as-fantasy of Reality TV was a worse nightmare than George Orwell had ever dreamed. Imagine not only consenting to this bullshit but auditioning for it, aspiring to it, queuing for hours with thousands of dewy-eyed hopefuls. Endemol has proven the most damaging export from the Netherlands since the Dutch East India Company.

When a Korean satire on this kind of voyeuristic entertainment, *Squid Game* (2021), was released, the response was to make a reality show inspired by it (*Squid Game: The Challenge* [2023]). Fluffy comedies like *Barbie* (2023) get pulled into the gravity well of gloom, playfully creating the Barbenheimer: a Cronenbergian Brundlefly of film culture if there ever was one.

This darkness is not only conceptual; it has become literal. In one article, *Variety* instructed its readers "Don't Adjust the Brightness: Here's Why TV and Movies are So Dark Now" (12 March 2022). Sasha Urban writes of how viewers of episodes of *Game of Thrones* and *Euphoria* struggle to see what is going on in scenes, partly due to poor viewing conditions at home or motion smoothing on their television sets. It is an article which is rewritten annually.

In the cinema, digital cinematography is not as good at revealing the darkness of celluloid. When Miloš Forman approached the production of *Amadeus* (1986), he told cinematographer Miroslav Ondříček that he wanted his blacks to look as black as possible. With streamers feeling pressure from their subscribers, many of whom watch films on their tablets or other relatively small devices, darkness was becoming a problem. A certain look was being called for, and Netflix drew up a list of the equipment that had to be used on their dedicated productions. No substitutions allowed.

Many filmmakers, including David Fincher and Darren Aronofsky, have made darkness both thematically and literally their raison d'être. The opposite of leitmotif? In 2022, *The Batman*, Matt Reeves' most recent (at the time of writing) rendering of the caped crusader, was dark to the point of pitch-black parody. As in Alex Proyas' *Dark City* (1998), day no longer exists. The murk has thickened to the point that we can't even be sure that there's anything out there. The Germans, always hoping to get straight to the point, created their most successful Netflix show, called, simply, *Dark* (2017).

Paint It Black
Jonathan Glazer has released four feature films as director: *Sexy Beast* (2000), *Birth* (2004), *Under the Skin* (2013) and *The Zone of Interest* (2023). He has also directed numerous commercials, as well as a handful of shorts and music videos.

Darkness is a key element in his films and work generally. It isn't there as a general Fincher-esque aesthetic choice; there is plenty of daylight as well as colour. Rather, darkness exists in Glazer's films as a tangible presence. It is, at times, visible. Neither is it a part of his philosophy or outlook. Glazer is assuredly not a nihilist. In his worlds, love is not just possible, it is vital and motivating. His darkest characters are striking for not being nihilists. His evildoers are not (at least by their own estimation) evil. And yet they do evil. So perhaps they are evil after all.

It is relatively easy to point to the visible darknesses in his quartet of films. The criminal underworld of *Sexy Beast* is a literal underground, where bodies are buried and creatures of the unconscious scrabble at the soil with long fingernails. In *Birth*, the bridge under which a man jogs is another underground, a tunnel in itself a gateway to the underworld between life and death. Is this a place from which you can return? That will be the mystery of the film. The black space of the alien honey trap of *Under the Skin* sucks light to an event horizon, a black hole made of goo. Musou black paint, developed in 2020, is now the world's blackest paint, absorbing 90 percent of light. Glazer's blacks are not that black, but they are still very black. His films are experiments in intensity. Outer space is an inner space: a gunk hole, anticipating the title of Charlie Brooker's TV show *Black Mirror*. And, finally, the darkness of *The Zone of Interest* is the theme of the film and its subject: the Holocaust. There are several moments where this is visualised, but none more clearly than the poster which advertised the film, and which features a garden party at the Höss family home. Everything beyond the garden fence—the sky, the camp, the surroundings—is blacked out as if redacted. This could almost be another of Glazer's science fiction films, with the family on some alien planet, living in a replica of family life. It is something Tarkovsky might have revealed at the end of *Solaris* (1972). Glazer's relationship with genre will be something we come back to, but for the moment I shall note here that he makes science fiction films like documentaries and realist drama like science fiction.

Darkness is not only visible in Glazer's films, it is also audible. His use of discordant elements and silences which swallow sound in his soundtracks adds an aural corollary to the darkness. The sound we hear frequently comes from things happening which we do not see or cannot see, like the noises off which Stanley Kubrick references in his spacey hotel room at the end of *2001: A Space Odyssey* (1968). The out of sight noises, the unseen voices—is this not also a sort of darkness? Arguably, the main drama of *The Zone of Interest* happens off screen, in our ears. Glazer's creative collaborations with composers Alexander Desplat and Mica Levi have intensified these experiments.

Thematically, Glazer's films present a universe of Manichean duality. Love can be a beautiful refuge from crime, hatred and violence, as in *Sexy Beast*, or it can be steeped in crime, hatred and violence. The return of the repressed, be it a nightmare bunny man (*Sexy Beast*) or smoke from burning bodies (*The Zone of Interest*), is always threatened and sometimes realised. Evil can be present as a source of darkness. *Sexy Beast*'s Don (Ben Kingsley) is a loud-mouthed, voluble vandal of chaos, an immediate terrifying danger to the domestic expat paradise that Ray Winston's Gal has created. But Ian McShane's Prince of Darkness in the same film is the glowering ultimate presence. The Höss household of is the *reductio ad absurdum* of Hannah Arendt's truism about the "banality of evil," which is so oft-repeated as to risk becoming, well, banal. The portrayal evokes empathy for the worst perpetrators of the worst crimes against humanity.

Darkness can evoke a universe, in the words of Friedrich Nietzsche, "beyond good and evil," where merely human ethical categories break down and are as radically and thoroughly dissolved as the bodies of Scarlett Johansson's victims in *Under the Skin*. Darkness can be death. The emptiness left by a human presence: a love-shaped hole punched in the universe by grief.

And yet—this is an important point to make early on—Jonathan Glazer's films are not dark. They are colourful, bright, sharply, often beautifully, photographed (6K digital) and scored, with humour and wit, all enriched with what one literary critic, referring to *Hamlet*, once called "a variety of incident."[*]

A teacher of mine at the University of Liverpool, Prof. Brian Nellist, told me, when I tried to fold mention of a novel I was studying into a predetermined political point I wanted to make, that "life is wider than argument." It's a phrase that has stayed with me. How easy it is to get an angle, an entry point, on an artist, then go in search of the evidence to shore it up, ignoring everything that is inconveniently contradicting you. It's something that Glazer himself referred to in an interview: "You don't write themes; themes come up through the cracks."[†]

This book is meant as an exploration and an appreciation, not an argument. I'm more interested in mapping the breadth of Glazer's cinema than in persuading you of a single thesis. If darkness occasionally slips out of sight—retreating into the shadows, so to speak—so be it. I'd rather be inconsistent than incomplete or insincere.

And yet, a kind of consistency does emerge across Glazer's work, despite the long silences between projects, the small number of films, and their shifts in genre: a gangster story, a quasi-supernatural thriller, a science-fiction parable, an experimental Holocaust drama. What binds them is a persistent darkness—one that circles the firelight, that threatens the family, that stalks

---

* John Dover Wilson, *What Happens in Hamlet* (Cambridge, 1935).
† "DP/30 Short Ends: Jonathan Glazer talks *Under the Skin*," 28 September 2013.

the individual. Sometimes it's historical, sometimes existential. It might come from the stars, cold and unknowable, or from within, raw and human. But it's always there, just beyond the edge of the frame.

The Life
On 10 March 2024, on the stage of the Dolby Theatre in Hollywood, Los Angeles, a somberly dressed man held his Oscar and his prepared notes in his hand. He did not look particularly happy, despite the fact he had just won the Academy Award for Best Foreign Language Film. He wore a dark blue suit, with black shirt and black tie. His hair was cut short at the sides above which sat an unruly mop of curls. He was thin, drawn, even, wearing glasses with transparent frames. He looked like he was attending a funeral rather than the glitzy annual award ceremony where the industry happily pleasures itself with tributes.

Having been handed the award by Dwayne "The Rock" Johnson (such deliciously incongruous moments make what George C. Scott once called "the meat parade" genuinely worthwhile), Glazer, flanked by the producers of *The Zone of Interest*, pulled out a folded piece of paper with his prepared remarks, his hands visibly shaking, and spoke.

> Thank you so much. I'm going to read. Thank you to the Academy for this honour and to our partners A24, Film4, Access, and Polish Film Institute; to the Auschwitz-Birkenau State Museum for their trust and guidance; to my producers, actors, collaborators. All our choices were made to reflect and confront us in the present—not to say, "Look what they did then," rather, "Look what we do now." Our film shows where dehumanisation leads, at its

worst. It shaped all of our past and present. Right now, we stand here as men who refute their Jewishness and the Holocaust being hijacked by an occupation, which has led to conflict for so many innocent people. Whether the victims of October the—*[applause]*… Whether the victims of October the 7th in Israel or the ongoing attack on Gaza, all the victims of this dehumanisation, how do we resist? *[applause]* Aleksandra Bystroń-Kołodziejczyk, the girl who glows in the film, as she did in life, chose to. I dedicate this to her memory and her resistance. Thank you.

When he left the stage, Glazer refused to go into the media room to pose for more photographs, and did no further press. He did not comment on the stories which came later, including letters of protest from pro-Israeli groups or letters of support, the signatories of which included many prominent Jewish figures in Hollywood. Nor did he clarify the speech, which was abbreviated by several publications, including *Variety*, to read "we stand as men who refute their Jewishness," rather than "we stand as men who refute their Jewishness and the Holocaust being hijacked by an occupation, which has led to conflict for so many innocent people." Regardless of whether this misquotation was accidental, or the result of an intrinsic piece of wobbly syntax in the remarks themselves, many used it to present a bad faith argument about where Glazer stood, and to portray him in the role of the so-called "self-hating Jew," unsympathetic to the cause of Israel.

In retrospect, it was small wonder his hands were shaking. In the polarised atmosphere which had followed the murderous Hamas attacks of 7 October 2023, which killed more than a thousand people, any criticism of the Israeli response, any pleas for humanitarian aid or a ceasefire, were being framed as somehow supportive of the Palestinian terrorist organisation. To use his moment on the global stage to issue a statement was an act of courage and determination. His statement included the victims of the 7 October attacks as well as the ongoing military response, but this was not considered by partisans for whom any dissent from the line being taken by the Israeli government of Benjamin Netanyahu was tantamount to treachery. The immediate silence in his defence (in the UK, Asif Kapadia was the lone fellow filmmaker who expressed his support) spoke to the riskiness of speaking out on the issue. In modern parlance, people seemed to be asking: is this the hill you want to die on? A letter was eventually published in support of his position, but the trades, which had provided a link to the first petition against Glazer, allowing readers to add their names to condemn his statement, did not provide one for readers who wished to express solidarity with Glazer.

It is ironic that this should be the first time that many people first set eyes on the director who, in a career spanning three decades, had made four films and had kept himself largely out of the public eye. Glazer is an intensely private man, who gives interviews during the round of junkets accompanying the (infrequent) release of his films but rarely talks in between jobs and hardly ever of his personal life. None of the films are particularly autobiographical. He doesn't do social media or television.

So, who is he?

Jonathan Glazer was born in 1962 and grew up in the northernmost reaches of London, in a leafy suburb called Hadley Wood. His family is Jewish, though observance was relatively light: synagogue a few times a year and Friday night dinners. His father was a graphic designer for a TV listings magazine as well as redesigning the trade journal *Screen International*. A film buff, Glazer senior introduced his son, who attended the Jewish Free School in Camden, North London, to a range of classic films as well as contemporary fare. "I spent time with him sitting in his chair, and I sat on the floor next to his chair," Glazer told an audience at the Cinema Ritrovato Festival in Bologna in 2025. "And we would watch films together." His first cinema experience was *Grease* (1978), but he didn't consider himself a cinephile, preferring motorbikes, skateboarding and music. He came to reading relatively late, preferring comicbooks. He would often draw his own: storyboarding as he later realized. As a teenager, he earned money working at a stall in Camden Market, not far from where he now lives. As part of the Givat Washington programme, Glazer spent five months in a religious boarding school in Israel.

Glazer finally discovered a form of cinema which was less traditional than his father's taste in the form of Lindsey Anderson's *Oh Lucky Man* (1973): "I remember seeing that and thinking it was illicit or something. It felt like he's a filmmaker who was doing something that felt somehow forbidden or from a place that I've never seen a film before. It shocked me, and it did awaken something, then many others followed that. But it was the first film I saw that rocked me."

At university in Nottingham, he shared a flat with boyhood friend and actor Paul Kaye, known in Britain for his Woody Allen-like interviewer Dennis Pennis. Glazer studied Art and Design and was drawn towards theatre design specifically. He dabbled in animation as well as directing plays for friends, music videos and commercials before getting work editing television and film trailers in London. In 1993, he joined Academy Films, where he made a series of stunning commercials which often foregrounded their own artistry beyond the needs of the client. His music videos for artists such as Radiohead and Jamiroquai won further acclaim, winning him an MTV award in the late 1990s. In 2000, he directed his first feature film, *Sexy Beast.*

Despite the lacunae, Glazer's work has been consistent and evinced a recognisable and frequently striking style, even while assaying different genres. He is a director who pushes visual storytelling and sound design over exposition and dialogue, although his first film is intensely scripted and dialogue heavy. His imagery can be impressionistic, even surreal, but his world is always grounded in an immediacy and connection to the quotidian reality of personal experience. He uses non-actors and movie stars who have been cast against type. The winner of an Academy Award for *Gandhi* (1982), Sir Ben Kingsley becomes an East End psychopath in *Sexy Beast.* Glazer's films take a long time to make. In this sense they resemble the work of Stanley Kubrick, who influences Glazer to the point of being almost a haunting. Like his cinematic hero, Glazer also tends towards literary adaptation.

Andrei Tarkovsky and Nicolas Roeg are two other influences, but Glazer also employs techniques from his music video work and the Reality TV world of *Big Brother.* Speaking to Raphael Abrams in an Italian restaurant not too far from where he used to sell hash pipes in Camden when he was 17, he spoke about his mission: "To me, cinema should be a radical political space in this day and age. That's the cinema I'm interested in. Be as bold as you can possibly be, as radical as you can be, be as political as you can be. That's the opportunity. You've got 200 people in the room, you've got their attention for two hours. What are you going to say? Because if you've got nothing to say, don't waste their time."*

---

* Raphael Abrams, "*Zone of Interest* director Jonathan Glazer" *Financial Times*, 23 February 2024.

This book will break down into four main chapters, each dealing with a feature film in chronological order. In between, there will be further chapters in roughly chronological order which will look at the commercials (in two parts, because they are legion), the music videos, and the shorts. Obviously, the shorts need no justification, but some might balk at the idea of commercials, and, to a lesser extent, his music promos being regarded in the same light as his films. But this isn't just filler to make up for an admittedly skinny filmography. Some of Glazer's most successful and popular work has come in the form of commercial advertising, where, in fact, he has made a name for himself above and beyond what he has achieved in film. The artfulness and ambition of his television spots reveal a filmmaker experimenting with form in as radical a way as anything he does in his features. They shouldn't be seen as simply complementary to the feature work either. At their best, they are works in and of themselves which deserve our attention.

Poetry survives "a way of happening, a mouth," as W. H. Auden once wrote. And likewise, the music videos and the adverts for beer and jeans do what they do: promote a group or singer, sell a product. They might survive the product they sell. The company might go out of business; the line is discontinued; the band breaks up—but the commercials and promos persist, a visual trace of their existence.

But something else too…

We watch all of this with the same mind, the same eyes, from the cinema to the thirty-second clip, and through it all, there's this darkness on the screen.

Darkness can be the canvas itself, or it can leak through the cracks, but it's always there as a threat or a promise.

ONE
"GOOD THINGS COME TO THOSE WHO WAIT"
Commercials, 1995—2006

From the late 1980s to the mid-1990s, the Belgian beer brand Stella Artois turned what had once seemed a drawback into a defining asset. Known for its high price—particularly in the UK, where a night out might involve ten pints of lager—cost was often a deciding factor for drinkers. Rather than shy away from this, the ads embraced it, building their campaign around a bold, two-word tagline: "Reassuringly expensive."

The words could just as easily describe Jonathan Glazer's career in TV commercials, as he directed three ads for the Stella campaign. When he made "The Surfer" for rival beer company Guinness, he became famous as the man who spent a million pounds on a hundred seconds. A year after its television debut, the spot was voted the best commercial ever made.[*]

Glazer speaks positively of his work as a commercial director, explaining that through his work in adverts, he received "a vital education. It's the discipline of condensing a story down to one minute. It's the economy you use to tell that story. And then it's about communicating more than that story. How do we multiply the story in that minute? It's a very exciting challenge, and you learn so much from it."[*]

There's no sense that Glazer simply graduated from commercials to feature films and never looked back. Given the sheer volume of his advertising work compared to his feature output, it would be more accurate to describe him as a commercials director who occasionally makes films, rather than the other way round. Many acclaimed filmmakers—Terrence Malick, Martin Scorsese, Pedro Almodóvar, Sofia Coppola—have turned to commercials to supplement their income, experiment with ideas, or test new equipment. For Glazer, advertising also offered a well-established pathway into cinema, particularly in the UK. Directors like Ridley and Tony Scott, Alan Parker and Adrian Lyne all refined their craft through the hundreds of commercials they made, at the same time earning serious money, mastering transferable skills, and helping to elevate the form into something akin to short-form cinema. By the time Glazer entered the field, high production values and bold, original concepts were already standard. Ridley Scott's Chanel campaigns and his iconic "1984" Super Bowl ad for Apple had become touchstones—works that pushed the boundaries of what commercials could do in terms of aesthetics, narrative ambition and cultural impact. In such an environment, directors could shift between genres and tones depending on the product, while still injecting personal style—and, as with the "1984" spot, even shaping the cultural conversation.[†]

---

[*] Patrick McDonald, "Director Jonathan Glazer Gets *Under the Skin*," www.hollywoodchicago.com 10 August 2014.
[†] Note also that the vast majority of television advertising is intentionally annoying visual and aural pollution, ear and eye worms designed like chemical warfare to do as much harm as possible to humans while leaving vital infrastructure intact.

It's also worth noting that, at the time, the internet had yet to make its mark. Ironically, it would be Apple—alongside Google, Facebook and the rise of social media—that would later help transform the media landscape, siphoning advertising budgets away from lavish TV and cinema commercials and toward viral campaigns and the baleful reign of influencers.

Throughout the 1990s and into the early 2000s, Glazer's commercials were a regular presence on television and in cinemas—though his growing reputation for bold ideas and large budgets was largely known only within the industry. Still, the work itself stood out, cutting through the noise of routine ad breaks with its memorable imagery and audacious concepts. It's important to note that Glazer operated within a highly collaborative framework, working closely with top-tier copywriters who often shared authorship of the campaigns—and who would later join him on his feature projects. Walter Campbell, for example, co-created the iconic "Surfer" commercial and went on to co-write *Under the Skin*.

Glazer's earliest commercials—for Pretty Polly hosiery and Kodak Fun Cameras—were sharp, well-crafted, and carried a certain narrative flair, but they had yet to establish a recognisable Glazer signature. These spots leaned more on clever writing and brisk storytelling, delivered with humour and panache, but felt more scripted than directed. His first ad for Kodak revisits the familiar scenario of a groom flashing back to his wild stag night—drunken antics and flirtation—only to breathe a sigh of relief that no one had a camera. That is, until his bride unwraps a wedding gift: a Kodak Fun Camera with "Develop Me!" written on it. Alongside his Sega Virtual Racer commercial, these early efforts revolve around themes of lost control, of things slipping just out of reach. But more revealing is what they say about Glazer's own development. They show how far he still had to go, both in mastering his material and refining his visual composition. His hand isn't yet steady, his eye not fully attuned. The work is restless, uneven, full of youthful fizz—as if he's just burst through the door, slightly breathless, asking, "Am I late? What did I miss?"

Glazer's distinctive style begins to surface in his commercials for AT&T, where he attempts the delicate balancing act of targeting a business audience while making the corporate world feel bold, witty and slightly offbeat. Black-and-white photography and a suggestive, slightly subversive narrative begin to signal the emergence of Glazer's signature style. His framing now centres the figures it observes, creating a symmetrical, almost architectural logic—borrowed from Kubrick— that will remain a constant throughout his later work. As budgets increased, so too did the boldness of his musical choices.

In 1996, Glazer directed the 60-second Club Med spot for Bartle Bogle Hegarty featuring Harry Nilsson's "Everybody's Talkin'" (used decades earlier in John Schlesinger's *Midnight Cowboy* [1968]) and the kind of desaturated, almost black and white photography, with specific moments of isolated colour (a child's red coat, a blue toy sailboat), that recalls Steven Spielberg's *Schindler's List* (1993). Connor Trinneer plays a business-suited young man still in the carefree thrall of his Club Med holiday. His view of Manhattan—the subways and traffic jams, a bank of television screens in a shop display— are seen from his outsider perspective, anticipating the off-kilter POV of *Under the Skin.* The story culminates with him stepping fully clothed into Conservatory Water in Central Park to retrieve a young boy's toy boat. "Is he mad? Or is everyone else?" reads the strapline.

That same year brought another New York-set spot, this time for Irish beer Caffrey's Ale. The ad opens in a lively, bouncing pub, where a game of pool plays out to the thumping energy of House of Pain's "Jump Around"—only for the soundtrack to dissolve into Carter Burwell's elegiac theme from *Miller's Crossing* (1990) as a pint is poured. The moment triggers a Joycean epiphany in the floppy-haired drinker, who drifts into a misty reverie of the old country, complete with a hurling team, a red-haired beauty framed by gorse, and a man in a pub cradling a whippet.

In 1997, Glazer was brought in to direct a new Nike campaign aimed at repositioning the brand ahead of the 1998 FIFA World Cup. He had already delivered an iconic ad for Nike's basketball line featuring Michael Jordan, where he captured in slow motion a series of spectators slipping into a trance-like state—"in the zone"—as Jordan makes his signature leap, a moment that became emblematic of the Air Jordan brand. Now football took centre stage with Nike's "Parklife" campaign. The concept was to pull the game out of the stadium and return it to its grassroots, quite literally, by showing star players ankle-deep in the muck of Hackney Marshes, a vast stretch of public playing fields in East London where hundreds of amateur footballers gather every weekend.

The guerrilla-style filmmaking that would later define *Under the Skin* was born of necessity here: the shoot had to take place in a real, working public space, surrounded by unsuspecting locals. Any hint of a film crew—or recognition of the football superstars on set—would have drawn a mob. To avoid this, the players were filmed as if they were just a group of regular blokes having a kickabout. Over it all, Blur's "Parklife" played on the soundtrack—fittingly, as the band rode the crest of their Britpop fame.*

Using freeze frames in the spirit of the Nouvelle Vague—Truffaut sells trainers—Glazer captures each

---

* The ad also serves as an alternate music video, selling the song as much as the sportswear. See also House of Pain's "Jump Around" in Glazer's 1996 ad for Caffrey's Ale.

footballer (Ian Wright, Eric Cantona, David Seaman, Robbie Fowler) in a gesture that playfully distills their persona: a sublime touch, a blistering strike, a bold save. The ad's strapline—"Whatever league you're in, Just do it"—melded Nike's iconic slogan with the inclusive spirit of Cool Britannia. A British bulldog trots through the frame, briefly sharing screen time with a women's football team and a vision of multicultural Britain that feels natural and refreshingly unforced, worlds away from the hooligan-stained image of the sport in the 1980s. The spot ends on a perfectly judged detail: a sucked and discarded quarter of orange. Unglamorous, instantly evocative, you can almost taste it—though you'd rather not.

Glazer's gift for dynamic motion was on full display again that year in his 60-second "Kung Fu" commercial for Levi's 501 jeans. I remember it vividly: one of those rare ads that people genuinely looked forward to, especially in the cinema. It hit a nerve, riding the wave of a kung-fu revival spurred by Tarantino's rapid-fire enthusiasm and a renewed affection for '70s fringed funk. Johnny Harris' "Stepping Stones" gives the spot its breathless energy, panpipes fluttering before launching into a hard-driving blaxploitation groove.

A young man, played by Vietnamese martial artist Dustin Nguyen, sprints through San Francisco's Chinatown pursued by a gang. He dives into a restaurant, fights his way through the kitchen, up onto a rooftop, down again, each sequence more acrobatic than the last. His final destination: a Chinese laundry. Dispatching the last enemy with comic precision— evoking the dry punchline of *Raiders of the Lost Ark* when Indy shoots the swordsman—he impresses the girl inside with an elegant series of *hai-ya!* moves, including the artful turning of a pair of jeans inside out. Then he's back on the street, still fighting. The final shot: a freeze frame of him mid-leap, legs split, airborne. The closing line: "Levi's 501s: Better washed inside out."

The fight and chase unfold with astonishing speed and wit, each shot delivering a perfectly timed burst of comic violence. Glazer matches the kinetic energy with a roving camera, yet resists any knowing winks or stylistic smugness. This is parody without irony: the performers play it straight, and the film never undercuts them with crash zooms or meta-commentary to signal that the director is somehow above the material. The spot also lets Glazer explore one of the recurring fascinations in his commercial work—the sheer dynamism of the human body in motion, whether dancing, fighting, or sprinting full tilt.

Just as the Levi's ad allowed him to riff on the Run Run Shaw and Bruce Lee martial arts productions of the Seventies, so the Stella Artois campaign gave Glazer the opportunity to evoke the European cinema of recent years, notably *Jean de Florette* (1986), whose use of Giuseppe Verdi's *La Forza del Destino* was echoed in the ads. After the campaign aired, that music became more closely associated with the Belgian beer than with Claude Berri's hugely popular film. The first Stella advert had appeared in 1989, directed by Michael Seresin, best known as the cinematographer for Alan Parker's *Bugsy Malone* (1976) and *Midnight Express* (1978). Glazer joined the campaign nearly a decade later, stepping in as director in 1998.

"Last Orders," 90 seconds in length and starring French actor/Leos Carax favourite Denis Lavant, is set in a Provençal village where the patriarch is on his deathbed. He has one last wish: a glass of the expensive lager. The gathered family collect their coins together and give them over to Lavant, who travels to the nearest town to buy the beer. On the cart ride back to the village, under the scorching sun, he succumbs to temptation and drinks the lot. With empty glass in hand, at the front door to the house he meets the priest who is preparing to enter in order to give last rites. Denis takes the man's hat and coat, and hands him the glass. The priest enters with Lavant in tow. The family immediately clock the empty glass in his hand. Lavant, with a bit of side eye, surreptitiously indicates that the priest drank every drop. It's a witty piece of work. The sight of Lavant's sorrow and love overcome by his wish for the beer is reminiscent of the kid eating the cream cake he promised to a potential girlfriend, as he sits on a step outside her door waiting for her, in Sergio Leone's *Once Upon a Time in America* (1984). Lavant's performance of simple innocence and eventual moxy is delivered with the subtlest flickers of expression, especially in the eyes.

"Devil's Island," Glazer's second spot for Stella Artois (2002), came with a $1 million budget and an epic scale to match. He spent weeks scouring Europe for the right lead and finally found an unknown Italian theatre actor called Antonio Rampino. Ron Perlman appears in a supporting role, alongside 850 extras dressed in 1930s costume, shouting, spitting and hurling abuse at a column of prisoners being marched through town to the docks. Four blocks of Buenos Aires were shut down for the shoot, and an 80-year-old ship, painstakingly restored, stood in for the prison transport bound for the notorious penal colony, as depicted in Henri Charrière's memoir *Papillon* and its film adaptation starring Steve McQueen. The script, written by copywriter Vince Squibb, follows a scrawny prisoner who stumbles across a bottle of Stella Artois. To keep it from the other inmates, he contrives to be thrown into solitary confinement, where he can savour his stolen prize in peace.

Glazer's final spot for Stella features a flock of "Ice-skating Priests" (2005) who send the youngest among them to fetch a crate of beer. When, in a scene reminiscent of *The Omen II* (1978), he falls through the ice, they chase after him as he swims beneath the surface, finally emerging empty-handed. Without hesitation, they send him back in to retrieve the bottles. As with the earlier adverts, Glazer demonstrates a near-silent-film mastery of visual storytelling. Each situation is set up instantly, character motives are clear, and facial expressions do all the work, most notably the deadpan gravity of the lead priest, who channels a kind of Buster Keaton stoicism, but without tipping into caricature.

The other beer brand Glazer became closely associated with was Guinness, the iconic black Irish stout that had long been at the forefront of innovative advertising, dating back to the era of the slogan "Guinness is good for you." As with Stella Artois, the creative brief was to transform a perceived drawback into a selling point. For Stella, it had been the cost; with Guinness, it was the wait. Unlike lager and most other draught beers, a proper pint of Guinness required patience: the glass had to be filled three-quarters of the way, left to settle, and only then topped up to the brim.

Glazer's first Guinness commercial tackled the issue of time head-on, depicting a man swimming from a buoy back to his brother's seaside bar in an attempt to beat the time it takes to pour the perfect pint. Visually striking and rich in atmosphere, it made the most of its setting — but it was merely a prelude to what came next: "The Surfer." Widely considered the apex of Glazer's work in advertising, "The Surfer" distilled his cinematic flair into a single, elemental metaphor. The production was once again lavish, cementing his reputation for delivering $1 million of visual impact in just 100 seconds. The soundtrack featured original music by electronic group Leftfield, later released as "Phat Planet" on their album *Rhythm and Stealth*.

The voiceover—delivered by *Sexy Beast* co-writer Louis Mellis—is a piece of street poetry with literary reach, laced with echoes of *Moby-Dick*. Visually, the ad takes its cue from Walter Crane's 1892 painting Neptune's Horses, transforming metaphor into motion. Shot over two and a half weeks in Hawaii, Glazer and his crew crisscrossed the island in search of the perfect wave—a restless process, ironically, for a piece devoted to patience. Legendary Polynesian surfer Rusty Keaulana played the lead. The horses were filmed separately and later composited digitally into the breaking waves. Glazer explained that he was uncertain whether the combination would work: "You're never 100% confident you're ever going to pull anything off. You only get there by the skin of your teeth each time. That was no different at all. The horses only really started to look like they made sense to those pictures very late on in the post-production process, but that's always the way. And there were conversations going on behind the scenes along the lines of, 'Why don't we just dump the horses? The ad's fine on its own.'"*

But Glazer's meticulous patience and perfectionism were yielding undeniably powerful results. Just a year after its release, "The Surfer" was crowned the winner of a World Cup of Adverts. It managed to be both popular and artful, visceral and intellectual. With its stark monochrome palette and arresting freeze frames, it had the feel of cinema, and in some parallel arthouse universe could easily have passed for an experimental short. How had someone managed to craft something so formally daring to sell creamy Irish stout?

"The Surfer" was bold, even beautiful, yet never lost sight of its brief: to refresh the brand. Those who already drank Guinness could feel affirmed, aligned

---

* Dave Calhoun, "Guinness was good for him," *The Guardian*, 5 October 2004.

with its aesthetic sensibility; those who didn't still came away moved, unsure why. And there was real darkness here—not just the visual chiaroscuro, but an edginess in tone that refused to pander to audience expectation. The black and white found its natural culmination in the stout itself, with its inky depths and luminous head. That final settling swirl carried a kind of yin-yang duality: darkness containing light, light containing darkness, motion resolving into stillness.

It was increasingly clear—even obvious—that a filmmaker capable of creating such cinematic, formally ambitious commercials would soon have to make a feature.

TWO
SEXY BEAST

"No! No no no no no no no! No! No no no no no!"

Life is a near-death experience.

Gary "Gal" Dove learns this the moment *Sexy Beast* begins. Jonathan Glazer opens his debut feature with Gal, played by Ray Winstone, sprawled on a sun lounger, roasting under a merciless sun. His body is inert, soft, almost grotesquely content. To describe it risks cruelty—but Glazer has a shortcut for that. Enter Don Logan, who storms in as the audience's unfiltered id and says what many might be thinking.

"Look at ya," he tells Gal. "You're disgusting."

And so Gal hangs there in a blinding white frame, as The Stranglers' "Peaches" kicks in on the soundtrack, a leering, post-punk anthem about men ogling women. "Sitting on the beaches, looking at the peaches."

Gal isn't exactly a peach. If anything, he might be the leering voice of the song himself: all swagger, all maaf, no trousers. But steady on.

According to Gal's voiceover, he is in a state of almost continuous bliss. He loves the sun, the heat. He loves his wife, Deedee (Amanda Redman). "I love her like a rose loves rainwater." He might be in exile, or hiding, but he prefers it that way. He is unrelentingly positive.

We are in what British tabloids used to call the Costa del Crime, a stretch of the Costa del Sol, in the southeast of Spain. In 1978, an extradition treaty between Spain and the UK expired, making the country — a mere two-hour flight away — perfect for career criminals wanted by British police. Nefarious characters like "Brown Bread" Fred, John "Goldfinger" Palmer and Ronnie Knight lived here with apparent immunity. But their time didn't last long. The loophole closed in 1985. From then on, fugitives who left Spain risked arrest and extradition the moment they returned. (Hence Gal's dread at the idea of going back to London.) A new treaty in 2001 — a year after *Sexy Beast* was released — streamlined the process further. But the region's ties to organised crime never went away. Italian journalist Roberto Saviano, chronicler of the Mafia, claims they now call it "Costa Nostra."* The part of Europe that fell off the back of a lorry.

Like many British expats, Gal prefers to stick with his own. His closest companions — Aitch (Cavan Kendall, who died before the film's release) and Julie (Julianne White) — seem less like friends than long-time associates. The banter between them is warm, familiar, and laced with the humour of shared history. Aitch, a touch more of a geezer than Gal, maybe a shade nastier too, delivers his lines with genuine wit, asking what colour water Gal plans to use to refill the pool, or riffing on the idea of the "everlasting haircut." It's the kind of patter you'd hear at a market stall flogging knock-off Chanel No. 5, or over pints on a Saturday afternoon with the match on.

Gal and Deedee live well. Their villa is spacious and sunny, though it sits beneath a sheer, threatening cliff face. The filmmakers struggled to find such a precarious location: "People just don't build swimming pools under

---

* "La mafia es un problema de toda Europa," *El País*, 4 February 2009.

rock faces that look like they're about to collapse,"* explained producer Jeremy Thomas. Eventually, they found one in Agua Amarga, in Almería.

Gal has a surrogate son of sorts, Enrique (Álvaro Monje), a local boy who he hires to help around the house and who he jokes with and who jokes back. They have an affection for each other that obviously runs deep. When Gal goes hunting with the boy and Aitch, Gal even loves the little rabbit, telling Aitch not to shoot it: "It's only a tiddler." Aitch's gun falling apart rather than killing the rabbit turns a potentially brutal moment into light comedy, but it also shows that these former hard men have gone soft. Their guns are not in good nick. And with that softness comes vulnerability.

But happiness is a precarious state of low entropy. It's like a glass vase. There's only one way to be that glass vase, but there are millions of different ways to be shattered shards of glass on the floor. There's only one way to be particularly happy, but a million ways that happiness can be destroyed.

The film's opening sequence, blasted through with a blaring pop track, feels like one of the music videos Glazer cut his teeth on: visually arresting, loaded with stylistic flourishes. It's dazzling, yes, but also a little eager to impress. You can feel it showing its influences: David Hockney's sun-splashed pool paintings come immediately to mind. It borders on self-consciousness — style for style's sake.

But *Sexy Beast* is very much the work of screenwriters Louis Mellis and David Scinto as it is Glazer's. Perhaps more so. As Glazer says: "My job on *Sexy Beast* was to calibrate my actors and put the camera in the right place and let the script govern."† Frequent collaborator, Walter Campbell remarked that if there were twelve "no"s in

* DVD commentary track.
† Cinema Ritrovato, Bologna, June, 2025.

the script, Ben Kingsley would say all twelve—word for word.*

The screenplay is unusually prescriptive, even visually so—something often frowned upon, as it steps on the director's toes. Painters are explicitly cited: Chagall is mentioned in the stage directions; camera movements are specified; entire visual moods are built from painterly reference points. The Gangster Trilogy (as the writers have referred to their three films) maps out like a gallery: *Gangster No. 1* (2000) is steeped in Francis Bacon, *Sexy Beast* channels Hockney, and *44 Inch Chest* (2009) draws on Magritte.

It wasn't just Glazer making his debut. Cinematographer Ivan Bird and production designer Jan Houllevigue were also first-timers. *Sexy Beast* isn't a singular vision, it's a collective arrival. A gang of new lads, kicking in the door.

The point-of-view shot of a tumbling boulder—something Sisyphus might have just rolled up the mountain—feels gratuitous at first. But here we go: rock 'n' roll. This visual jolt sets a pattern the film will return to, as sky and earth blur into chaos, tumbling down the cliff toward Gal, who sits below, fanning himself with a dinky battery-powered fan like a Roman emperor who's just been to a tacky souvenir shop. The boulder bounces over his head and lands in the pool. The splash hits Gal, not the other way around. Gal doesn't go to the water; the water comes to him, just as Muhammad didn't go to the mountain—the mountain comes to Muhammad. The whole sequence teeters on the edge of cartoonishness, like something out of Hanna-Barbera. It flirts with the ridiculous. But it's also deadly.

A near-death experience indeed. The film might have ended right there.

---

* In conversation with the author.

And even though it doesn't, we're left with the temptation of one of those tedious fan theories, that the protagonist actually dies early on and the rest of the film is a dream-state reverie. Bruce Joel Rubin borrowed it from Ambrose Bierce for *Jacob's Ladder* (1990), and it's been trotted out ever since. Death, in fiction, is rarely final. Bobby Ewing steps out of the shower in *Dallas*, Jon Snow rises from the dead in *Game of Thrones*. And what about Don? At the end of *Sexy Beast*, he smiles in his grave. We rewind to the beginning. The boulder rolls again—only this time: SPLAT.

Except we don't.

The rock is now in the water. Beneath the surface, Gal and Enrique exchange exaggerated gestures, miming what just happened before mouthing up to Deedee, watching from above: "Boulder!" The moment is comic, almost slapstick—but it foreshadows the climax of the film. Wordless. Underwater. A silent choreography of danger. In fact, everything in the opening sequence serves as prelude. Earth (the boulder), water (the pool), fire (the punishing sun) and wind reduced to a feeble puff from Gal's battery fan. The four elements are all present, all conspiring. The proximity of death to pleasure. The unseen arrival of chaos.

Something's off. The air is charged. The world is restless. That evening, at a barbecue with Aitch and Jackie, it happens again: fire leaps suddenly from the grill, singeing Gal's shirt. Everything, it seems, is trying to get him. Deedee's visible burn scars on her might lead us to speculate as to a violent encounter with fire, but these are actually Redman's real scars from a scalding when she was a child.

The boulder. The fire. These things come in threes. The third is a phone call from London—the real harbinger of doom. It's not even for Gal directly. Maybe he doesn't have a phone. Maybe he's made himself deliberately unreachable, hiding from the past, from people like Don Logan. But the name alone is enough to ruin the evening. The moment it's spoken, the mood dies. You see it in the faces around the table—Gal, Deedee, Aitch, Julie—all stricken with the same sick recognition. Whatever Don Logan is, he's no ordinary acquaintance. He's fear incarnate. Violence, in human form. Death with a boarding pass. And he's getting on a plane tomorrow.

"The Mafia? I shit 'em!"—The Short, Sharp Rise of the British Gangster Movie

The British gangster film came into its own relatively late. Earlier British crime cinema focused less on organised syndicates and more on lone criminals—master thieves or Jack the Ripper–style murderers—as in Alfred Hitchcock's *The Lodger* (1927). While Charles Dickens had conjured a vivid underworld in *Oliver Twist*, with Fagin and the Artful Dodger leading a gang of juvenile delinquents, it wasn't until *Brighton Rock* (1948) and *Pool of London* (1951) that British cinema began to seriously explore criminal gangs on screen. Richard Attenborough's Pinkie in *Brighton Rock* is the Artful Dodger gone psycho: a baby-faced scumbag who embodies post-war fears of aimless, lawless youth.

These young thugs would return in more overtly sociological films like Joseph Losey's *The Damned* (1963) and Stanley Kubrick's *A Clockwork Orange* (1971), while the traditional gangster remained a sporadic figure. In *Villain* (1971), Richard Burton channels both Kray twins into a single character, flanked by a young Ian McShane, who would later appear in *Sexy Beast*. Meanwhile, *Performance*, shot in 1968 and released in 1970, reveals a deep ambivalence about the genre itself. Directed by Donald Cammell and Nicolas Roeg, it is less a gangster film than a psychedelic breakdown masquerading as one. British filmmakers have long treated the gangster film with suspicion, as if it were too American a genre to embrace unironically—almost as unthinkable as making a British Western.

Performance was financed by a major studio on the promise of a *Hard Day's Night*–style Rolling Stones vehicle. What they got instead was something far stranger: a hallucinatory gangster-reverie in which James Fox—who also appears in *Sexy Beast*—plays a criminal on the run who hides out in the London townhouse of a reclusive rock star, Turner, played by Mick Jagger. Drugs are taken. Boundaries blur. Reality and identity begin to unravel. The film captures a moment when Sixties optimism is already beginning to curdle into something darker, an Altamont-fed pessimism that would soon take hold. Violence, *Performance* seems to suggest, will never let the flower children flourish. They shall be destroyed from the outside, by rednecks and shotguns (*Easy Rider*, 1969), or from within, by charismatic psychopaths like Charles Manson. Either way, the dream is doomed.

Roeg's use of genre as a vehicle for radical experimentation would prove a lasting influence on Glazer. *Sexy Beast* and *Under the Skin* both echo Roeg's bold reimagining of form and tone, and can be thematically and generically paired with *Performance* and *The Man Who Fell to Earth* (1976), films that twist genre conventions into something stranger, more unsettling, and entirely their own.

Two of the most influential British gangster films— Mike Hodges' *Get Carter* (1971) and *The Long Good Friday* (1980)—arrived a decade apart, each tipping its hat to American noir while forging something distinctly British. Michael Caine's vengeful antihero in *Get Carter* reads Raymond Chandler and bears more than a passing resemblance to Lee Marvin's taciturn Walker in *Point Blank* (1967), itself directed by a Brit, John Boorman, in Hollywood. *The Long Good Friday*, meanwhile, riffs on Chandler's *The Long Goodbye* (filmed by Robert Altman in 1973) and centres on a London gangster, Harold Shand (Bob Hoskins), who dreams of legitimising his empire by luring investment from the American mafia to redevelop the Docklands. Seen today, Shand's entrepreneurial vision feels eerily prescient. His fury at the Americans' withdrawal — "The Mafia? I shit 'em!" — is both a howl of betrayal and a flash of hubris. But his downfall doesn't come from a rival gang; it comes from a different kind of organisation altogether: the IRA. In the end, the political turbulence of 1980s Britain proves more volatile, more lethal, than Harold's underworld ambitions.

Stephen Frears' *The Hit* (1984) has more in common with *Sexy Beast* than just its Spanish setting. It was produced by the same person (Jeremy Thomas) and shares an ambition to be as much an art film as a crime film. John Hurt and a young Tim Roth play hitmen dispatched to retrieve Terence Stamp's character, a former gangster turned supergrass, now hiding out in rural Spain. As the story drifts through sun-scorched landscapes, picking up hostages along the way, the two killers are increasingly unsettled by their target's calm acceptance of his fate and his philosophical detachment. *The Hit* is less concerned with action than with ideas — destiny, freedom, the illusions of control. It's a meditation on mortality wrapped in a crime film's clothing. And in keeping with the Thatcher-era mood of mid-1980s Britain, it offers a far bleaker worldview than Glazer's film. There's more existentialism than gunplay, more quiet dread than violent confrontation.

Real-life villains continued to provide material for British crime films — and vehicles for middle-of-the-road pop stars with acting ambitions. Phil Collins took the lead in *Buster* (1988), playing Great Train Robber Buster Edwards, while Gary and Martin Kemp of Spandau

Ballet starred as the murderous Kray twins in *The Krays* (1990). On paper, it was ideal casting—real-life identical twins playing the most infamous twins in British criminal history—but neither Kemp brother proved especially adept at acting, and the film leans more on surface likeness than emotional depth.

The British gangster film received a major jolt in 1998 with the release of Guy Ritchie's *Lock, Stock and Two Smoking Barrels*. Riding the wave of Quentin Tarantino's revival of American crime cinema (*Reservoir Dogs*, 1992; *Pulp Fiction*, 1994), Ritchie infused the genre with black humour, hyper-stylised violence, real-life underworld references, and a twisty, ensemble-driven narrative. Its runaway success triggered a flurry of imitators and variations. Among them were Paul McGuigan's *Gangster No. 1* (2000)—written by *Sexy Beast*'s screenwriters Louis Mellis and David Scinto—*Love, Honour and Obey* (2000), and Ritchie's own follow-up, *Snatch* (2000). The early 2000s saw further entries like Nick Love's *The Business* (2004) and *Layer Cake* (2004), directed by Ritchie's former producer Matthew Vaughn and starring a pre–James Bond Daniel Craig.

Ray Winstone's career is closely entwined with the evolution of the British crime film. His breakout role came in *Scum* (1976), Alan Clarke's brutal television play about life inside a borstal. Winstone plays a young inmate who learns to survive—and rise—through violence, eventually becoming the "daddy" of the institution. The film's unflinching realism and raw aggression proved too much for the BBC, which shelved the original broadcast. Clarke was later forced to reshoot the screenplay for theatrical release.

Winstone's on-screen persona seemed tailor-made for hard-man roles, yet his baby-faced softness lent him an unusual empathy. Even when he's sharpening a shiv, you want to put an arm around him. He brought that same mix of menace and vulnerability to *Quadrophenia* (1979), a film that stirred controversy with its semi-romanticised depiction of violent clashes between Mods and Rockers on Brighton Beach. Cinema owners feared their seats might get slashed. The film played like *A Clockwork Orange* meets *Brighton Rock*, set to a soundtrack by The Who — who also financed it.

By the late '90s, Winstone was a mainstay of the genre, co-starring with Robert Carlyle in Antonia Bird's underrated *Face* (1997), and appearing in *Final Cut* (1998) and *Love, Honour and Obey* (2000). He later crossed the Atlantic for Martin Scorsese's *The Departed* (2006), holding his own opposite Jack Nicholson. Yet despite a string of high-profile Hollywood roles, his full range was rarely tapped.

His most searing performance remains Raymond in Gary Oldman's *Nil by Mouth* (1997), an alcoholic, abusive husband — a shattering deconstruction of the violent masculine ideal he had so often embodied. He returned to similarly grim territory in *The War Zone* (1999), the directorial debut of Tim Roth, portraying another monstrous patriarch in a film of relentless bleakness.

More recently, Winstone appeared in *The Gentlemen* (2024), a TV spin-off of Guy Ritchie's seemingly endless crime universe. That same year saw the release of a small-screen prequel to *Sexy Beast* (2024), though none of the original film's cast returned. One notable connection: Paul Kaye, once Jonathan Glazer's flatmate, appears in a supporting role.

Sexy Beast began life as the middle chapter of a proposed trilogy of plays titled *Gangster No. 1*, *Gangster No. 2*, and *Gangster No. 3*. The first was staged in Islington,

London, and quickly caught the attention of producers and agents.

Author Louis Mellis, born in Edinburgh, had moved to London as a teenager and drifted through a string of jobs—from rat catcher to zookeeper—before training as an actor. He gave up acting in 1991, but at a party met David Scinto, another aspiring actor, originally from Stratford. The two bonded over a shared love of art and theatre and decided to collaborate. Rather than basing their gangster scripts on research or reportage, they began by improvising in character, recording their imagined dialogue, and writing it down. The result was stylised, theatrical, and deliberately heightened—eschewing the kitchen-sink "gritty realism" that often masquerades as naturalism. Their work sounded like no one else's: jagged, profane, almost musical.

The writers adapted their stage play into a screenplay and approached Nicolas Roeg to direct. The script was densely novelistic in its scene descriptions and extravagantly baroque in its dialogue, with profanity deployed as much for rhythm and emphasis as for vocabulary. But producer interference soon derailed the project. The script was heavily revised, and when a dispute erupted over casting—producers pushing for Peter Bowles to reprise the role he originated on stage, even though the writers had imagined it going to someone very different—the attached director, Jonathan Glazer, and the writers walked away.

Still determined to collaborate, and furious about how their first venture had been handled, Scinto and Mellis quickly wrote a new script in just three weeks. They changed the title from *Gangster No. 2* to *Sexy Beast* to distance themselves from the earlier project, which they no longer felt connected to. They also removed their names from *Gangster No. 1*, leaving the final screenplay credited to a single writer, marked only as "adapted by," with no mention of what it had been adapted from.

Sexy Beast and *Gangster No. 1* were released in the same year—2000—effectively going head-to-head while also contending with the higher-profile *Snatch*. Guy Ritchie's film had Hollywood muscle behind it: Brad Pitt, Benicio del Toro, and a lineup of regulars including Jason Statham and Stephen Graham. The star power made a statement. But amid the glut of British crime films at the time, *Sexy Beast* initially struggled to stand out.

Its reputation, however, grew steadily in the U.S., where it was reappraised as a cult classic, eventually gaining enough cachet to spark a belated prequel TV series nearly two decades later. Scinto and Mellis became sought-after script doctors in Hollywood and attempted to mount *Gangster No. 3*—retitled *44 Inch Chest*—as their joint directorial debut, but creative tensions proved irreconcilable and the partnership dissolved. *44 Inch Chest* was eventually released in 2010, starring *Sexy Beast* veterans Ray Winstone and Ian McShane.

"Calamari. I'll have the calamari."
There are two kinds of trauma for a first-time filmmaker: the trauma of failure, and the trauma of success. *Sexy Beast* was widely praised upon release, but Glazer remained ambivalent. The film didn't immediately find its audience, and it was the only one of his features where the development was relatively swift—and from a script he didn't write.

Though Glazer arrived with a formidable reputation from music videos and commercials, he had limited authority on set. The writers, cinematographer and production designer were all newcomers, but the cast were seasoned, and the producer, Jeremy Thomas, was a heavyweight, known for his work with

Bertolucci, Cronenberg, and for producing *The Hit*, a film with striking tonal and thematic parallels.

The screenplay was filmed largely as written, though a few sequences—particularly Gal's surreal rabbit nightmare—were cut for budgetary reasons. It was the script that first drew Jeremy Thomas in; he read it over a weekend and made an offer the following Monday. The same script attracted major talent, including Ben Kingsley, who took on the role of Don Logan—a part that had previously been considered for Anthony Hopkins, and, at one point, even Ray Winstone himself.

Kingsley was inspired casting. Born Krishna Pandit Bhanji in Yorkshire and raised in Lancashire, he began his career on stage before achieving global recognition in *Gandhi*, winning both a BAFTA and an Academy Award for his portrayal of the pacifist leader who challenged British colonial rule through non-violence. A decade later, he appeared in Spielberg's *Schindler's List* as Itzhak Stern, the quiet, steadfast accountant who helps Oskar Schindler rescue Jews from the Holocaust. Though Kingsley had played a wide range of roles, he remained most publicly associated with these real-life figures—men of moral clarity and inner calm who demonstrated immense courage in the face of unimaginable violence.

Enter Don Logan.

Kingsley's view of the role provides a succinct description of the film: "I've done a lot of interviews for *Sexy Beast* with the press. It's a wonderful film to talk about, and I try to reduce the film to a sort of one-line myth. I came up with: 'Once upon a time, there was a man who thought he was very happy, so the Gods sent to him the unhappiest man in the world.'"*

As the unhappiest man in the world, Don is a violent inversion of everything audiences associate with Kingsley. This is no Gandhi, no Stern. Don would beat them both

---

* From the DVD commentary.

senseless and spit on their twitching bodies without a flicker of remorse. With his machine-gun delivery and a head like an alopecia-stricken testicle, he doesn't just embody toxic masculinity—he weaponises it. And yet we can't look away. He's all drive, all intent. When he first appears, slicing through the airport terminal, he's like a shark or a missile—unrelenting, purpose-built. The crisp white short-sleeved shirt is his only nod to the climate. He carries his own suitcase—no trolley.

The rest of the cast had been in Spain for over a week, tanning and, in Winstone's case, downing vodka and piling on pasta to bulk up. Kingsley, delayed by other commitments, arrived late, and with his Oscar-winning reputation acquired an almost mythical presence before he ever stepped on set.

First to be shot was the restaurant sequence with Gal, Deedee, Aitch and Jackie—a tough opening, with four principal characters speaking across each other, a logistical nightmare of blocking and eyelines. Originally, it was meant to be filmed later in the schedule, giving the actors time to settle into their roles and allowing Glazer space to find his rhythm. But a clash over location availability pushed it to the top of the shoot.

It's a superb scene. Gal's character, and his warm, easy rapport with Deedee, is instantly clear. The performances have a natural, unforced rhythm; the realism feels lived-in and instinctive. "What are you having? I think I'll have the calamari," Gal says. "I love calamari." It's a small moment, but it gestures toward some-thing bigger: a reminder that the British gangster film is the Mr. Hyde to the Jekyll of British social realism—Ken Loach, Alan Clarke and, to some extent, Mike Leigh. But even Loach, with the debt collectors in *Raining Stones* (1993) and the gangsters in *Looking for Eric* (2009), isn't without his monsters. People who live at the sharp end of life are vulnerable to the predation of such chaotic figures.

Don is a genre unto himself—fully embodied, fully unhinged. His impact has been lasting, inspiring a wave of British actors to try their hand at foul-mouthed, feral sociopaths: Ralph Fiennes in *In Bruges* (2008)—a film that owes a clear debt to *The Hit* and *Sexy Beast*—and Hugh Grant and Colin Farrell in Guy Ritchie's *The Gentlemen* (2019) among them.

Don's arrival is foreshadowed by a clever misdirection. Gal assumes Aitch and Jackie are mid-domestic, something that clearly happens often enough for him to slip straight into peacemaker mode. But that's not what's happening.

This isn't a spat. This is the worst news imaginable. The unhappiest man in the world is coming for Gal.

The Job or Job

God had a gambling problem. In The Book of Job, He takes a bet with Satan, that Job—a blameless, God-fearing man—will keep the faith even if stripped of everything he loves. Satan is given free rein to destroy Job's life, with one condition: he can't kill him. And so begins the onslaught. Job loses his wealth, his children, his health. Broken and bewildered, he demands an explanation. How can a just God allow such suffering to befall a good man? His friends insist he must be guilty of something, some hidden sin he's unaware of. But when God finally shows up, He sidesteps the question entirely, launching into a majestic monologue about the grandeur of creation. Essentially: "Can you do this?" It's like a magician pulling endless ribbons from your ear while ignoring the rigged game that caused all the pain in the first place. This is God at his most Zeus-like, the same capricious deity Dylan invoked on *Highway 61 Revisited.*

Criminal protagonists in movies are not good men—they're criminals after all—but they are *trying* to be good men. As Samuel L. Jackson as Jules, the hit man, says in *Pulp Fiction*: "The truth is you're the weak. And I'm the tyranny of evil men. But I'm tryin', Ringo. I'm tryin' real hard to be the shepherd." The "one last job" trope is so pervasive it's outgrown cliché and become a subgenre of its own. *The Asphalt Jungle* (1950), *The Killing* (1956), *Thief* (1981), *Carlito's Way* (1993), *Heat* (1995), *The Town* (2010) and *The Fantastic Mr Fox* (2009) all hum the same tune, that this time next week we'll be out of this dump, sipping something cold on a beach in Acapulco. It's a narrative absolution. As long as the criminal is reluctant, as long as he wants to go straight—just not yet, as Saint Augustine put it— we can forgive him. We'll watch him get the old crew back together, plan the perfect job, recruit the sketchy insider, fall for the woman in the museum, fine-tune every detail, dodge the heat. And then, more often than not, watch it all fall apart. Because someone's always more wounded than they let on.

That looming sense of tragedy becomes the audience's get-out-of-jail-free card for empathy.

Gal has already done his "one last job." But now he's being dragged into one more. As Al Pacino laments in *The Godfather Part III* (1990), "Just when I thought I was out, they pull me back in"—a line that captures the soul of the genre so perfectly it's become self-parody, most memorably in *The Sopranos*, where the crew delights in Silvio Dante's (Steven Van Zandt) hammy Pacino impression.[*]

Gal's last job is going to be a black box to us—until it happens. And then it'll be a literal black box. We'll be lost. Underwater. But first, Gal has to accept the job, and

---

[*] It's one of the many pleasures of *The Sopranos* that it is one of the shows in which the characters are themselves enthusiastic consumers of popular culture, whether it's Carmella Soprano's love of *Casablanca* or Christopher Moltisanti's encounter with Martin Scorsese, where he shouts "*Kundun*, Marty! I loved it!"

he won't. He wants nothing to do with it, but he has to make that clear to Don, who simply won't take no for an answer. It's a key scene, a tour de force, a gale-force blast of vociferous verbals. It's ingenuity and humour, psychosis and poetry, gassing and gaslighting.

"Why are you swearing? I'm not swearing," says Don, the sweariest there ever was. At one point he lets out a throaty guffaw mid-flow—"A monkey could do it, that's why I thought of you"—corpsing, to use the theatrical term: the performer breaking with the performance, undone by his own wit and ferocity. But it's not Kingsley breaking character, it's Don himself.

There's something vulnerable about Don, who is seething with need and emotion. Compare and contrast to Gal's contentment: "Lapping it up." Gal is stationary, on his lounger, exactly where he wants to be. Don, on the other hand, is all movement: an Exocet missile fired from London, through the airport, always wanting to go somewhere else: a nightclub, the beach, back to London. Even on a plane, he's itching to move, and gets off before it departs. Even when he's sitting still, his intensity is that of a man ready to move forward at full speed.

He needs Gal. Above and beyond Gal's skills as a thief, he likes him; loves him in fact. "You're lovable. Big lovable bloke. Lovable lump," he says, words Don could never apply to himself. He's estranged from his brother, Malky. (In an earlier draft, Malky was Don's identical twin and part of the heist. Still, Malky's name lingers; he is listed as one of the crew, ghosting through the margins of the film, just out of frame.)

Even Don's closest allies—those who should mourn him, or avenge him—barely pretend to care: "If I gave one solitary fuck about Don…" It's not grief, just a shrug wrapped in profanity.

Don is all yearning, all need. He loves Jackie too—desperately, possessively. But that's a story for later.

Don's disappointment at Gal's refusal isn't just logistical. It's not like the job hinges on him. All they need are "eight men... strong... ain't afraid to graft." A solid crew, sure—but not a delicate operation of specialists. Gal isn't a safecracker or explosives expert; he's muscle, filler, one of the bodies in the room. During the heist, he does what everyone else does, nothing singular, nothing irreplaceable. In this world, no one is indispensable. Not even Don. When the job goes ahead without him, his absence is noted, but barely an inconvenience.

The stylised flashbacks showing the job's preparation echo a device from *Gangster No. 1*, with overlapping voices, characters finishing each other's sentences, words ventriloquised by Don's narration. Don "knows a bloke... who knows a bloke... who knows a bloke." He's third-hand, with Stan as his contact. But the real puppet-master is Teddy Bass, "Mr. Black Magic, hisself," as Don puts it. The rabbit from your nightmares, Gal.

Mr Black Magic, hisself

Don might be a demon, but Teddy Bass is the devil. Where Don rants and raves, Bass listens. He hears what you're not saying. He never raises his voice. His words are spare, his meaning precise, slipping out in fragments— unfinished sentences that leave no doubt. If you've been wondering where the "visible darkness" is in all this, here he is, in the flesh. He dresses in black: coat, suit, shirt, tie. He drives a matte grey car that seems to absorb the night as it moves through it. Even in broad daylight, he brings the dark with him. Wherever he is—there is darkness, and darkness is where he belongs, to misquote Marlowe's Mephistopheles.

For British audiences, the shock of Bass' entrance was doubled. Ian McShane, the actor, was best known at the time as Lovejoy, the mullet-haired, roguish antique dealer and amateur sleuth from cosy Sunday-night telly.

Lovejoy, the Jeremy Clarkson of crime-solving, worked his way through bloodless mysteries with a pint and a wink, alongside his pickled sidekick, Tinker. And now here he was: sodomised in a shower at an orgy, radiating cold menace. It was as jolting as seeing Gandhi turn mobster.

In the script, that same shower scene resolves into the film's title—*Sexy Beast*—a phrase previously used in the stage directions to describe Deedee. But before Lovejoy, McShane's film career had included darker turns: *Villain*, with Richard Burton, and *Sewers of Gold* (1979), another crime film involving a tunnel job not unlike the one in *Sexy Beast*. His return to the underworld was both a revelation and a reckoning.

The orgy is an off-screen affair and has an *Eyes Wide Shut* (1999) ambience of high-class decadence. As the devil incarnate, Teddy moves effortlessly through every layer of society. One of his marks is Harry, played by James Fox, another veteran of British gangster lore, his presence a quiet echo of *Performance*. Harry is a toff, drawn to Teddy's charm and menace, so much so that he carelessly invites the wolf into the vault at Imperial Emblatt, the elite banking firm where he works.* It's a fatal act of trust. The camera circles the building's revolving door in a slow, deliberate arc, mirroring the spinning rock that tumbled into Gal's pool. Once again, the wheel turns. Fate is in motion. And this, finally, is the job: a heist. The moment Gal tried to evade has arrived, right on schedule.

Gal wants no part of it. He's heard the "no risk" pitch before, and the last time it cost him nine years inside. But Don doesn't recognise refusal. An immovable object meets an unstoppable force.

---

* The name of Harry's company can't help but put me in mind of Imperial Leather, a soap that was a prime brand through my upbringing before edible sounding shower gels took over.

"You're just going to have to turn this opportunity 'Yes'!" Don tells Gal nonsensically. The persuasion and badgering continue in different settings as day turns to evening turns to night, like a video for a boy band lip-synching to their hit in four different locations, wearing different clothes. In a club, Don lets something slip: he likes Jackie. Maybe that's why he didn't go straight to Gal, but circled through Jackie and Aitch—any excuse to see her, to speak to her. Uncomfortable with the admission, Don doubles down, oversharing with an obscene story of being anally penetrated by Jackie's finger during intercourse, something that baffles and disgusts Don, but that also—very obviously—has left an impression.

Sexual fluidity runs throughout *Sexy Beast*, as it does across the work of Louis Mellis and David Scinto. *Gangster No. 1* pivots on a charged, unresolved desire between two men; in *44 Inch Chest*, Ian McShane's Meredith—a flamboyantly gay provocateur—delights in needling John Hurt's crusty, homophobic Peanut. In *Sexy Beast*, the undercurrents are messier, stranger. Don spins a surreal tale of being sexually assaulted on his "front bottom"—a euphemism typically reserved for vaginas—before bristling at what he calls Gal's "innsinuendos." The word itself, mispronounced, becomes another layer of confusion and deflection.

We know Teddy Basso is gay, though I'd bet a pony he's pansexual.

When he asks Harry, the chairman: "Men or women?" Harry replies with the deliciously non-committal, "Oh, definitely." Teddy instantly clocks the Turkish baths, which will provide them with access via a tunnel to the vault. All those robbers in their speedos, big bulky criminals, squeezing through tight spaces. All that liquid and squelching.

Don's relationship to women is purely transactional and degrading. His first comment about Jackie is "big tits"—affection reduced to anatomy. With Deedee, he tries to shame her history in porn, rebranding her "Dirty Deedee" to drive a wedge between her and Gal.

And Don will ultimately be fucked by Aitch, though this fucking has a different fatal element attached.

"Yes, yes, yes, yes, yes, yes, yes."
Don is trying to wear Gal down. He appeals to comradeship, to money, to the thrill—the buzz, "the sheer fuck-off-ness of it." He shifts tactics with dizzying speed. "I'm a good listener," he says, but when Gal continues to turn him down, the charm vanishes: "You fat cunt." The violence begins on the beach, where Don punches Gal. Such is Don's status and menace that Gal doesn't even try to defend himself. Like the state, Don holds a monopoly on violence. Back in the car, Don stares at him—rigid, silent. The evening that follows is excruciating. One by one, Gal, Deedee, Aitch, and Jackie peel away, leaving Don alone in the living room while they take refuge in the kitchen. The women do what they can to protect their men. Jackie freezes Don out with elegant hostility. Deedee pushes back more openly and earns a surreal, thinly veiled threat in return: "You got very nice eyes, Deedee. Never noticed them before. They real?"

Don knows he can bully and cajole, manipulate and berate. But he's also aware that his sharpest weapon is a double-edged sword. "Still giving too much of yourself away with your fucking mouth," he mutters at his reflection—like Gollum lashing out at Sméagol in *The Two Towers* (2002). Or perhaps he's closer to Iago, circling his own motives without ever fully grasping them. He moves through conversations like Travis Bickle, talking more to himself than anyone else. Don doesn't have friends he can trust and is estranged from his brother. In the script, he has a wife, but she's wisely dropped from the film (who on earth could put up with him?). When we first see him at home, he's alone, watching television, taking the call about the job. At first, he wallows in wounded pride, but it quickly curdles into violence. He attacks Gal as he sleeps. Deedee intervenes to protect Gal. She's the one who drives Don out, the real "sexy beast in the jungle," the one, as the script once described her, who defends her mate.

Don will try twice more before giving up, at least temporarily. First, he attempts a kind of mini-seduction, cooing over how lovable Gal is. When that fails, he explodes in the kitchen, hurling insults like headbutts and kicking the cabinets in fury. Finally, he says the quiet part out loud. A lonely, bitter man, appalled by contentment: "I won't let you be happy," he shouts.

Once upon a time, there was a man who thought he was very happy, so the Gods sent him the unhappiest man in the world.

Don rides away in the taxi, seated dead centre in the back, like a strange child who's never been in a car before and wants an unobstructed view of the world. There's a brief interlude, a pause for breath. He boards the plane, cigarette in hand, flouting social norms, basic manners, airline regulations—none of it matters to Don. Nothing stands a chance against the vitriolic verbal vandalism of Don Logan. Aitch can be reasonable. Gal might claw back his confidence. But we already know Don has stormed off the plane, outmanoeuvred authority with the force of his furious, ungovernable will. We're drawn to him—if not admiring, then at least unable to look away—because of his absolute freedom. But like anything absolute, that's all he has. It consumes everything else.

Gal knows he's coming back. His face collapses with the same dread that struck him in the restaurant when Don's name was first mentioned. It's the oh-fuckiest of oh-fuck moments. Ray Winstone's baby face was made for those quiet implosions.

And now Don is back. The choices are simple, if unspoken: either do the job, or kill Don. Ironically, it ends up being both.

As well as Iago, there is something of King Lear in Don: the nihilism, the collapse of reason, the inability to connect with another human being. He confuses domination for love, destruction for meaning. Compare:

> Not this time, Gal. Not this time. Not this fucking time. No! No, no, no, no, no, no, no, no, no! No! No, no, no, no, no, no, no, no, no, no, no, no, no! No! Not this fucking time! No fucking way! No fucking way! No fucking way! No fucking way! You made me look a right cunt! Like a right fucking Mr. Confused.

A Right Fucking Mr. Confused could be an alternative title of *King Lear*.

Now this:

> No, no, no life!
> Why should a dog, a horse, a rat, have life,
> And thou no breath at all?
> Thou'lt come no more,
> Never, never, never, never, never.
>   (King Lear)

> No, no, no, no, no, no, no, no, no!
>   (Don)

Language has broken. It's no longer up to the job. "I will do such things — What they are yet I know not, but they shall be The terrors of the Earth!" says Lear, blustering through the fog of senility, impotence, and grief. He is edging closer to the white cliffs of death, and covering the collapse with noise.

Don has similarly come to the end of the road. He can't leave without Gal, and Gal won't go. He can't get Jackie to look at him — did they ever actually have sex? — let alone convince her to leave Aitch. Maybe that's why she stuck her finger up his bum. To make him come. Get it over with. Like she was pressing the button on a talking doll.

Don has become Mr. Confused. He can piss on the bathroom carpet and attack Gal in his sleep, but none of it will change Gal's mind. Gal isn't going to London. Gal isn't doing the job. And Don has no plan. He has no more sense of the future than a child in the middle of a tantrum. He wants what he wants and can't imagine a universe in which he doesn't get it. That universe is inconceivable. So he screams, smashes, lashes out — until reality breaks, or he does.

This is why the sudden arrival of young Enrique as a kind of *deus ex machina* makes more psychological than narrative sense. It's a child standing up to another child. Don may be violent, dangerous and terrifyin, but at root, he's throwing a tantrum. And kids understand tantrums. Enrique bursts out of the night with his broken blunderbuss, a toy-rifle in all but name. He wants to protect his father, Gal, from the bully. We already know the gun won't work, but that's beside the point. What matters is the instinct. Has he been circling the house for hours, lurking just out of view, ever since Gal banished him when Don arrived? His intervention triggers the final collision. But by now, the rock is already rolling downhill. The damage is done. Deedee has gone to fetch a real weapon.

England...What a shit hole.

Does Gal miss England?

"What, England? Nah. Fucking place. It's a dump. Don't make me laugh. Grey, grimy, sooty. What a shit hole. What a toilet. Every cunt with a long face shuffling about, moaning, all worried. No thanks, not for me."

And the film agrees.

The first shot of England shows rain pouring down as Gal steps out of the taxi and enters the Grosvenor Hotel, booked under the name Mr. Rowntree—"like Shaft, like Smarties." Even his nudity feels cramped in the hotel room. On the bed, he's not sprawling but curled like an apostrophe, a foetus. England has shrunk him.

Now he goes through the motions Don had already outlined. He's collected, driven to a meeting with Teddy. But Teddy wants a word first. Gal walks through plastic curtains into ever darker rooms—descending layers of menace. Stan and Teddy want to know where Don is. Not a deal-breaker, they say. But it's a concern. A worry. And these are men who don't like worries.

Later, Gal and the crew are briefed on the job. But the next morning, Teddy shows up again—quiet, surgical— as Gal is eating breakfast. The balance has shifted. Don is gone. Teddy's the Rabbit now. We know Don never made it to London. His fate plays out in flashback, even as Gal lies about it in real time. Teddy doesn't interrupt. He listens. Watches. He doesn't accuse Gal; he lets Gal accuse himself.

"I'm not lying."

Teddy is everything Don wasn't. Controlled. Graceful. His voice soft, his movements precise. Where Don ranted and fidgeted, Teddy radiates stillness. He belongs in a glass tower, drinking whiskey in silhouette, the anti-Don—a Michael Mann figure of quiet authority. He doesn't fumble or flap. He watches Gal, calm as a monk, staring not just at him but *through* him—into the flashbacks, into the truth.

"Okay," he says, once he's understood everything. "Alright then."

Teddy's "Okay. Alright then." isn't an acceptance of Gal's story. It's not belief—it's permission. A signal: *That's your version. Fine. I can work with that.* Gal knows he hasn't fooled him. The best he can hope for is that his usefulness outlasts Teddy's suspicion. That's why his bag is packed. He plans to vanish the moment the job is done.

The gang itself is little more than background noise. A bunch of loud blokes—shouting, laughing, eating Chinese food, smoking, carrying on. They're the table in the restaurant you pray you won't get seated next to. No character development, no complexity, just a many-headed beast of blunt noise, a stark counterpoint to Gal's frayed interiority.

While they shout, Gal slips away to use the pay phone. He calls Deedee and tries to say he loves her. But how can he find the words, after everything he's just endured? On one side, Don's relentless verbal assault—filthy, chaotic, unstoppable. On the other, Teddy's volcanic silences—controlled, sulfurous, waiting to erupt. Between those two poles, Gal has been battered by language. And yet he manages to speak. That moment, small and fragile, is what grounds the film.

Gal doesn't want to do "one last job." He really doesn't. There's no secret itch, no buried thrill. The myth of the "One Last Job" is often a death sentence anyway. These men are already dead, in a way, so bound up in their criminal identities that dying during the job or retiring afterward makes little difference. Like the people who work all their lives, save for the dream house abroad, and drop dead the week after they get there.

But Gal has already retired—*successfully.* He's dodged the cliché. This isn't the usual "one last job" narrative. If Gal dies in a hail of bullets, it won't be a blood-soaked consummation, a noble blaze of glory à la *The Wild Bunch*. It'll be a fucking tragedy. He'll be furious. He has something to lose. His love for Deedee is real—mutual, grounded, adult. He's seen her porn films, and he doesn't care. It's not a problem because he doesn't love an illusion. He doesn't love an idea of her. He loves *her*—biography included. Her whole life comes with the deal, and he accepts it, no edits.

"I love you like a rose loves rainwater, like a leopard loves its partner in the jungle, like… I don't know what like."

The words fail, but not out of weakness. They fail out of strength. Out of the need to say something utterly sincere, utterly true, about a feeling too large, too deep, too hardcore to be captured in language. His love isn't ornamental. It's foundational. It's the still point in the chaos. It is, as Marx once said of religion, "the heart in a heartless world."

All Gal needs from Deedee is the sound of her voice saying his name.

The heist itself is fiddly, inelegant. Gal complains about the cramped space. There's no glamour here, just middle-aged men in swim trunks, wielding oversized rock drills in a steam bath, "digging tunnels like Charles Bronson in *The Great Escape*," as Mr. Brown puts it in *Reservoir Dogs*. (In Tarantino's scene, "digging tunnels" is also slang for fucking.) The steam bath, thick with sweat and hissing steam, pulses with homoerotic overtones. No wonder Teddy clocked it instantly.

When they finally breach the vault, the rewards are sordid and strange. Imperial Emblatt, the bank's name, proves apt. The deposit boxes yield colonial detritus: photographs of imperial officers, tokens of violence and domination, bondage paraphernalia, alongside the expected haul—cash, diamonds, bonds, heirlooms, secrets. The vault itself, now half-submerged, echoes Gal's swimming pool back in Spain. But this one is wrong. A night-pool. Enclosed, unnatural. Someone opens an urn and ashes bloom across the water like a shadow taking shape. The past, literally and metaphorically, refuses to stay buried.

The job done, the others celebrate. Gal wants out. He's already halfway gone, bag packed. But his urgency reads as guilt. He knows the jig is up. Maybe he hopes to slip away unnoticed, but Teddy doesn't believe in "unnoticed."

"I'll give you a lift," he says, smooth as ever.

Teddy is a two-birds-one-stone kind of man. He wants to deal with Harry, who can link Teddy with the job, and also implicate Gal further—have him present at a murder, maybe even touch a whiskey glass he'll forget to wipe. A detail, but damning. Teddy isn't just settling scores; he's tightening nets. When he pulls the car over and slashes Gal's cut from a hefty percentage to a measly £10, Gal feels not outrage, but relief. It's over. He's still breathing. To make it absolutely clear to Gal and leave a lingering threat, he says that he might pop in to "pay his respects," signalling he knows Don is dead. And he knows Gal knows he knows.

Before he leaves him on the roadside, he delivers the final line, sharp and cold: "If I cared, Gal. If I fucking cared. If I gave one solitary fuck about Don… Get out of the fucking car."

"More rabbit than Sainsbury's"

In 1980, a single called "Rabbit" by the pop duo Chas & Dave broke into the UK top ten. Flat-capped throwbacks with a pint in one hand and a piano in the other, Charles Hodges and David Peacock invented a genre they dubbed Rockney. Cockney rock. "Rabbit" was a comic love song about a girlfriend who won't stop talking. Despite protests from feminists at the time, it became their biggest hit to date. The intro and outro are nothing but a verbal barrage:

"Yup yup rabbit yup yup yup rabbit rabbit bunny jabber yup rabbit bunny yup yup yup rabbit bunny jabber yup yup yup rabbit bunny jabber yup yup bunny jabber rabbit."

It would be unfair—and dangerous—to say Don Logan sounds like this. Not least because it's unfair to Chas, Dave and the unfortunate girlfriend. Don's language may be relentless, but it's not babble. There's a poetry to it. Not Virginia Woolf—too clipped and sharp for that. More like James Joyce. *Finnegans Wake*, not *Ulysses*: language pushed to the edge of coherence, an assault of rhythm, rage, and association. Still, if you were safely out of earshot and felt brave, the Chas & Dave song could pass for a mocking imitation of Don's spiel.

"Rabbit," of course, comes from Cockney rhyming slang: "rabbit and pork" = "talk." The rhyme is dropped, leaving just the code word. Same principle with "Barnett Fair" (hair), "butcher's hook" (look), and so on. You can decode the culture by listening to what gets abbreviated. There is, appropriately, a rabbit—or rather a *hare*—that haunts Gal's dreams. In Melville and Scinto's screenplay, the animal has a name. Its appearance is grotesquely detailed and faithfully realised in the film:

> The figure is hairy, mangy, skinny, slightly humped, bare topped—it is a 6ft tall, man-sized hare… it wears black, dusty, silver studded, Mexican trousers… battered, tooled, Cuban-heeled boots… it smokes a cheroot… flies hum around it's [sic] licey head. One ear, broken, buckled, slightly flopping… the other—the good ear—chewed and tattered… we think his name is HERMAN?

"Chewed and tattered." It sounds like a child's toy left too long at the bottom of the bed. Usually it's a teddy, but with Teddy Bass in the picture, we'll avoid that association. Could "HERMAN?" come from some private memory? The name has no obvious Cockney lineage, though one could imagine a new bit of slang: Herman Munster = youngster. "There were a couple of Hermans hanging around the bus stop."

Where do dreams come from? A mincemeat of anxiety, indigestion, memory, and the residue of the day. So what did Gal do that day? He went rabbit hunting. He ate calamari. He heard that Don Logan was on his way. Enough to summon something monstrous from the depths.

Herman?—the question mark is part of the name throughout the script—might be the "tiddler" Aitch failed to kill: "Prepare to meet your maker." Or maybe he's one of the rabbits from *Watership Down* (1972), Richard Adams' traumatising tale of a doomed rabbit warren fleeing the advance of man. Or the March Hare, Carroll's jittery symbol of madness, all wild eyes and nonsense logic.

He's very obviously a man in a costume. Cowboy boots, six feet tall, smoking a cheroot. Not trying to pass for real. A spectral presence with staccato movements, awkward and uncanny, like the film is running in reverse—a nod, perhaps, to Cocteau. It calls to mind another man-sized rabbit: Frank from *Donnie Darko*, released a year after *Sexy Beast*. "Why are you wearing that stupid bunny suit?" Donnie asks. The reply: "Why are you wearing that stupid man suit?"

The outfit evokes the spaghetti Westerns Sergio Leone shot nearby, in the arid hills outside Madrid. From Gal's villa you can see the kind of landscape Lee Van Cleef and Clint Eastwood once rode across. Aitch dresses up cowboy-style to go hunting, carrying a

Winchester that falls apart in his hands, as fantasy often does.

But Herman? He's no cowboy. He carries an Uzi, the Israeli submachine gun made famous by Chuck Norris in *Invasion U.S.A.* (1985). In the script, he unleashes a hail of bullets at the table and around Gal, forcing Gal to hold it up as its legs are shot out. Herman? begins as Don, later becomes Teddy, but throughout the film he is also something else entirely: Gal's dread made flesh. He's the fear of prison, the terror of losing Deedee, the collapse of everything Gal has built in Spain. Killing Don doesn't kill Herman? He lingers on, alive and malignant, haunting the Grosvenor Hotel. Maybe he always has. Like a charred child's toy, Herman? is something Gal's carried for years, a comfort object turned demonically possessed.

Let's pause on Don's murder, revealed to us in jagged fragments. It recalls *Murder on the Orient Express*, where the question isn't whodunit but who didn't. Don is first shot by Deedee, then punched by Gal, kicked and battered by Jackie, shot again by Deedee, and finally finished off by Aitch—using what? In the script, it's a barbecue. On screen, it might be a speaker. Whatever the weapon, the scene unfolds like a sacrificial rite. It's a Revenger's Tragedy, an ancient justice. Like William Wallace in *Braveheart* (1995), Don's crimes are carved into his body.

He brutalised Gal, so Gal beats him. He mocked Jackie, so she tears into him. He violated Deedee's sanctuary, so she shoots him in the heart. And still he lashes out. "I fucked Jackie," he says to Aitch, bleeding, knowing it will land harder than a fist. So Aitch delivers the coup de grâce: "Well, I've fucked you now, haven't I?" What goes around comes around. Rabbit, rabbit, why don't you give it a rest?

The murder is revealed to us as the heist unfolds. The film drills down, excavating a single pool while plumbing memory. Don's death coincides with the breakthrough—not just into the vault, but into trauma. Gal still has to face Teddy, but the job is done. Don's dying wish, fulfilled. The final image is idyllic: Enrique, Aitch, Jackie, Deedee, and Gal, back in Spain, lounging around the pool—repaired, refilled, and covering Don's grave. Aitch is off on one of his bullshit jags—"he's at it," as Jackie would say—spinning some nonsense about monkeys with different haircuts. Then Don's voice cuts through, rising from the soundtrack like a curse: "Told you you'd do the job." Gal answers in voiceover: "But you're dead. So shut up."

Darkness has been present all along, even in the sun-drenched frame. Like the blistering light of New Mexico in Billy Wilder's *Ace in the Hole* (1951), or the washed-out desert glare of the same state in *Breaking Bad* (2008–13), brightness here is a cousin of darkness—just as capable of blinding. Gal doesn't see what's coming, whether it's Don or the falling boulder, both burning in the sun. And now, down beneath the pool, through the tunnel, the rabbit paces, clawing at a wooden crate. Inside lies Don, perfectly at ease, smoking a cigarette. This is where the darkness resides—for now.

The Flitcraft Parable

In *The Maltese Falcon* (1930), Sam Spade tells a story omitted from John Huston's otherwise faithful 1941 adaptation, a parable about a man named Flitcraft. Spade had once been hired to find him after he vanished without a trace, leaving behind a wife and children. Five years later, Spade tracks him down in another city—remarried, living a life almost identical to the one he abandoned. Flitcraft explains: one day, walking down the street, a beam fell from a construction site and narrowly missed him. In that moment, he saw how random and meaningless the world could be. The ordered life he had built suddenly felt out of step with the chaos of the universe. So he left, walked away without a word. After drifting for a while, he settled down again, remarried, and resumed almost exactly the life he had fled. Spade's conclusion? The meaning is simple. Flitcraft "adjusted himself to beams falling, and then no more of them fell, and he adjusted himself to them not falling."

Gal was happy. Then the unhappiest man in the world came to visit. And now he's gone. For now.

THREE
SOUND AND VISION
Music Videos

Post-David Fincher and Spike Jonze, and later Mark Romanek and Anton Corbijn, the idea of a director moving from music videos to feature films no longer seems unusual. It's simply one of many routes into filmmaking. But in the 1990s and early 2000s, there was still a stigma attached. Established directors like John Landis and Martin Scorsese might direct a pop video — lending their prestige to Michael Jackson's "Thriller" and "Bad," respectively — but being known as a music video director still carried a faint air of dismissal. It suggested something flashy and insubstantial, associated with glossy, if loveable, fare like Russell Mulcahy's *Highlander* (1986).

But Jonathan Glazer was forthright about being classed as a music video director. "If someone calls me that, I won't take offense to it," he told Anthony Kaufman for *Indiewire* in 2001. "I've tried to use the film and video mediums to my own advantage, and to my own learning. I've actually done them to push the limits each time. I think the actual leap from commercials and music videos to film — even though it's a massive learning curve and the tasks are magnified a million times—is not that big; there is a connection."*

Magnified a million times, but not that big.

"Karmacoma"—Massive Attack (1995)

Glazer's career in music videos began shortly after he started working in advertising. Massive Attack, formed in 1988 in Bristol, were pioneers of what came to be known as trip hop. "Karmacoma," the third single from their second studio album, was Glazer's first music video.

Cinematic pretensions are evident from the start. The video opens with a tracking shot down a hotel corridor, as a man in a short leather coat, carrying a gun, appears to be on the run, like a 1970s undercover cop caught in a 1940s film noir. His muttering can be heard over the music, an unusual technique Glazer will return to throughout his career. It marks the soundtrack as part of the video's narrative fabric, not just the song laid over visuals.

Band members Tricky and 3D rap directly to camera. In one room, a man lies on a couch, bleeding from a gunshot wound, evoking Tim Roth in *Reservoir Dogs*. Other rooms are occupied by eccentrics engaged in strange activities: a man covered in black motor oil photographs himself using a rigged camera setup; a Barton Fink–like figure with towering hair types the word "armacoma" repeatedly, omitting the letter "K." The typing echoes *The Shining* (1980), while the missing "K" might be a nod to Kafka's *The Trial* (1925) and its protagonist. Dialogue from the video bleeds into the song: "I'm a dangerous person," says a bearded man. Two sex workers face an older man, who asks, "Who's going to be a bad girl tonight?" The film references

---

* Anthony Kaufman, "Shooting the *Beast*: Jonathan Glazer Tames the Gangster Genre," *Indiewire*, 12 June 2001.

accumulate. 3D shrinks—*The Incredible Shrinking Man* (1957). The oiled man withdraws a finger from his belly—*Videodrome* (1983). Twin girls stand in the hallway—*The Shining*, again.

The atmosphere and set design evoke a seedy gangster aesthetic reminiscent of *Performance* (1970), especially the musical sequence where Mick Jagger sings "Memo from Turner." A man in underpants stands on a plastic-covered bed, suggesting golden showers. A child, dressed like an adult, sits watching television and mimics a newsreader reporting on a heist, presumably the one involving the bleeding man and the gunman in the corridor.

The twin girls hand the gunman a key from a typewriter—the missing "K." His feet stick to the floor as though glued. Atmosphere dominates. There's a ghost of narrative, but Glazer is more interested in weaving references and creating startling images. As Massive Attack's brand is firmly rooted in counterculture—they are outspokenly political—the depiction of a transgressive world aligns with their ethos, if that's not too cynical a way of putting it. It also grants Glazer the freedom to portray decadence and imminent threat without worrying about consumers or clients, as he would in his advertising work—though, as we'll see, pushing those boundaries will eventually land him in trouble.

"The Universal"—Blur (1995)

If *The Shining* was only hinted at in "Karmacoma," then Kubrick's *A Clockwork Orange* is screamed from the rooftops in Glazer's video for Britpop band Blur. A golf ball-like speaker stands in a concrete plaza, evoking Malcolm McDowell's neighbourhood from the film—a space familiar to readers of J. G. Ballard. It's a late-1950s, early-'60s vision of the future, devoid of greenery, designed by men with unhappy marriages, sharp pencils, and little imagination.

The camera slowly tracks in, moving with the same stately pace as the intentionally dreary ballad. Then, matching that rhythm, it tracks out from Damon Albarn's eye—made up like Alex DeLarge—to reveal him and the band, his Droogs, seated in a pristine white version of the Korova Milk Bar. The original, of course, was black. Here, they double as the house band, playing with studied indifference, far from their usual kinetic style. Albarn occasionally strikes a David Bowie-like theatrical pose, wearing the crooked, malevolent smile of a demonic ventriloquist's dummy. Guitarist Graham Coxon sits on the floor. The audience comprises a strange, elite group: a priest and a young man, an opera singer surrounded by admirers, two old men in tanning goggles. Meanwhile, outside by the speaker, people gather like inmates from *The Prisoner*, the cult TV show from the late 1960s starring Patrick McGoohan.

Dystopia is also present in the song's lyrics, with their vision of a future already arrived—satellite television, karaoke, "but the words are wrong." This "Universal" is something that "really, really, really could happen." Part threat, part promise.

Compared to "Karmacoma," Glazer's work here feels more controlled and consistent, more recognisably a pop video. It's less fragmented, more immediately striking, but also antiseptic and cynical. It's MTV-ready. Albarn's sneer is mechanical—not the rage of punk, nor a genuine emotional response—and that artificiality permeates the entire video.

Kubrick's vision was of a future steeped in chaotic violence, rape, and moral decay—meant to shock and provoke. But its afterlife has been oddly cosmetic. The most superficial elements—the clothes, makeup, and poses—have become iconic. The anti-heroes have been recast as plain heroes. The nightmare future is now available on mugs and T-shirts.

A revival of *A Clockwork Orange* came in the 1990s with a Royal Shakespeare Company stage version starring Phil Daniels, star of *Quadrophenia* and guest vocalist on Blur's "Parklife" (also the soundtrack for Glazer's Nike ad). The production premiered at the Barbican and featured music by Bono and The Edge. With screenings of the film banned in the UK by Kubrick himself, it acquired the aura of forbidden fruit. Many—including me—first watched it on poor-quality VHS transfers from the Netherlands. It was one of those films that was watched but not seen, engaged with more as an artefact than as cinema. Alex and his Droogs became countercultural figures, anti-heroes with the emphasis on "hero." Malcolm McDowell gave endless interviews about that one film, rarely ending a story without the line, "but that was Stanley all over." Alex became a fashion icon. A pop star.

What other cultural context could make a pop group say, "Hey, you know those rapists in that film? Let's dress up like them"?

"Street Spirit (Fade Out)" — Radiohead (1996)

Jonathan Glazer's collaboration with Oxford rock band Radiohead began in 1996 with the video for "Street Spirit (Fade Out)," from their commercially successful second album *The Bends*. It's beautiful music, but Cher (Alicia Silverstone) in *Clueless* (1995) nails it when, upon hearing Radiohead, she exclaims: "Yuck! What is it about college and cry-baby music?"

"That was definitely a turning point in my own work," Glazer says. "I knew when I finished that, because they found their own voices as an artist, at that point, I felt like I got close to whatever mine was, and I felt confident that I could do things that emoted, that had some kind of poetic as well as prosaic value. That for me was a key moment."*

Shot over two nights in the desert outside Los Angeles, with Stephen Keith Roach as cinematographer, the video is presented in stark black and white. A rumble of thunder sounds before the arpeggiated guitar begins. Lead singer Thom Yorke stands on the roof of an old trailer, looks behind him—checking there's no safety net—and falls backwards, like a trust exercise gone wrong, the goal being not to be caught, but to hit the earth as hard as you can. As he falls in slow motion, we brace for impact, but the cut arrives before he hits the ground.

The other band members jump, fall and run, but their movements are manipulated. Lights flicker. Time reverses. Images fade in and out, in sync with the lyrics: "fade out, again." Speed-ramping—abrupt changes from slow to fast motion—permeates the video, with figures moving at different speeds within the same frame. There's something of Jean Cocteau's experimental cinema here, especially *Beauty and the Beast* (1946) and *Testament of Orpheus* (1960): simple, poetic effects, executed with real flair.

There are also echoes of *Eraserhead* (1977) and the deep-focus cinematography of Gregg Toland on *Citizen Kane* (1941), especially when a snow-globe-like shower falls around a bare tree. A shirtless boy stares directly at the camera. Feathers drift. Locusts hover. A tin of black paint is thrown and dodged.

You can imagine the video functioning almost like a sketchbook for Glazer: an opportunity to test out bits of kit and in-camera effects. There's no narrative. Just a setting, a few props, the band, some dancers, and the camera.

---

* Anthony Kaufman.

The darkness (visible) of the background feels total—consuming, absorbing—but not threatening. The music lends the images a magnetic glamour, just as the images imbue the music with a series of falls and yearning gestures. In the final moment, Thom Yorke leaps into the air and hangs there—not soaring, not falling, just suspended.

"Virtual Insanity"—Jamiroquai (1996)

When talking about his award-winning video for "Virtual Insanity," it's telling that Glazer focuses on the budget. The original concept came from Jamiroquai's frontman, Jay Kay, who imagined himself dancing in a room while the walls and furniture moved around him. He believed this could be achieved using travelators—the pedestrian conveyor belts found in airports—as the floor, moving him while the set remained stationary. But Glazer had a different idea: he wanted the entire set to move using hydraulics. This would have proved far too expensive—costing £280,000, well over the £150,000 budget—so an alternative had to be found.

That alternative came from a crew member whose name has been lost to time and is never credited in interviews. His idea was brilliantly simple: keep the floor clean, unmarked, and stationary, and instead mount the set on wheels. Furniture pieces sat on coasters, so they could either glide with the moving walls or remain bolted to the floor, appearing to move independently. If needed, items could also be attached directly to the walls, allowing them to move in various directions depending on the choreography. The camera was bolted to one wall, creating a fixed perspective and the illusion that Kay was sliding around the room along with the furniture, while everything else appeared still. Each of the four walls was assigned a cardinal direction—north, south, east, west—and the crew were instructed accordingly: "East fast, south slow," and so on.

This elegant and low-tech solution allowed the video to be choreographed in a single day and shot the next. In post-production, a bird and a bug—both reminiscent of *Naked Lunch* (1959) by William S. Burroughs, filmed in 1991 by David Cronenberg—were added. The camera tilts down to the bug or up to the bird to disguise the cuts between the four takes that made up the final video.

The set design is steel grey and institutional light blue. The walls, made up of square panels, could be safety deposit boxes—*Sexy Beast*'s vault?—or perhaps morgue drawers. One thing is clear: under the harsh fluorescent lighting, "We all live underground," as one lyric puts it. Against this stark backdrop, Kay's smooth, seemingly effortless dance becomes the central focus. He weaves through gliding furniture with ease, embodying the song's theme of navigating an unstable future—only to conclude with surprising optimism: "It's all alright."

Wondering where the Kubrick reference is? Don't worry. Toward the end of the video, blood appears, leaking from a sofa, just as it pours from the elevator in *The Shining*. And the smooth, pale minimalism of the room itself evokes the stark hotel suite from *2001: A Space Odyssey*.

The video won several awards, including "Best Video" at the 1997 MTV Awards. "I may not love Jay Kay particularly as an artist," Glazer later remarked, "but I admire what he does. That was just a good stage for his talent."*

Only a year after "Karmacoma," "Virtual Insanity" established Glazer as an award-winning director and a

---

* "The Making of Virtual Insanity," Play UK, https://www.youtube.com/watch?v=MzwY7ii582Y.

leader in the field of music videos—a huge leap forward from his first foray.

"Into My Arms"—Nick Cave and the Bad Seeds (1997)
Emerging from the Australian post-punk band The Birthday Party, Nick Cave gradually cultivated a more mainstream appeal—a trajectory that would eventually see him invited to the King's coronation, featured on *Desert Island Discs*, and regularly described as a "national treasure." It's quite the journey for a singer who, in John Hillcoat's *Ghosts... of the Civil Dead* (1988), played a psychopath who smears his cell with his own excrement. A key step in that transformation was *The Boatman's Call*, a stripped-back album of elegiac, beautifully sung songs. "Into My Arms," its lead single, is the album's most extreme example of minimalism: just piano, bass, and a quietly devastating lyric that begins, "I don't believe in an interventionist God."

The video is similarly minimal. Superficially, it resembles Glazer's earlier work on Radiohead's "Street Spirit (Fade Out)." Cave sings—sometimes three-quarters turned, sometimes directly to camera—lit in stark black and white, surrounded by a darkness so complete it feels existential. Like the void at the edge of town in "Street Spirit," but deeper, more Lynchian: the kind of darkness from which either monsters or beautiful women might emerge.

Intercut with Cave are a series of close-ups—people responding to the song, or so the video implies. They are visibly upset, wrestling with emotion, or crying openly. Tears in a music video can be powerful. Godley & Creme's "Cry" (1986) is an early example, with faces cross-fading in close-up, which Glazer's video clearly echoes. Sinead O'Connor's spontaneous tears in "Nothing Compares 2 U" (1990) helped cement her international profile.

But here, the emotion feels oddly disconnected from the song's quiet, redemptive tone. In fact, Cave himself disliked the video. Not much happens, and what does feels oddly contrived. The inclusion of random children, for instance, seems like a calculated attempt to add visual poignancy, with little behind it but the assumption that it will "look good."

It's a shame, because Cave has a genuine relationship with cinema — as actor, screenwriter and composer — and "Into My Arms" is a deeply evocative song, inspired by a visit to a church while Cave was in rehab. The video, however, never quite earns its emotion.

"Karma Police" — Radiohead (1997)

The follow-up to "Street Spirit (Fade Out)" came with a song from the seminal album *OK Computer*: the single "Karma Police." The idea for the video first emerged as a short film, dreamed up while a hungover Glazer dozed through a Los Angeles screening of David Lynch's *Lost Highway* (1997), waking with the image of a road rushing toward him in the dead of night. The concept was initially pitched to Marilyn Manson for his song "Long Road Out of Hell," but Manson passed.

We open inside a car furnished in plush retro upholstery the colour of uncooked veal, then turn toward the windscreen to look out into the dark. The blackness of night, the road lit by headlights, and the green verges drawing the eye to the vanishing point all foreshadow the poster design Glazer will later use for *The Zone of Interest*. An internal light flashes on as an unseen passenger enters the car, then clicks off again. The motor starts. We begin to move.

We appear to be in the driver's seat. From the edge of visibility, a man emerges, running hopelessly away as we gain on him. He's wearing a shirt and trousers, his shoes and cuffs caked in mud. Is this a gangster film chase scene, *Performance*-style? Are we Droogs enjoying "real country dark, my brothers," in *A Clockwork Orange*?

Just as it looks like the man is about to be run down, the camera turns. Thom Yorke is in the back seat, lazily lip-synching a few lines before the camera—with smooth, CCTV-style detachment—returns to the pursuit. The car moves at a leisurely pace, but the man never tries to leave the road. There's an uncanny sense that some strange rules are being followed. When the camera shifts again, Yorke is disturbingly close, leaning over the front passenger seat to watch. He's not engaged in the chase—if chase it is—any more than he is in his singing. It's dream logic.

Unlike "Street Spirit," this video has something like a narrative—it's a chase, a journey—but halfway through, the action reverses. Two and a half minutes of the running time (so to speak) are made up of a single shot. We cut to the man running: Lajos Kovács, a Hungarian actor with an extensive filmography—including *Wings of Desire* (1987)—and who will later appear in one of Glazer's Guinness ads. The headlights flare as he runs in close-up. He collapses onto his hands and knees. The shoot was physically punishing. His legs cramped, and he badly burned his thumb.

The car draws closer. He turns and glares at it, prompting it to reverse—maybe to accelerate for a final blow, maybe as a show of mercy. Maybe it's just prolonging the cruelty. The car, backlit and fuming, recalls the demon vehicle from John Carpenter's *Christine* (1983). Then the man spots a trail of leaking fuel. He pulls a matchbook from his pocket, the kind you might get at a hotel or bar. Its cover shows the silhouette of a foetus (a nod to the Star Baby from Kubrick's *2001: A Space Odyssey*?). He strikes a match and lights the petrol. The car reverses as the flame races toward it. The hunter becomes the hunted. The fire engulfs the front of the car. As the camera swings from side to side—malfunctioning, it seems—we see the back seat is now empty. Thom Yorke is gone. The song collapses into grinding noise as we burn alone.

Once again, Glazer begins with darkness. If he were a painter, he would start with a black canvas. The video anticipates three of his later films: the gangster world of *Sexy Beast*; the vehicle-as-predator perspective of *Under the Skin*; and the obsidian aesthetic of *The Zone of Interest.* All of this years before any of them were made.

There's also the idea that the camera itself can commit acts of violence. This isn't new. *Rear Window* (1954) and *Peeping Tom* (1960) both explored cameras as accomplices in crime, implicating the viewer in voyeurism. A camera can place us in control, watching others suffer unseen. Just as quickly, it can fix us in place, passive before the spectacle. James Stewart in his wheelchair, helpless as Raymond Burr approaches. Karlheinz Böhm behind the lens, forcing his victims to watch themselves die.

For all that, Glazer wasn't satisfied. "I regard 'Karma Police' as a complete failure, because I decided to do a very minimalist, subjective use of camera, and tried to do something hypnotic and dramatic from one perspective, and it was very hard to achieve, and I feel that I didn't achieve it."[*]

"Rabbit in Your Headlights" — Unkle (ft. Thom Yorke) (1998)

With the video for UNKLE's "Rabbit in Your Headlights," Glazer took the opportunity to try again, describing it as a companion piece to "Karma Police." "I did the UNKLE video because I felt I had missed

---

[*] Anthony Kaufman.

emotionally and dramatically from a simple craft point of view," he later said.*

Coincidentally, Thom Yorke was providing vocals for the British electronic trip-hop duo, and Glazer cast one of his favourite actors: "Denis Lavant has an incredible pathos to him. But he's also a funny man. He flips between comedy and pathos."† Glazer had previously worked with the French actor on a series of commercials—the aforementioned "Last Orders" for Stella Artois, and another, unscreened, for Cadbury's Flake. Lavant was already known for his extraordinary physicality, distinctive appearance, and collaborations with Leos Carax in films like *Mauvais Sang* (1986) and *Les Amants du Pont-Neuf* (1991), and later in Claire Denis' *Beau Travail* (1999). The scene of Lavant running to David Bowie's "Modern Love" in *Mauvais Sang* plays like a music video in itself, while his final dance in *Beau Travail* transforms his character into something strange and newly born.

In "Rabbit in Your Headlights," Lavant wears a blue parka with the hood up, a snorkel coat familiar to many British kids of Glazer's generation. He trudges through a tunnel: a liminal, inhuman space where pedestrians don't belong. It's a close cousin to the bank vault/swimming pool tunnel in *Sexy Beast* and the tunnel connecting Rudolf Höss' house to the death camp in *The Zone of Interest*.

Lavant seems completely unaware of his danger. Cars flash their lights, honk their horns, and swerve to avoid him. He mutters to himself, wrapped in an internal monologue that occasionally flares into something louder, more passionate, oblivious to the universe surrounding him. Eventually, one of the cars clips him. It feels like an impatient shove—petty, but devastating to

---

* Ibid.
† Anthony Kaufman.

the human body. Lavant lies prone on the road, maybe dead. Then his eyes open. He stands and continues. Then he is hit again.

The collisions become more frequent, more violent. He flips like a ragdoll. What was only threatened in "Karma Police" becomes a bone-breaking reality: man versus machine. The dread builds. Lavant sheds his coat without breaking stride, revealing a bruised, wounded body. How long has he been walking this road? Finally, he stops. Arms raised. Head lifted. Is it surrender, or pure defiance? A car slams into him from behind at full speed, but this time, the machine crumples. Lavant stands, unmoved. Smoke surrounds him. Arms outstretched, he accepts the grace of survival.

The setting—the tunnel—was particularly reso-nant. A year earlier, Princess Diana had died in a car crash in a similar Paris tunnel, pursued by paparazzi. As noted before, Glazer's tunnels are thresholds: between life and death, between comfort and annihilation. In *Birth,* a park underpass becomes a birth canal; tunnels also appear in *Sexy Beast* and *The Zone of Interest.*

"Rabbit in Your Headlights" marked a more ambi-tious turn in Glazer's music video work. The narrative is fully realised. A character is introduced and sustained. The video feels so strong, so self-contained, that it's easy to imagine the soundtrack was composed for the short film, rather than the video made to promote the song. As in "Karmacoma," diegetic sound overtakes the track: Lavant's muttering, the horns, the shouts. At one point, a car full of young men pulls alongside to taunt him, their dialogue interrupting the music.

There are three major ideas from Philip K. Dick's *Do Androids Dream of Electric Sheep?* (1968) that didn't make it into *Blade Runner* (1982): the Mood Organ, Buster Friendly, and Mercerism—three tools designed to console the last humans on a ruined Earth. The Mood Organ allows users to dial up any emotion. Buster Friendly, a relentless TV personality, may be an android, since his nonstop presence on air exceeds human capacity. The final idea, Mercerism, offers a kind of communal spiritual therapy. By gripping the handles of an Empathy Box, celebrants are drawn into a virtual reality in which they walk with a stoic, battered old man—Wilbur Mercer—climbing a hill while unseen forces hurl rocks at him. In feeling Mercer's pain, participants experience connection, which translates into spiritual elevation.

Denis Lavant in "Rabbit in Your Headlights" recalls Wilbur Mercer. He is a human figure battered by modernity, all too vulnerable in a world of steel, speed, and exhaust. And yet he keeps going—stoic, solitary—until he becomes something triumphant: a figure of resistance, a man wreathed in smoke and headlights, walking straight into transcendence.

"A Song for the Lovers"—Richard Ashcroft (2000)

Pop promos are a chance to build up a musician's persona beyond the concert stage—to give them a glow of cinematic reality while offering the audience a closer, more intimate view. Richard Ashcroft's band The Verve had broken up, and although "A Song for the Lovers" was originally written for them, it became his first single as a solo artist.

Playing up Ashcroft's rockstar persona, Glazer makes a short film that only intermittently uses the song it is meant to promote. It's playful in the way the film takes over, letting diegetic sound—sound occurring within the scene—dominate the soundtrack. The setting is one of the most clichéd in offstage rock iconography: the hotel room. But here it's reduced to banality.

The video opens with a loud flickering neon light—like the one in Leon's bathroom in *Blade Runner*—as we follow a shirtless Ashcroft into his hotel suite, towel around his shoulders. He sits on the bed, slips on his rings, grabs the remote, and turns on the music.

The rest of the video shows Ashcroft doing mundane things—phoning room service to complain about a missing order ("It's been thirty minutes"), washing, fiddling with his hair, picking at a sandwich. The drama, such as it is, is hilariously low-stakes. There's a banging at the door while he's in the bathroom, drowned out by running water (and the song). It sounds menacing, but turns out to be room service.

This is a Lynchian hotel: subdued lighting, crackling neon, and the unsettling sense that even in the most ordinary spaces, something lurks—Bob from *Twin Peaks*, the demon from the dumpster in *Mulholland Drive*. The camera glides through the rooms. Does it have malign intent?

Ashcroft is bored, yet also contentedly singing along with his own song. But something feels off in this temporary home. He pauses the music, as if to insult it one final time, and listens carefully. Has he heard something? Is he alone? How did the tray of limp sandwiches get into the room? We didn't see anyone bring it.

He approaches the bathroom. The shower curtain, closed from the start, remains drawn. What's behind it? The old woman from another Kubrick film? He gazes at something off camera, and then—puncturing the tension—the silence is broken by the splash of his piss hitting the toilet bowl. The song resumes. As it plays out, the camera retreats from the bathroom in a slow tracking shot, leaving Ashcroft framed in a doorway of light—a reverse monolith in the surrounding dark.

The film works as a short. It's less clear how it functions as a music video, except by subverting the form—literally taking the piss. The song is interrupted twice, muffled behind a door, and has no privileged place on the soundtrack. It becomes one among several ambient noises.

We watch Ashcroft wander his underlit, oversized hotel suite, shirtless, the song playing in the background. His movements are a slouch, just as Jay Kay's are a slide and Denis Lavant's a trudging march toward something greater.

The story turns out to be nothing. The sense of dread, unfounded. The film ends—an exercise in style, well executed, but self-consciously unimportant. If anything, it satirises and deconstructs Ashcroft's rock god image. This star isn't trashing the room or tossing TVs out the window; he is complaining about room service and unimpressed by the sandwiches.

"Live with Me" — Massive Attack (2006)

A decade had passed before Jonathan Glazer directed his second collaboration with Massive Attack, and his growth as a storyteller in the interim was significant. In that time, he had made a string of music videos and two feature films. Gone was the scattergun approach to pop culture references. As in "Karma Police" and "A Song for the Lovers," the song becomes a prompt for Glazer to tell a story, one that aligns with the soulfulness and heartbreak of the track, but that does not perform the usual function of a pop video. It plays instead like a piece of social realist cinema, reminiscent of Claire Denis or the Dardenne brothers.

The promo opens on a coughing town crier, silhouetted in spotlights, calling: "Oyez! Oyez! Roll out the barrel, we'll have a barrel of fun." It's a deliberate misdirection. The jubilant tone is completely at odds with what follows.

Exterior. Night. London. A professionally dressed young woman, played by Kirsty Shepherd, walks into an off-licence on a busy street to buy what looks like enough alcohol for a large party. A couple of men outside make comments to that effect, sharing a laugh—a joke among strangers. She then moves through the city's night-time streets, the camera tracking her from a distance, picking her out from the crowd with long lenses, in a style Glazer will later use in *Under the Skin*. The people around her seem unaware they are being filmed.

Inside her flat, she begins drinking almost immediately—starting with a can of beer before she's even unpacked, then swigging vodka straight from the bottle while still in her coat. She tosses the cap away. This bottle won't be set down until it's empty.

The rockstar intimacy of "A Song for the Lovers" now becomes something uncomfortable. There, the man was confident, only slightly perturbed. Here, we are intruding. We don't know what's happening. Her phone is flashing. The flat is tidy, well-kept. But she drinks with the discipline of experience. Is this a "raging alcoholic" or a "binge drinker"?

Language around alcohol itself begins to slur. It gets squiffy on its own fumes, staggering toward meaning and bumping into the furniture. Has she suffered a crisis? Is her heart broken? How does any of this relate to the love song being sung over her slow collapse? Is this realism— or a life concertinaed into a single moment?

It is an uncomfortable watch, and the context— a music video—feels almost inappropriate. We see her urinating. In "A Song for the Lovers," Richard Ashcroft's piss was a punchline. Here, she sits with her underwear around her knees, drinking still, as if she has become nothing more than a tube, running from bottle to toilet. It's as far from *Eyes Wide Shut*'s pristine image of Nicole Kidman on the bathroom floor as you can imagine, and yet there's the Kubrick connection again.

Now trouserless—what's the point of pulling them up just to take them down again, in booze logic—she staggers. In the kitchen, several empty bottles are visible. She admires a necklace (perhaps a gift from a relation-ship now lost) in the mirror.

When she ventures outside again, she is visibly vulnerable. Strangers passing recognise her distress. Some seem inclined to help. Others look like they might take advantage. It anticipates the scene in *Under the Skin* when Scarlett Johansson's alien collapses on the street, prompting real, unscripted acts of compassion from those around her.

She lies down on a park bench. She also falls — endlessly — down a spiral staircase with a golden hue. Suddenly, realism is revealed to have always been meta-phor. The table in the flat held an impossible number of bottles. Now she tumbles through a staircase without end. This is a nosedive without a bottom. A fall that doesn't stop. On the bench, she looks up at the sky, and we cut to a striking, impossible view: a bright starry night over London, undimmed by light pollution. It's science fiction again.

The song, with vocals by Terry Callier, is a soulful plea: "I've been thinking about you, baby/Come live with me." It's lushly orchestrated, with a bluesy electric piano and swelling bass. Comments under the video on YouTube often say the same thing: "This song helped me stop drinking. I am 15 months clean." "Today is my first day clean in months. I don't know why, but I needed to revisit this." "28 months today. Feel solid. Need to revisit this once in a while."

"Treat Me Like Your Mother" — The Dead Weather (2009)
The opening shot: what looks like an old-fashioned cartoon anarchist bomb, spinning on the ground. Cut to a tracking shot of Jack White walking. Alison Mosshart, lead singer of White's supergroup The Dead Weather, is seen in a separate shot, striding forward with equal

purpose. The setting is a nondescript suburban landscape (it was filmed in Lancaster, California) behind some houses. White and Mosshart are dressed in black leather jackets, evoking a *Near Dark* (1987) goth vibe, and both are armed. : White with an M4 carbine, Mosshart with a Heckler & Koch MP5. They load their weapons, and, at a preordained distance, turn.

Apparently, they have been walking away from each other all this time, as if pacing out the ground for a duel—machine guns at dawn—and now, facing one another, they begin to fire. They land hits and take them, bleeding, but continue undeterred, closing the gap while peppering each other at point-blank range. Despite multiple wounds, neither shows pain. Like Denis Lavant in "Rabbit in Your Headlights," they exist in a universe beyond injury. As they run out of ammunition, Jack White stumbles away. Sunlight pours through the bullet holes in their bodies—another visual echo of *Near Dark*.

The video looks good. It's built on effective minimalism: one location, two characters, long takes. There's integrity in its refusal to cut away to the rest of the band or a performance setup. The action-movie aesthetic—part Spaghetti Western, part Peckinpah—is unique for Glazer and feels like an experiment. He's trying something out, not necessarily aiming to make a feature in this register. There's exaggeration, even pastiche. As in "A Song for the Lovers," we're in a world of rock gods and posturing, but played with a dry wit.

If there's controversy, it lies in the gunplay: a violent power fantasy built on stylish nihilism. But in a country where school shootings are routine, this kind of imagery now passes without comment.

At the time of writing, it's been sixteen years since Glazer last directed a music promo. The ten videos he made show a director capable of creating polished, iconic works ("The Universal," "Virtual Insanity"), while also undercutting the pomposity of the format ("A Song for the Lovers"), and pushing the medium into entirely new realms ("Rabbit in Your Headlights," "Live with Me"). His impulse to go beyond the genre's expectations is clearest in his repeated use of diegetic sound to interrupt or undermine the track, and in "A Song for Lovers," to treat the song with complete indifference.

Only *Sexy Beast* and *Birth* were made during the years he was still occasionally directing music videos, and even then, he worked infrequently—just four promos between 1998 and 2009. Glazer's ten music videos are a modest tally compared to the directors mentioned earlier in this chapter: David Fincher has directed thirty-four, Spike Jonze thirty-five, and Mark Romanek forty-five. And yet, Glazer's collection includes some of the best examples of the form. As with his films, his quality control rests on a tight grip over how much product reaches the world.

So what can we learn from them?

First, there is range. It's hard to isolate a single signature Glazer move. Perhaps it's what they *aren't* that becomes the defining feature as his work matures. With the exception of "The Universal" and "Virtual Insanity," most of the videos downplay performance. Many actively undercut the persona of the band or singer. In "Rabbit in Your Headlights," the star is Denis Lavant, not the band, not even the vocalist.

These videos operate more like short films, where a single narrative thread is played through to conclusion. A journey is undertaken, often quite literally, and often back and forth: "Karma Police," "Treat Me Like Your Mother." There's dynamism, but only "Virtual Insanity" turns that movement into a performance of the song itself. In the others, movement comes as meandering, marching, tumbling, being hit by cars.

Like his work in advertising, Glazer's music videos grow bolder and more confident as they go. It's instructive to compare "Karmacoma" and "Live with Me," both made for Massive Attack a decade apart. In the first, the band is prominently featured; in the second, they are entirely absent. The story is complete, independent. It's a film with a great soundtrack, not a music video selling a single. That—rather than the stylish but slight "Treat Me Like Your Mother"—feels like the true culmination of Glazer's music video career.

FOUR
BIRTH

Death is a near life experience
At the end of Chapter Two, the Flitcraft Parable from
Dashiell Hammett's *The Maltese Falcon* taught us that
sometimes beams fall and almost kill us—and then
they don't fall anymore, and life reverts to the mean.
Both realities must be reckoned with. You can die, but
life goes on. There are tunnels you run through. Some
you enter and emerge from the other end. Others you
enter... and never come out. Is there even an end to the
tunnel? Or is the tunnel simply all there is?

At the beginning of *Birth*, Jonathan Glazer's second
feature-length film, Sean (Michael Desautels) runs into
one such tunnel and never comes out the other end.

We have seen tunnels before in Glazer's work.
They're transgressive. They take you into bank vaults
where secrets and treasure, death and money, are kept.
And they're dangerous. If you can tunnel in, other
things can tunnel out. Like Don Logan in *Sexy Beast*.
He hasn't quite surfaced yet, but that rabbit doesn't look
like it's going to stay underground for long.

In Glazer's 1995 music video "Rabbit in Your
Headlights," Denis Lavant trudges heedlessly through
the hostile confines of a traffic-choked tunnel, enduring
a series of brutal collisions he somehow survives.

In *Birth*, a tunnel becomes a birth canal to the grave. Pozzo's final lines Samuel Beckett's and *Waiting for Godot* (1952): "They give birth astride of a grave, the light gleams an instant, then it's night once more." Can we invert the image and see the dead falling back into vaginas, tunnelling their way back to the womb?

We never properly meet Sean. A quick Google search turns up a photograph of an actor who looks very much like a stock image of "young man," and *Birth* appears to be his only credit. We hear him before we see anything. He's giving a speech to what sounds like a room full of students. It's the end of a Q&A following a lecture, and he is responding to a final question we didn't quite hear. The speech begins while the New Line Cinema logo is still twirling into existence, already wrong-footing us. Watching that logo, I'm thinking of *The Lord of the Rings* (2001). Others might be thinking of horror movies. Has the film already started? Are we already too late? Did I miss something coming in? Are we *in medias res*?

I live in Italy and teach English at the University of Ca' Foscari in Venice. One of my small delights is casually mentioning my imminent death and watching my students recoil in superstitious horror. Italians are still very, very superstitious. I'll say something like, "I'll see you next Wednesday, unless I die this weekend." And as they gasp—unless they've heard it before and are already bored of my shenanigans—I'll push it a bit further: "Imagine how cool it would be if I actually did die this weekend, and you could all say, 'He was joking about it the other day, and now he really is dead.'"

Sean seems to be doing something similar. He's speculating that if his wife died and then came back as a little bird, perched somewhere saying, "Hi, I'm Anna. I've come back," that might shake his otherwise scientific worldview. But otherwise—no. He's a man of reason, and he has no time for that sort of guff. I don't do space crystals, homeopathy or other forms of magical thinking either. (Short of a talking bird showing up to contradict me.)

Then he says he has to go for a run. To the Prokofiev-lite notes of Alexandre Desplat's jaunty prologue music, he jogs through a snowy Central Park as the camera follows him with the smooth, controlled certainty of Stanley Kubrick's opening shot in *The Shining* (1980). The shot goes on just long enough for us to notice it—long enough for our expectations to rise. It holds the same pace, keeping Sean's dark figure centred in the frame. It follows at a high, giraffe-like angle. Not quite a God's-eye view, but something powerful and interventionist. A hawk.

The talk of death, the winter cold, and the run through slippery Brueghel snow leave us subtly unsettled, despite the brightness of the music. The presence of the camera makes us wary: cameras don't usually follow people to whom nothing happens. Sean runs into one tunnel and emerges at the other end. Phew.

Then a cut—to a more conventional long shot, an establishing shot of sorts, even though it lands in the middle of the scene. We see Sean in the distance. We're no longer following him. We slowly realise, as he draws closer and the camera begins to retreat, that we're waiting for him. The frame is overtaken by the frame of another tunnel—one we're already in. Lurking? And now he enters. Something happens.

Death happens.

Sean staggers, bends and collapses.

What does it feel like?

We can't know until we do. And then what good will it do us? As Louis Cyphre (Robert De Niro) says in Alan Parker's *Angel Heart* (1987): "How terrible is wisdom that brings no profit to those who are wise!"

Sean dies, alone. No last words, no opportunity to settle his affairs. Cut off in the prime of life, in the full flood of his sin. As the ghost of Hamlet's father puts it: "No reckoning made, but sent to my account with all my imperfections on my head." Sean leaves behind only confusion, misunderstandings—the mess. There is no closure. We move in, but his face remains in deep shadow. A close-up that reveals nothing.

The only witness is this camera.

And who is behind that camera?

Initially, it was Harris Savides.* Savides made his name in the 1990s shooting high-profile music videos for the likes of Madonna, working with directors such as David Fincher and Mark Romanek. He went on to shoot films for Noah Baumbach, Gus Van Sant (notably the "Death" trilogy: *Gerry* [2002], *Elephant* [2005] and *Last Days* [2005]), and Sofia Coppola, and later reunited with Fincher for what may be his masterpiece: *Zodiac* (2007). For Zachary Wigon, Jonathan Glazer's *Birth* represents the pinnacle of Savides' career: "I think *Birth* is Savides' greatest work. The creaminess of the film, of the texture, which persists despite a definite grain, is a great counterintuitive feat of cinematography."†

Savides was known for working at the absolute limits of what could be captured on screen. What directors sought and admired, says Wigon, was his ability to achieve a "vivid creaminess" while preserving the grain and texture of the image. On *Birth,* he achieved this by underexposing two stops and then pulling an additional two in processing—yielding a surprising level of detail in the darkness while still embracing the shadows. This method also gave him a lower-contrast image, with milky

---

* Garrett Brown, inventor of the Steadicam and one of its best operators, also contributed to filming this sequence.
† Zachary Wigon, "The Toenail of the Curve: Remembering Harris Savides," *Filmmaker*, October 2012.

blacks that are really more dark browns and purples than true black. (Savides often cited Rembrandt and Georges de La Tour as key influences.)

Stops are relative measures of light: if a single candle is one stop, then two candles are two stops. Underexposing or overexposing film allows the cinematographer to pull or push stops—decreasing or increasing the amount of light that registers on the finished image. It's the cinematic art of rendering darkness visible. In Fincher's *Zodiac*, San Francisco becomes a nocturnal chiaroscuro of murderous spaces where the killer might be hiding. Savides was known for pushing the envelope—or closing it entirely—on how little light could be used while still registering an image on film. Sometimes his light metre wouldn't even register a reading. To achieve these edge-of-oblivion results, Savides had to experiment relentlessly—testing lenses and film stock, lighting setups and chemical processes.

These extremes were not only tolerated but encouraged by his director. "The margins were so narrow," Glazer said, "but once we'd seen the promise of those early camera tests—that luminosity—we went all out."[*]

Savides put it more simply: "It's purely about evoking the feeling. What feels better is that creaminess, that softness—it's a dreamier picture while you're watching. It just takes you a little bit away from reality, and more into your mind."[†]

Studio executives responsible for *Birth* were less impressed with what they were seeing in the dailies. A crew member, Jason McCormick recalls that Savides "was about to get fired from *Birth*, 100 percent true. They were tripping on how thin the negative was. There was a screening, it was shown the way it was intended,

---

[*] Chris O'Falt, "The Best of the Best," *IndieWire*, 15 August 2014.
[†] Ibid.

and everybody was in the room. And when they saw it, he said you could hear the breath escaping people. It ended and they turned and said, 'Just keep doing what you're doing.'"*

Savides died of a brain tumour at the age of 55. It may seem a gratuitous detail in the context of a film he worked on, but the camera implies a kind of immunity. As Christopher Isherwood writes at the start of *Goodbye to Berlin* (1939), his memoir of Germany's Nazification in the thirties: "I am a camera." Isherwood's aloofness, his sense of immunity, his neutrality and to some extent his privilege (though his homosexuality would become potentially fatal under Nazi rule) are encapsulated in this modernist, mechanical image.

In *Birth*, the camera watches steadily, and then sees something else, even as Sean collapses and dies. The camera outlasts everyone. But the cameraman doesn't. The camera survives; the eye doesn't. The tunnel, a low oval, looks like an eye. Think of how it must have felt for Homer's listeners to hear the deaths of all those Greeks and Trojans before the spears of Achilles and Hector, each warrior thudding to the earth, bronze armour clattering around them. Each listener member could imagine those heroes. They could even, at the death of mighty Hector, think: "Well, I'm still alive. I'm still here. I'll lie in my bed tonight and wake up tomorrow morning."

It's only a temporary triumph though. Death takes all.

Death is the disrupter, the interrupter, but life goes on, a fact some find comforting and others find even worse. When a loved one dies, shouldn't we, as Auden wrote, "stop all the clocks"? And yet even that is temporary.

Asked about the strangeness of the film's concept, Nicole Kidman told Glenn Whipp of *The Los Angeles*

---

* Chris O'Falt.

Times: "I never found it strange. I found it profound, the way it deals with grief and how people will fill holes to explain things, needing to explain things and then being incredibly open to all possibilities when you're in a deeply vulnerable state... Grief isn't finite because it most definitely isn't. Grief never ends."*

And yet something else happens immediately after Sean's death:

A birth.

The birth of Birth

It was a simple, absurd idea. Glazer remembers the exact moment it came to him. It happened while he was making *Sexy Beast*: "I was in my kitchen with a friend, walking over to the kettle, talking about something completely unrelated. And I said to him, 'I just had a really good idea for a film. There's this little kid and he tells a woman he's her dead husband. And he's ten.' And then I finished making a cup of coffee."†

Glazer expanded the concept from a sentence into a paragraph and brought it to Jean-Claude Carrière, the screenwriter who collaborated with Luis Buñuel for nearly two decades on films such as *Diary of a Chambermaid* (1964), *Belle de Jour* (1967), *The Milky Way* (1969) and *The Phantom of Liberty* (1974), and who also wrote *The Return of Martin Guerre* (1983) and *The Unbearable Lightness of Being* (1988). The Carrière film closest in spirit to *Birth* is *Max, My Love* (1986), which he wrote for Japanese director Nagisa Ōshima. It stars Charlotte Rampling as a sophisticated Parisian mother and wife who falls in love with a monkey from the zoo. With its understated treatment of an extraordinary situation—though a scene in which Max performs

---

* Glenn Whipp, "Nicole Kidman on Making *Birth*," *Los Angeles Times*, 25 April 2024.
† *Dazed and Confused*, December 2004.

cunnilingus on his human lover was excised—it peels back the artificiality of bourgeois life in a surreal fashion reminiscent of Carrière's work with Buñuel. With its portrayal of the untrammelled nature of love and desire pushing into areas forbidden by society, it's easy to see why Glazer might have responded to Carrière's tone and approach. After checking in an encyclopaedia of film to see if Glazer's idea had been done before, Carrière decided it hadn't. He liked it and began writing with Glazer, who occasionally headed over to Paris on weekends to lend a hand.

At the same time, Glazer was also developing an adaptation of Michel Faber's novel *Under the Skin* with Walter Campbell—a friend, collaborator, and self-described "troubleshooter" from Glazer's advertising days. Campbell had written the famous Guinness "Surfer" advert, among many others, and had also maintained a close working relationship with Tony Kaye, another British director who transitioned from advertising to cinema, with *American History X* (1998), starring Edward Norton.

Carrière's version of *Birth* was said to be excellent, good enough, certainly, to attract A-list actresses. Initially, Glazer had his sights on Robin Wright, but then Nicole Kidman read the script and wanted to meet. "I knew I'd recognise if she was right pretty quickly," Glazer told David Thomson. "There was also concern about the exposure her celebrity would bring, and whether I was happy with that." It was one thing to have Charlotte Rampling—an arthouse, off-beat actress—fall in love with a monkey. But could Nicole Kidman fall in love with a child? How would audiences respond? "She got the script almost entirely," Glazer said, "and she had a very peculiar response to it; she talked about it as if she'd written it herself."*

* Roger Clarke, "Grief Encounter," *Sight and Sound*, November 2004.

With Kidman on board, the European setting—London or Paris, which Carrière had originally written—was no longer viable. Milo Addica, screenwriter of *Monster's Ball* (2001), was brought in to revise the script, primarily to relocate the story to New York. Addica's draft soon diverged from the lighter, more verbal version Carrière had produced. Glazer and Addica went back and forth through twenty-one drafts. Meanwhile, *Under the Skin* was put on hold as preproduction on *Birth* continued. A nervous Glazer asked Carrière for advice on his first studio movie. He received two gems: 1. When in doubt point your camera at Nicole Kidman, and 2. Clarity is mystery.

Weeks before filming was set to begin, Glazer realised the script still wasn't ready. Working late into the night, he and Addica shifted the focus from Sean—the boy, to be played by newcomer Cameron Bright—to Anna, the woman, played by Kidman. This was an obvious choice. Star power has its own gravitational pull, bending a project around it. It also would have been a risky gamble to place the dramatic weight of the film on an untested child actor.

As filming began, the writing continued. Pages were drafted overnight and rushed to the cast first thing each morning. Tensions with Miramax executives escalated, becoming what Glazer described as "fucking vicious." "We didn't write the ending until we were walking around a supermarket buying biscuits two days before shooting it," he said. "We could still be writing that film. No question. It's a non-stop series of conundrums. You can constantly put layer onto layer."*

The film opens with a variation on the initial idea that came to Glazer in his kitchen, now twisted into something even more absurd. Instead of a 10-year-old

---

* *Dazed and Confused.*

boy approaching a woman and claiming to be her dead husband, it's a small bird at the window. The premise becomes more supernatural, more transgressive. Not merely a crossing of generations, but of species. A faint echo, perhaps, of Carrière's *Max, My Love*? Or is the bird a fleeting allusion to that beautiful image of life evoked by the Venerable Bede: a sparrow flying through a mead-hall, "passing from winter to winter again"?

From coffee to biscuits, the film took shape — conceived in a kitchen, refined in a supermarket. It is part metaphysical riddle, part thought experiment, part absurdist poem, part practical joke. A hallucination? A delusion?

The "birth" that follows Sean's death is the emergence of another Sean from his mother's birth canal. It appears to be a water birth. The camera is intimately, omnisciently close. Human life, seen this close, looks strange and alien. (Is that a leg?) Bursting through the water, the child transitions from one element into another, like the children in Terrence Malick's *The Tree of Life* (2011), who swim up toward reality, born from their underwater antenatal chambers.

Sean's birth is followed by a title card: "Ten Years Later." We see Anna for the first time, leaning against Sean's grave in a cemetery. She is a Hamlet figure on the battlements of Elsinore, already waiting for the ghost before it appears — manifesting it, to use a term of popular magical thinking. In a 2004 interview with Charlie Rose, Glazer remarked that "she never really leaves the cemetery for the whole film, in a funny way." But rather than mourning a father's death, Anna mourns her husband's; and instead of her mother's wedding, it is her own. Her Claudius — Joseph, a name rich with religious resonance as the holy cuckold, stepfather to Jesus and husband to the Virgin Mary — is played with unctuous charm by

Danny Huston. As the son of legendary director John Huston, he adds another layer of ghostliness, one of the film's many hauntings by old Hollywood.

With a single "Okay" — her first word — Anna signals that it is time to "cast [her] nighted colour off." Unlike Hamlet's mother, she has waited a considerable time, and the delay invites speculation. Was she institutionalised? Is that why her family treats her with such anxious solicitude, surrounding her as if to prevent a sudden escape? Has her hair been shorn by authorities rather than styled in homage to Mia Farrow or Jean Seberg?

Joseph's speech at the engagement party outlines a courtship that stretched over several years. Courtship is a curious thing. The assumption that a woman should be wooed — worn down over the course of three years — suggests that "no" doesn't really mean no in this world. What might once have been seen as romantic now feels dated and unsettling, even predatory. Yet the party itself is a period piece, suspended in aspic. This is old money: quiet conversation and polite mingling, tasteful music, heavy furniture, canapés and wine served by Black staff. It could be a scene from Edith Wharton's Gilded Age New York. The atmosphere is funereal. Dressed in black, Anna seems to dissolve into the shadows, only ever half present, her face a pale ghost haunting her own body. Has she left the cemetery? No. She has brought the cemetery with her.

We first see Sean — the boy — as an outsider: small, waiting in the lobby, engulfed by negative space. He spends much of the film in liminal zones — corridors, lobbies, waiting rooms. Are these extensions of the tunnel? And that parka has more than a hint of Denis Lavant. He observes Clara (Anne Heche) and Clifford (Peter Stormare) as they wait for the elevator. We don't yet know who they are. Clifford, we will learn, is Sean's brother, an uneasy presence at the engagement of his sister-in-law to another man, a further erasure of his dead brother. Claudius' words about Gertrude could just as easily be Clifford's about Anna, or ours about Nicole Kidman: "Our sometime sister, now our Queen."

Clara is his wife. Clifford and Clara. Their names have the alliterative ring of light comedy, like something you might see emblazoned across the windscreen of a camper van. Clara leaves, claiming she needs to rewrap their engagement present with a nicer ribbon (a bizarre excuse), and Clifford heads upstairs alone. Clara is all pent-up energy; Clifford, doleful and slow. We follow Clara to the park. The camera slows her movements, lending her an ethereal quality, as though she's operating in another dimension governed by different laws. The box she buries there will become the film's MacGuffin, though it's too early for us to register its significance. We're still orienting ourselves, trying to understand who's who, and may not yet realise how important it is.*

As Clara shops for a replacement gift—a wicked queen mirror, slyly hinting at her duplicity—we cut back and forth between her and the engagement party. The party glows with golden light, rich browns and greens, while the park is a world of darkness interrupted by the occasional gleam of traffic.

Clifford gives Anna his blessing: "This is a good thing," he says firmly, even as Joseph looms possessively behind her. Yet between Clara's strange errand, Sean's unexplained presence, and the stiff, uneasy atmosphere, a creeping sense of dread settles in.

To contradict Clifford: this is not a good thing.

---

* There's a certain anxiety that comes with starting any book, play, TV show or film. How am I supposed to follow this? Remember all the names, all the relationships? As I got older, I realised that wasn't my job; it was the writer's. If they were doing their work, they would guide me through it. And if, like Gabriel García Márquez or Emily Brontë, they wanted me to feel lost for a while, then that confusion was intentional, and something to be embraced.

"They have money"

In the weak light of a winter's day, Sean's school friend calls out for him. He lives in a clapboard house, far removed from the Central Park penthouse of Anna's wealthy family. Even in his bedroom, Sean seems to exist within a kind of tunnel. As Christopher Marlowe wrote in *Doctor Faustus* about clinical depression—or Hell: "Where we are is hell,/And where hell is, there must we ever be."

So, is Sean a reincarnation of Sean, or simply a delusional little boy?

Each hypothesis raises further questions. If he's delusional, what is the nature of his illness? Why would his fixation fall specifically on Anna? And if he is Sean reborn, what chain of coincidences has brought him back to her? Why does his awareness surface only at age 10—why not earlier, or later? If the explanation is magical, are further explanations even necessary? Once you accept a world governed by magic—as Anna does—mechanisms and causality become a black box. Magical thinking. Things happen not through logic, but through proximity, through symbolic resonance. The mere co-presence of two things can suggest a causal link.

The term "magical thinking" entered sociology in the 1930s and was soon adopted by psychologists. Joan Didion's memoir *The Year of Magical Thinking* (2005), written after the sudden death of her husband, popularised the concept in relation to grief—though it applies more broadly: to superstitions, astrology, homeopathy, even voting in general elections.

Anna's life unfolds through a sequence of social occasions; the next time we see her she is at her mother's birthday party. The family's oldest member is celebrating her youngest day. Sean is drawing nearer—approaching like a vampire who must be invited in, slipping inside this time with the party's late arrivals. He enters with uncanny confidence, removing his coat as if he's been coming to this house for years. The lights go out, and in a dazzling shot—Savides pushing boundaries, pulling stops, likely inspired by the candlelit photography of *Barry Lyndon*—Anna appears in the distance, a glowing apparition.

She progresses like a Faerie Queen down the corridor, her image doubled in the glass of the framed pictures along the walls, until she arrives before her mother, Eleonora (more Hollywood royalty, Lauren Bacall), with the birthday cake. With her sister Laura (Alison Elliott), the family seems, momentarily, at its most content and united. The brothers-in-law, Joseph and Bob (Arliss Howard), are relaxed and at ease.

But Sean doesn't falter. His preternatural self-possession remains intact. "I need to talk to Anna," he says. He summons her into the kitchen, then tells her plainly: he is Sean.

"Are you going to play a trick on me?" Anna asks—her first acknowledgment of the absurdity of the situation, an uncertainty that lingers throughout the film. Is this all a joke? Are we, the audience, going to be tricked? Anna and her sister burst into laughter after she recounts what Sean has said. Even Sean's father struggles to keep a straight face. Sean's real powerlessness—as a working-class child navigating a world of wealth—is laid bare when the doorman, Jimmy, is given money to put him in a taxi but instead pockets the cash and sends him home on the subway.

Again, the family laughs when Anna receives a note from Sean urging her not to marry Joseph. But beneath the laughter is a flicker of curiosity. Are they simply bored, craving a touch of magic in their orderly lives? There's even the implication, in a scene where Anna and Joseph have sex, that Sean's presence has added some spice to their otherwise missionary-position-centric routine. "It's probably just some prank," Joseph says. But he's clearly irritated when he discovers Sean still loitering in the lobby. With a pointed, sarcastic jab, he tells Anna: "I think your husband's downstairs."

But in confronting him, Joseph at least manages to resolve part of the mystery. Sean is the son of a music teacher (Ted Levine) who gives lessons to tenants in the building. Although Room 202 is mentioned twice, the confrontation takes place not inside the apartment but in the in-between space of the corridor. The adults have uncovered Sean's identity, his origins, his connections. That should settle it. He has a father, a home, a school. He isn't miraculous or magical. He's explainable. And yet, even in the face of this, he refuses to abandon his story. When his father orders him—"Promise you'll never see or bother her again"—he stubbornly refuses.

Anna, meanwhile, appeals to him on an emotional level. It's already a concession: she's taking him seriously, treating him as a peer capable of empathy. "You're hurting me," she says.

Joseph, too, begins to sense Sean as a real threat—though not consciously, and never in terms he would admit. He's unnerved by the boy's stare, brushes past him in the corridor, nudging him aside with barely concealed irritation. In the elevator, he tells Anna, "Well done"—a patronising little jab—even as she is visibly shaken by the sight of Sean collapsing behind them. Joseph misreads the situation entirely. His victory is pyrrhic. For Anna, witnessing Sean collapse triggers not just pity but love. From that moment on, according to Kidman, she knows exactly how things will unfold—but she chooses to go through with it anyway. Such is the depth of her feeling.*

The music has begun, and Anna has just seen Sean collapse, an image that lingers as she and Joseph hurry off to yet another social engagement: Wagner's *Die*

---

* Charlie Rose, 28 October 2004.

Walküre, the second opera in the *Ring Cycle* and nearly six hours long if she's attending the full performance. If so, she'll be watching a story about a woman forced into marriage, rescued by a man she loves, who is then killed by the man she was meant to marry.

Arriving late, Anna and Joseph must shuffle past a row of black-tied opera-goers. The camera closes in on Anna in an unbroken shot. Glazer asked Danny Huston to whisper something improvised to Kidman—"to give her a nudge or two," as he put it, "to knock her off balance, out of her reverie." Anna listens, startled. She's shocked he's still there, so far away from her now. She's on a different plane entirely, her mind with Sean. The music mirrors the passion that's been reignited, now charged with a dangerous, transgressive energy.

Her face is transparent: we see her heart racing, her thoughts spinning, an entire world opening before her as she begins to believe her lost love has returned. Her grief, it seems, is over.

The world is reborn.

Béla Balázs once described the closeup as a "silent soliloquy."[*] Here, it would be more accurate to call it wordless—but a soliloquy it remains, and unquestionably the centre of the film: its crux. "It was only two takes," Kidman said of the shot. "That's how bold Jonathan was. 'Great. We got it.' It wasn't always that way with him." Glazer described watching Kidman as "like watching a trapeze artist on a high wire, poised gracefully in midair."[†]

---

[*] Béla Balázs, *Theory of the Film: Character and Growth of a New Art*, trans. Edith Bone (London, 1930): "The language of the face cannot be suppressed or controlled. However disciplined and practisedly hypocritical a face may be, in the enlarging close-up we see even that it is concealing something, that it is looking a lie. For such things have their own specific expressions super posed on the feigned one. It is much easier to lie in words than with the face and the film has proved it beyond doubt."

[†] Glenn Whipp.

The music carries over into the next scene, and we find ourselves in Sean's home, where his father is explaining the situation to his mother (Cara Seymour). Levine can't help but laugh: "It's not funny," he scolds himself, but still chuckles. "He wrote her a letter telling her she can't marry this guy." As for the people involved, he doesn't really know them. "They have money," is all he offers. Levine is one of those character actors who always seems to come at you from an unexpected angle. His Buffalo Bill in *The Silence of the Lambs* is both more terrifying and more darkly funny than Anthony Hopkins' Oscar-winning Hannibal Lecter.

There's also a second layer to the dilemma: Sean's parents are losing their son to something. A delusion? Mental illness? A predator? A form of psychological kidnapping?

But they're not rich, and more crucially, they're not Nicole Kidman. As a result, we don't truly care what happens to them—except insofar as it might threaten Anna.

At first, Sean's mother seems relaxed, even playful with him, suggesting a warm relationship grounded in shared imagination and private jokes. His father, too, finds the situation absurdly funny. This is a family that can absorb a little weirdness. But Sean isn't joking. He snaps, rebuking his mother harshly: "I'm not your stupid son anymore."

The Opera

While making *Birth*, Nicole Kidman won an Oscar for her portrayal of Virginia Woolf in Stephen Daldry's adaptation of Michael Cunningham's novel *The Hours*. The film weaves together Woolf's writing of *Mrs Dalloway* (1925), the life of a 1950s housewife and reader played by Julianne Moore, and a modern-day "Mrs Dalloway" figure portrayed by Meryl Streep.

Kidman's performance is a textbook Oscar-winner—bravura, transformative, and, crucially, very good. She nails the accent and, aided by a prosthetic nose, renders herself nearly unrecognisable. At the very start of the film, she enacts Woolf's suicide, while her voice on the soundtrack reads Woolf's farewell letter—an effort to sound calm, even hopeful. The words "happiness" and "happier" recur with unsettling insistence.

The film is a study in female disintegration and the paradoxical forms of resilience that can accompany it. It also returns to a theme we have already noted: the vulnerability of those behind the camera, or in this case, behind the typewriter. The novelist is falling apart even as she writes about falling apart. As Marcus Aurelius observes in *Meditations* (Book IV): "Hippocrates, after curing many diseases, fell sick and died."

No one is immune from death or grief.

Born in Hawaii and raised in Sydney, Kidman began her film career precociously in the 1980s, appearing in titles like *Bush Christmas* and *BMX Bandits* (both 1983). Due to her tall frame, pale complexion, and red curls, no stunt performer could convincingly double for her, so she often performed her own stunts. She gained international attention with Philip Noyce's excellent thriller *Dead Calm* (1989), based on the novel by Charles Williams, a story Orson Welles had famously spent years attempting to film. Acting opposite New Zealander Sam Neill and American Billy Zane, Kidman delivered a performance that was notably mature for her age. Even in this early role, she portrayed a character marked by trauma: a woman injured in a car accident that kills her child. She was 22.

Dead Calm put her on Hollywood's radar, and she soon became Tom Cruise's girlfriend both on-screen in *Days of Thunder* (1990) and off. Her career quickly took on a ping-pong rhythm between studio-pleasing fare—

Batman Forever (1995), *The Peacemaker* (1997)—and more challenging artistic work, including Gus Van Sant's *To Die For* (1995) and Jane Campion's *The Portrait of a Lady* (1996).

Following the filming of *Eyes Wide Shut* (1999) with then-husband Cruise, the couple separated. Kidman's career did not suffer from the split; she continued to pursue daring and diverse projects, notably Baz Luhrmann's *Moulin Rouge* (2001) and Lars von Trier's *Dogville* (2003). As noted earlier, she was not Jonathan Glazer's first choice for the role, and there were initial reservations.

Kidman's appearance in the film is distinctive. Her short hair recalls Mia Farrow's page-boy haircut in Roman Polanski's *Rosemary's Baby* (1968), a Manhattan-based horror film that unfolds in a series of enclosed apartments. Her voice is a small sound—something Kidman herself found strange. It was as if her character had retreated into herself, giving as little as possible back to the world. Novelist William Styron, in his memoir about depression *Darkness Visible*, describes how, with the onset of his illness, his voice "degenerated into a rasp which barely broke the silence."* She wears black and other dark colours, allowing her to slip easily into the shadows. By contrast, for the opera scene and her momentous confrontation with Sean, she wears a flesh-toned dress that renders her utterly vulnerable—naked in a way that foreshadows the nudity of the bath scene.

She is oral, we might notice. She bites her thumb. She often stares off, lost in thought. Her reactions are slow. She's often interrupted. The world pounces. A letter is delivered into her lap; a work meeting is interrupted by an announcement of family news. Her sister stands in her way. Her mother threatens to call the police. She's

---

* "I had begun to develop that ancient voice myself": William Styron, *Darkness Visible: A Memoir of Madness* (Knopf, 1989).

not quite there. "She's still in the cemetery," as Glazer said.* Her eyebrows are feline. When she leans down to tell Sean—"You're hurting me"—she has never looked so bewitching (she filmed *Bewitched* a year later), and yet she will be the one who is cast under a spell: utterly consumed by it.

The opera marks the moment when she chooses to believe. There's a sense that she has always been waiting for Sean to return, for the grief to lift.

And let's take a moment to consider who Sean— the dead Sean—is, or was. The disembodied voice over the studio logo, the structuring absence, the dark figure moving through the snowscape: he is also the obscure object of desire. As a betrayer, he cannot be trusted—nor can anyone associated with him. Anna believes he was the love of her life, and that the strength of that love was powerful enough to defy death itself.

But Sean's sister-in-law Clara believes *she* was the love of his life, and that the proof lies in his returning to her the love letters Anna had written—unopened and unread. His proof to Clara is one of devastating betrayal and cruelty. So, one conclusion we might draw is that Anna is mistaken about his feelings—deluded, even actively deceived. However, that doesn't necessarily mean Clara is right. She, too, is caught in the grip of her own passion. She believes that Sean not coming to her proves he isn't Sean—not *her* Sean.

But the real motive is that she knows the McGuffin, the black box through which the child accesses the secrets. Maybe Sean was betraying Clara as well. Who knows how many lovers he might have had? And who gets married in thirty churches in thirty days? It's not a romantic gesture; it's unhinged. *The lady doth protest too much.* Talk about putting a hat on a hat.

---

* Charlie Rose.

Isn't that a clue to how fundamentally meaningless he considered his marriage to Anna?

Incidentally, Sean has, to varying degrees, betrayed others. His brother Clifford has been cuckolded by him, despite Clifford's evident devotion. Sean and Anna have had sex on her sister's couch, an act that feels more than a little hostile, and is experienced as such when recounted. It's embarrassing, awkward. Not something one generally does.

Lauren Bacall, as Anna's mother, tells Joseph: "I never liked Sean." It's hardly a surprising revelation. She may not have seen through him entirely. Perhaps it was just some old-money prejudice against someone a bit too flash. Or maybe she distrusted her daughter's surrender to him.

And what exactly is his job? Young Sean says he works "with the atom," yet he seems to drift between roles, including one at his brother-in-law's hospital. Generally speaking, medicine doesn't operate at the atomic level. There's a dash of Emmanuel Carrère's *The Adversary* (2000) here, a book that tells the true story of a man who pretended to be a doctor for eighteen years before murdering his entire family. It's about the human capacity for deception and how a lie, once begun, can snowball over decades. It's also about the terrifying lengths a man will go to in order to protect a false self-image from being exposed to those he loves. It isn't enough for him to die; he must ensure that his family die believing the lie.

And speaking of work, what is that lecture Sean is giving, the one that ends with the hypothetical about Anna dying and coming back as a bird? And why does the example involve imagining his wife's death? What is that about? Returning to my own ghoulish jokes with my students, I didn't kill off loved ones or family members. My dark humour was purely self-inflicted.

To be clear, adult Sean is a slippery figure. Not only is he a source of deceit, he's also someone others seem willing to deceive themselves about—Clara as much as Anna. Even 10-year-old Sean, having read only Anna's letters to the original Sean and knowing him solely through her eyes, has conjured a version of Sean worthy of such love.

Your Shining is showing

Another sudden death occurred one Sunday in March 1999, back in England. The man—like Sean—suffered a massive heart attack: myocardial infarction, coronary thrombosis, and atheroma. But he wasn't jogging in a park. He was reaching for an oxygen tank by his bed when it struck. His body was taken to Luton and Dunstable Hospital for a postmortem, and the news was soon announced to the world: Stanley Kubrick was dead. To paraphrase W. H. Auden, the director had become his films.

If there is a supernatural element to *Birth*, it is the ghost of Stanley Kubrick.

As we have seen, Glazer had long been influenced by Kubrick. His video for Blur's "The Universal" is such a loving pastiche of *A Clockwork Orange* that it turns Anthony Burgess' rapist hoodlums into pop stars and style icons—Damon Albarn sneering with unironic delight in a spruced-up version of the Korova Milk Bar. More importantly for our purposes, it reveals Glazer's clear and publicly acknowledged debt to Kubrick. The American director, who made England his home for the latter half of his career, casts a long shadow across all of Glazer's films. Kubrick's influence is especially evident in Glazer's aesthetics: the symmetrical, meticulously composed frames; the slow, deliberate pans and tracking shots; the clinical precision that suggests an inhuman, omniscient gaze. Glazer has never met a corridor he didn't love—those parallel lines stretching toward a vanishing point where, eventually, they will converge.

On a philosophical level, Glazer's universe suggests a similar sense of hopelessness. Human beings are prey to larger forces, operating mysteriously from outside. In *Sexy Beast*, dark fate dictates the groove Gal's life must follow—through the nightmare hare (the night-hare?) and, of course, through Teddy, the Prince of Darkness, not unlike Lloyd the barman in *The Shining*. Dark humour abounds. From Don's psychopathic ranting, it's only a short lunge to Gunnery Sergeant Hartman (R. Lee Ermey) in *Full Metal Jacket*. Even the name—Hartman—suggests the heartless bastard, the brute, the bully, who is nevertheless ultimately shot in the heart.

Birth is the most overtly referential of Glazer's films in relation to Kubrick. From *Barry Lyndon*, it borrows the candlelit photography (seen in the birthday cake scene) and the elaborate interior décor. It shares the theme of the interloper: Sean/Barry, and to some extent Joseph/Barry. The violent outburst at the wedding rehearsal, which leads to Joseph's downfall and his spanking of Sean, directly echoes Barry's beating of his stepson Lord Bullingdon (Leon Vitali, who would become Kubrick's longtime assistant), and Barry's subsequent ostracism. The casting further deepens the connection, with former Kubrick alumni Nicole Kidman and Arliss Howard. Kidman, of course, starred in *Eyes Wide Shut*, while Howard—who played Cowboy in *Full Metal Jacket*—appears here as Anna's brother-in-law, Bob.

The tunnel where adult Sean dies bears more than a passing resemblance to the underpass where Alex and his Droogs assault a drunk in *A Clockwork Orange*. The use of classical music (the Wagner prelude and Mendelssohn) also draws from Kubrick's dystopia. That aesthetic choice echoes a broader tendency in Kubrick's work: the juxtaposition of classical music with unsettling imagery, a tendency that includes contemporary composers like György Ligeti, whose influence can also be felt in Mica Levi's scores for Glazer.

Kubrick's *Lolita* is another clear influence on *Birth*, with its paedophiliac undertones and taboo-breaking subject matter. The film places the audience in the deeply uncomfortable position of accomplice or enabler to someone who is, at least in part, contemplating the grooming and kidnapping of a child. How are we meant to respond when Anna begins to adopt the tropes of the romantic comedy—a dinner date, a horse-drawn carriage ride through Central Park—later in the film? Humbert Humbert's flight with Lolita in the second half of Kubrick's film finds a parallel in Anna's plan to flee with Sean. The crucial difference, arguably, is that while Lolita is a "nymph," a girl on the cusp of puberty, Sean, 10 years old, is unambiguously prepubescent. In this sense, *Birth* pushes the envelope even further than Kubrick's adaptation of Nabokov, and the disturbing scenes that follow would contribute to the film's polarising reception.

Eyes Wide Shut is another key reference, not only due to the casting of Kidman, but also in *Birth*'s Christmas-adjacent setting and its depiction of an upper-class New York milieu. Though shot in England, *Eyes Wide Shut* is set in the same rarefied Manhattan world. Its exploration of deviant, potentially family-destroying sexuality also resonates powerfully with Glazer's film.

However, if there is one Kubrick film that haunts *Birth* more than any other, it is *The Shining*. The first tracking shot of Sean jogging through the park clearly recalls Jack Torrance's drive to the Overlook Hotel in the opening sequence of Kubrick's film, as well as Danny's eerie rides through the hotel corridors on his pedal car. In both cases, the camera exudes a cool, threatening presence—a sense of something lurking, an unseen pursuer. We, the audience, are placed in the position of predator, complicit in the act of watching.

Both films are, in their own way, poems to snow. *The Shining* is filled with artificial, powdery snow, and famously recreated the blinding light of snow glare through hotel windows using lamps so hot they caused a fire on set, delaying production. In contrast, Glazer appears to be working with real snow—sludgy, slippery, unstable. No one—not Anna, adult Sean, or Clara—is sure of their footing in the sleet. Snow lends the film a fairytale quality. The outside world becomes a wilderness, even in the heart of Manhattan. Note how Central Park and the cemetery Anna visits at the beginning of the film seem like one and the same place, unified by the anonymising white blanket of snow.

The interior spaces in both films—the Overlook Hotel and Anna's duplex—offer protection, but only of a tenuous kind. They are retreats, not sanctuaries. In *The Shining*, Native American motifs have been incorporated into the hotel's décor—an aesthetic gesture toward rendering safe, or at least acknowledging, the dark history of the land: burial grounds, massacres, hauntings. In Anna's apartment, the wallpaper is striking, suggestive of the outdoors—a dark forest, a pastoral world where grandmothers are eaten by talking wolves. It hints not only at the danger outside, but at a potential wildness within Anna herself. Those feline eyes.

The large building, with its clear social stratification—"We're from upstairs," Joseph tells a fellow tenant in a not-so-subtle flex—and its excess of corridors, recalls the labyrinthine depths of the Overlook Hotel, with its contrast between the gilded public spaces and the cramped quarters of Jack's family. It is in these empty, liminal spaces that Sean can exist: the lobbies, elevators, corridors, and bathrooms. His father is a tutor—"his father has always been the tutor," one is tempted to add—a music tutor, and Sean will later be attacked by a piano. Like Jack, Sean can bounce a ball in the lobby when no one is there.

But Jack Torrance is most clearly echoed in Joseph, with his widow's peak hair and his slow descent into madness. When Anna stands him up at an apartment viewing, he glowers out the window with that unmistakable chin-down, eyes-up expression known as the "Kubrick stare"—shared by Alex DeLarge, Private Pyle, and Jack Torrance himself.

Chef Hallorann (Scatman Crothers) is the lone black figure in *The Shining*, problematically positioned as a sacrificial character whose sole function is to ensure Danny and Wendy's survival. He brings the Snowcat they will escape on, one he himself will never use, having been killed with an axe.

Lee, the family housemaid, is played by Novella Nelson, an actor whose film work largely comprises unnamed bit parts—unlike Crothers, who was already a star as a musician, actor, and the cartoon voice of Hong Kong Phooey. Here, she has a quiet authority within the household and acts protectively toward the family, much like Chef Hallorann, as if they were her wards. She warns Sean, "Don't touch that," when he approaches a vase, and later tells him, "I won't let you hurt this family." He—somewhat—disarms her by using her name and by thanking her when she hands him a glass of apple juice, something perhaps no one else thinks to do.

At the same time, Lee is another signifier of the family's wealth and privilege. Her presence feels like a throwback—a remnant of an older film and an older chapter in American history. But unlike Hallorann, she is not a "magical negro." She has no supernatural powers to deploy, no special insight to offer, and she will not become a victim. After the chaos of the ruined wedding rehearsal, she sits amid the wreckage and replies to Clifford's polite "How are you?" with a flat "Okay." One wonders if the vase survived the commotion.

Ultimately, she can only care so much.

Danny Torrance and Sean are both child protagonists, each marked by an unfashionable haircut—Danny's bowl cut and Sean's buzzcut (which also mirrors Anna's cropped hair). Both serve as the apparent locus of supernatural phenomena. But where Danny is the unwilling conduit of a telepathic gift, Sean is either a fraud or deluded, rather than the genuine reincarnation he initially claims to be.

Both boys are in danger. Danny is attacked by the woman in Room 237 and Sean is violently assaulted by the unhinged Clara, who, in her self-confessed willingness "to explore this," effectively admits to being a potential child abuser. He will also be attacked by Joseph in a later scene. And, of course, there is Anna, whose intentions become increasingly suspect. She openly expresses her plan to wait until Sean is of legal age before marrying him—but the kiss, the bath, and the fervent look in her eyes as she imagines what he might look like in eleven years suggest she may not be able to wait.

Sean also places himself in physical danger. After his confrontation with Clara, in a moment of extreme crisis, he climbs a tree in the park as high as he can. Later, he runs into the darkness of Central Park to escape the police. That he is white, at least, means he is probably at less risk of being arrested—or shot—by them.

The Bath
One scene that provoked much of the controversy surrounding the reception of Jonathan Glazer's second film takes place in a bathroom.

Bathrooms are a favourite setting in horror films, largely because they are where we are most vulnerable. While we may be asleep in the bedroom, it's only in the bathroom that we can be caught truly exposed—pants around our ankles, naked in the shower, or drifting off in the bath, as Freddy Krueger's claw emerges between our legs. The bathroom carries its own peculiar taboo; it is a room of dual function, a space where we cleanse ourselves and where we perform the basest of bodily functions—purity and soil in the same space.

It is also the ideal setting for murder—or for cleaning up its aftermath. *Psycho* (1960) famously features a brutal killing in the shower. While censors objected to that scene, Hitchcock had artfully constructed it so that blood and nudity were more implied than explicitly shown. What truly troubled the censors, however, was something else: the shot of the torn pieces of paper Marion Crane flushes down the toilet. That single image was in direct contravention of the Hays Code. It marked the first time a toilet had been shown in a mainstream Hollywood film. So great was the taboo around toilets that it wasn't until the 1970s that a toilet was first heard flushing on American television. Ever the boundary-pusher, Hitchcock had long tried to incorporate toilets—if only the sound of one flushing—into his films. It was one of his many cinematic obsessions.

Kubrick, too, returns frequently to the bathroom. General Jack D. Ripper kills himself in the bathroom in *Dr. Strangelove*, as does Private Pyle (Vincent D'Onofrio) in *Full Metal Jacket*. That scene—featuring a row of exposed lavatories and Pyle's fresh, strawberry-red blood and cream-coloured brains splattered across white tiles—forms a nakedly obscene tableau. Part Goya, part *Tiswas*. The only joke in *2001: A Space Odyssey* comes when Dr. Heywood Floyd (William Sylvester) anxiously studies the instructions on how to use a zero-gravity toilet. In *A Clockwork Orange*, Alex DeLarge takes a long, enthusiastic piss, mercifully with his back to the camera. In *Eyes Wide Shut*, Nicole Kidman's character urinates and wipes herself in front of her husband, a stark signifier of both marital intimacy and sexual indifference. The same shot is echoed in Glazer's music video for Massive Attack's "Come Live with Me," stripped of any trace of eroticism. Later in *Eyes Wide Shut*, Bill Harford (Tom Cruise) treats a woman who has overdosed in Sydney Pollack's bathroom. Elegant artwork adorns the walls, but the woman—naked and beautiful—is similarly objectified, disarranged. We will see her next at the masked orgy, and finally, in the morgue.

In *The Shining*, bathrooms are everywhere. They are the film's hidden chambers, its secret spaces. Jack is seduced and then horrified by the beautiful woman in the bathroom of the cursed Room 237. The distance from bath to toilet is just a few steps. In the public bathroom of the Overlook's bar, Jack has his pivotal conversation with his demonic double, Grady—a man who urges him to kill his family and admits to having murdered his own. The urinals line the background. And when Jack finally does attempt to kill Wendy and Danny, they hide in the bathroom—but the flimsy door is made to be axed through.

In *Birth*, bathrooms are spaces of revelation and confession, of seduction and—once again—repulsion. Clara takes Sean into the bathroom to wash her hands; she has just unearthed the spot where she buried the letters and discovered they are gone—though we don't yet know this. When she writes her number on his hand and tells him she has moved house, Sean replies, "Don't tell Anna," as if he knows exactly who Clara is, showing no sign of awareness that he has finally been exposed. Is he improvising? Making one last gambit? What, exactly, is going on in that opaque head of his?

The bathroom will also be the site of the most controversial scene in the film, when Anna is taking a bath and Sean comes into the room and takes off his clothes before getting into the bath with her. They have already alluded to the question about how he— a 10-year-old boy—would satisfy her sexual needs when they go on their after-school date. The danger is that this moment could cross into the territory of a sex scene. The exchange of looks, and the sense that Anna and Sean are perceiving more than the audience is shown, already breaches multiple taboos—not only the sexual, but also the familial. Anna is engaged to Joseph, who stands helplessly on the other side of the door, a hopeless cuckold. And Anna is not Sean's mother—the only context in which sharing a bath with a child might be considered innocent by societal norms.

The scene was filmed on a closed set, with only essential crew present, along with Glazer and Cameron Bright's mother. Both Kidman and Bright wore flesh-coloured underwear. And yet, the scene remains suggestive of paedophilia. It raises the emotional and philosophical stakes of the film's premise. If reincarnation is real, how should one behave in light of that knowledge? In adult Sean's earlier thought experiment—imagining Anna returning as a little bird—it's clear that no one would consider bestiality. The species boundary is firm. But if the reincarnated being is human, does it matter that the body is that of a child?

When Sean is asked if he's ever made love to a girl before, the answer might well be, "not in this body." But if he is to be believed, he remembers making love to Anna—on Bob's green couch, to be precise. He would remember what it felt like, what it looked and tasted like. His interior life would be sexually mature. And even when we learn that he has gleaned this information from Anna's love letters, more questions arise. How sexually explicit are those letters? How has a 10-year-old boy absorbed and reimagined those images within his own developing mind? Does he have a genuine urge to — as Clara puts it — "explore this"?

These are deeply uncomfortable questions — queasy-making, in fact — and it's understandable that many critics, upon the film's release, avoided pursuing them with any real diligence. It is easier — it comes as a palpable relief, in fact — to dismiss the film as silly or absurd. And to be clear, I've used the word absurd several times in this chapter, and indeed throughout this book.

But silliness doesn't disqualify something from being taken seriously. If it did, we could safely disregard politics as an area worthy of scrutiny — when, in fact, the sillier it gets, the more urgently it demands our attention. There is a streak of absurdity running through all of Glazer's films, and *The Zone of Interest* is no exception, suffused as it is with a galling, cosmic absurdity.

With his actions in the bathroom, Sean is taking the active role. He is undressing and getting into the bath with Anna. He is seducing her. Of course, this plays horrifically with our instincts. We can hear the voice of the paedophile, pleading that the child led him on. Children are not as innocent as they seem, Humbert Humbert says.

And if Sean is a fake, then where did this sexuality come from? How did this 10-year-old boy learn these moves? Is he really in love with Anna? Does he really want to have sex with her?

Both versions have ramifications of the purest ick.

"I'm looking at my wife," Sean says.

This male gaze is possessive and demanding; it lays a claim. Sean is saying: I have every right to do this. It is a denial of transgression. Joseph cannot compete; he has been displaced. From this moment on, the wedding cannot proceed, because Sean has asserted his right, as the husband, to object and not hold his peace. Joseph and Anna, by this logic, would be committing bigamy. In the ultimate obscenity, Sean has become the law.

The cut that follows leaves us with more questions than answers. What happened next? What did they do in that bathroom?

In fact, we know they didn't do anything because we are film-literate, and we understand the grammar of narrative order. The disrobing and the shared bath read as foreplay; the kiss outside the apartment is the first act of mutual, conscious consent, and arguably even more controversial than the bath itself. Anna's declaration of love and her revelation of the plan (also delivered in a bathroom) serve as the emotional and narrative climax of the affair. Yet at the very moment of her total surrender, she does not know that Sean—having just learned of adult Sean's betrayal—has already decided to betray her in turn.

At this point, Joseph and Sean have swapped roles. Joseph is now the interloper; Sean is the one who belongs. His insolent, insistent kicking of Joseph's chair is a territorial gesture, a provocation that Joseph cannot respond to without ceding ground, like the crow with the cheese in Aesop's fable.* Yet to leave it unanswered is to accept the new status quo.

The violence that follows is the film's only real moment of physical action. It's notable how otherwise still the film is. Characters walk from one place to another. They sit in rooms. Sean jogging is about as fast as it gets—and we've seen where that leads. Joseph's dramatic pushing of the piano (he had earlier spoken to Bob about regretting not keeping up his piano lessons)

---

* The Crow is outwitted by the Fox's flattery. Fable number 124.

is an attempt to trap Sean, to keep the others at bay long enough to deliver the boy a proper spanking. He wants to hurt him, yes, but more than that, he wants to reassert Sean's traditional role as a child—to humiliate him. But he won't succeed.

Joseph's outburst is revealingly not even about Sean: "He has no clue how to make something happen. He's living in a land where he's pretending to be something instead of doing the job. And that's the real problem. I'm the one who should be respected, but obviously not."

What on Earth is he babbling about?

In his rage, Joseph reveals himself to be insecure and dependent. When he storms out, it's to go to Bob's apartment, as he has no place of his own. We're never told how much money he has, or what his social standing is. Why doesn't he go to a hotel, or stay with a friend? Is Bob actually his friend, independently of Anna and her family? Or is this some wannabe brothers-in-law collective?

The Kiss and Clara

Sean has also left, but unlike Joseph he will be called back. And he'll be called back by Anna. And they kiss. Is this kiss a continuation, a beginning, or a consummation? Again, what happened in that bathroom?

We see the kiss through Bob's eyes. It's in slow motion and close-up, unambiguously adult and sexual. It's not a peck. From a technical standpoint, you wonder how a 10-year-old actor could legally perform such a scene. Did the filmmakers use forced perspective, so the actors never actually touched? As with pornography, the question arises: can an act of physical intimacy be acted— performed without being done? It's why Macbeth trails so many superstitions. You can't just pretend to do spells. Pretending and doing are the same thing. They yield the same results.

Bob is the audience inscribed in the film. He turns away in surprise and embarrassment. He is complicit in his inaction, uncertain about what he has seen, but all too certain. Sean, too, seems to realise they've been caught, and his embarrassment feels strangely more adult than the kiss itself. It's the reaction of a confederate, a peer.

"Uh-oh, Bob saw us," he seems to be saying.

Now they're in it together. His and Anna's pact is complete.

Anna had asked Clifford to come and convince her that Sean isn't Sean—to send him away—but now it's too late. That's Clifford's role: he always arrives too late. And Clara, not to be outdone, is always even later. They're outsiders. But Clara is still an insider, in a way no one else understands, except her and the dead Sean.

When Clifford meets Sean, he tells Clara clearly and unambiguously: "That's not Sean."

But then we see Sean sitting in the corridor, waiting, turning his head this way and that, while superimposed images create multiple versions of him. It's a rare moment of overt cinematic trickery. Glazer has been stylish throughout, but rarely in a way that so openly reminds us we're watching a film capable of such visual magic. Take, for example, the use of slow motion when Clara enters the park to bury her letters and later crosses the road: it's subtle enough to go unnoticed. Something feels slightly off about the speed of her movement, but we register this only subliminally. The manipulation is felt rather than seen.

By contrast, the moment with the multiplied Seans is literal and striking. It suggests indeterminacy, perhaps even indecision on the part of Glazer and his co-screen-writers, Jean-Claude Carrière and Milo Addica. Or are we witnessing a palimpsest of all the drafts, layered onscreen as Glazer deliberates between his own conception, Carrière's version, and Milo's rewrites?

This is the film's moment of greatest ambiguity. At this point, the boy could be Sean reincarnated, a malicious fraud, a mentally disturbed child, or some combination of all three. Or we may never know the truth. This is the final moment when all these possibilities remain genuinely open. It's the cinematic equivalent of quantum superposition, before the cat is revealed to be dead or alive, before the box of letters is unearthed, before the observer's gaze collapses the waveform into a single version of reality. Adult Sean, we were told, works with atoms.

Clara arrives at this exact moment, and her fervid, staring eyes—her eager, domineering presence—impose themselves on the rest of the narrative. As the other woman, she brings disruption and power, though it's a power wielded from the margins: wounded, desperate, teetering on the edge of madness. In a reversal of roles, she commands Sean into the bathroom. At first, she treats him like a child, barking orders, until her dominance takes on a darker, more adult tone when she tells him to dry her hands. Is this how she once ordered Sean around during their trysts?

The moment is layered with betrayal. Sean has betrayed Anna and his brother; Clara has betrayed Anna and her husband. Is Sean now betraying Clara too? Clara's hunger for affirmation is extreme, even cruel. She demands complete betrayal, insisting he give her Anna's unopened love letters. The whispered exchange in the bathroom is itself a betrayal, taking place while Anna and Clifford remain in the kitchen, believing they're the ones deciding what to do. Anna has summoned Clifford—not Clara—to help her solve this crisis, but it is Clara who speaks to Sean, who gives him her new address. Joseph once endured the humiliation of standing outside his fiancée's bathroom, listening at the door. Now Sean is inside, with Clara.

Later, Sean will lie naked in bed, waiting for Anna as if nothing has happened, as if his conversation with Clara had never taken place.

"Don't tell Anna," he has already whispered to Clara, making himself complicit. The betrayal continues.

Why? Because he's Sean, and that's what Sean did?

We learn the truth in a flashback that anticipates Clara's interview the following day. Once again, we see Clara in the park, Sean following her, Clara burying the box. But this time, we also see Sean reading the letters in his room. What's going on?

When someone acts out of character, we ask: what possessed you to do such a thing? This is that moment— a moment of magical possession. Sean is being possessed by Sean. He falls in love with Anna through the letters addressed not to him, but to his namesake. *What if I am him? What if she is writing to me?* In some unfathomable yet real way?

The ancient Greeks, when they encountered a foreign name that resembled a familiar god or hero, assumed they were one and the same. It wasn't just a coincidence—coincidence itself was evidence of something metaphysically true. Sean makes the same mistake. *If we share a name, we must be the same person.* I had the same instinct as a child: I could relate to John Wayne, John Lennon, and John Travolta—but not to John Denver, for some reason.

Sean is a confused, disturbed young boy. Clara, by contrast, is a vengeful hypocrite. "You can't go around pretending to be someone you're not," she says— the same woman who betrayed her husband with his brother. She has spent the entire film posing as someone she is not.

If this were a noir—and all of Glazer's films are, in some way—then Clara is the black widow, the femme fatale, the woman at the center of intrigue, the one holding the cards. And (adult) Sean clearly is too, despite Eleanor seeing through him.

Anna's mother, Eleanor, is the only one who sees the situation with any clarity — or humour. "Does Mr. Reincarnation like his cake?" she asks young Sean. She tells Anna, bluntly: "I will tell his mother, and she will call the police." Later, at the maternity ward, peering through the glass at her first grandchild, she deadpans: "Maybe that's Sean."

Like Bob, earlier, Eleanor helps inscribe the audience into the film. She signals that at least one person recognises how absurd and destabilising this story is. But her clarity doesn't make her voice any more persuasive. Anna is still in the grip of passion. It will take Sean himself to shake her free.

Clara assigns the roles: "I'm your lover. Anna's your wife."

Note the use of *your*, even as she's effectively disproved Sean's identity. Is it irony? Or the stubborn persistence of delusion? She knows he's not Sean, and yet she doesn't. She openly says she wanted to believe. She admits she would have explored it, if only.

Rewatching the film — and all Glazer films reward rewatching, but this one especially — we can track Clara closely. After burying the letters in the park, she buys a mirror. Her face fills the screen, until it tilts and pulls back: we've been watching her reflection. It's an early sign of her duplicity. The slow motion that surrounds her movements makes her feel spectral, as if she's operating on a different register from everyone else.

But there's something else here. The camera participates in Clara's deceit. The film does too. The filmmakers are her allies. She seems to know the backstory, the full script — the MacGuffin, the twist, the truth about Sean. Eleanor is the one who asks, *How does he know what he knows?* Clara knows how he knows.

She never makes it to the party at the beginning of the film. She never appears in the kitchen with Clifford and Anna later. She's always arriving late to events we never actually see her attend. It's not a trivial kind of power: to remain permanently imminent, to skip every social occasion simply by never quite arriving.

When Anna visits Clara's apartment to speak with her and Clifford, Clara watches her hungrily. Her plan—to return the letters in order to prove that Sean loved her more—has been in place for ten years. That she accepted the invitation to Anna's engagement party just to execute that plan is both cold-blooded and astonishingly bloody-minded. Anna's love and grief have persisted all that time—but so have Clara's love for Sean and her resentment toward Anna. That Roger Ebert, in his review, mistakes Clara for Anna's best friend speaks to just how slippery Clara is. The film gives us no indication of such a relationship, but the more colour we can add to the betrayal, the more devastating it becomes.

Well, why not Anna's best friend? It's not as if that would have stopped Clara. And the fact that we can now add Ebert to the long list of her dupes only proves how good she is.

Anne Heche plays Clara brilliantly. A gifted actor, Heche rose to prominence in the 1990s with standout roles in *Donnie Brasco* (1997) and *Six Days, Seven Nights* (1998). The day before the release of the latter, news broke of her relationship with sitcom star Ellen DeGeneres. Though hailed by many as one half of the first openly gay Hollywood power couple, Heche faced severe backlash. She later blamed industry bigotry for the abrupt decline of her career in major studio films; from that point forward, she mostly found work in independent productions.

After her breakup with DeGeneres, Heche suffered a series of psychotic episodes and published a memoir — *Call Me Crazy* (2001) — in which she alleged that her fundamentalist Christian father had sexually abused her from infancy, an accusation her family swiftly contested. In the same book, she wrote that she believed she was from a fourth dimension — a being named Celestia — and, at times, Jesus himself. This was three years before *Birth*.

One night in 2022, Anne Heche was involved in a series of incidents while driving erratically through a residential neighborhood in Los Angeles. The final incident proved fatal: she crashed into a house, which quickly caught fire. Firefighters battled both the blaze and the wreckage to reach her. It took forty-five minutes to extract her from the vehicle and administer medical attention. She had sustained multiple injuries, including severe burns and smoke inhalation. She died in hospital some time later. An autopsy confirmed that no active drugs were in her system at the time of the crash.

Heche's troubled life and tragic death neither diminishes nor enhances her performance in *Birth*, but it has become part of my experience of watching the film. I can't unknow what I now know about the circumstances of her death — the pain, the violence, the suffering. I add it to the premature death of the film's cinematographer, Harris Savides. Together, they cast shadows over the film: a darkness created by people who were here and are now gone.

Heche gives Clara a piercing intensity, driven by a willingness to embrace a delusion she knows is a delusion. She stands in opposition to Anna — a counterpoint. Where Anna hesitates, Clara charges forward. Her fervour, even fanaticism, allows her to see through Sean immediately. She tests him and finds him lacking. She chases him to the door and seems fully prepared to beat him if necessary. Her breezy greeting to the neighbours in the hallway—interrupting her assault on Sean—is a chilling reminder of her skill at deception. She can slip effortlessly into the role of Clifford's wife, Anna's sister-in-law, the pleasant neighbour, all while keeping her gaze fixed on Sean, her next victim.

"A little boy in my bathtub"

The collapse of the wave function happens, for Anna, in the bathroom. It has already happened for Sean—and for us. The spell, so often spoken of, is now definitively broken. Sean begins to behave like the child he is: he runs away, climbs a tree. Eventually, he slouches back to Anna's bathroom—he can't very well go home to his own mother and father now—to soak in the tub and await the denouement. As children, we often find temporary refuge in a home that isn't ours but feels preferable. A friend's house, a cousin's place—where the parents are more indulgent, the toys newer and cooler, the towels fresher. For Sean, Anna's duplex has become that place. Why not? Look at the location. Look at the furniture. They even have a maid, like in the movies.

As his father said, bluntly, right at the beginning: "They have money."

We, as the audience, have been ahead of the characters for some time—but only just. We've been misled, confused, then allowed to feel momentarily superior, gaining insight just minutes before the characters catch up. We may realise, in hindsight, that we had the pieces from the start: Clara heading to the park at night, the flashback to the buried box, and then the final image, Sean reading the letters. That's when it all falls into place.

Now we understand how Sean knows. "Well... I can't be Sean," he tells Clara, "because if Sean was in love with you, and I'm in love with Anna, then I'm not Sean."

This irony needs untangling. Young Sean believed he was the reincarnated Sean, and so believed he loved Anna. But in believing, he truly fell in love with her. Now that he realises the original Sean didn't really love Anna, he reasons that he cannot be *that* Sean. And so he isn't. He's simply Sean.

Anna doesn't know any of this, and so we arrive at a classical moment of irony—Greek tragedy irony, not postmodern winking irony. As she speaks of their future together, as she tells him she loves him—words that would have meant everything to Sean just hours earlier—we, the audience, know the truth: Sean is not the Sean she believes him to be. He can't keep up the deception. He's not that Sean. So he tells her plainly: "I'm not Sean."

Anna's collapse is sudden and, after a flicker of denial, absolute. *Of course he can't be Sean. What the fuck was I thinking?*

"You certainly had me fooled," she says, her eyes glassy as she recoils against the bathroom wall. The sheer madness of the premise crashes down on her. *I thought you were my dead husband... but you're just a little boy in my bathtub.*

By the time she leaves the room, not only has she fallen entirely out of love with him—she has lost all interest in him. She drops a towel by the side of the tub, not out of contempt, but indifference.

He means nothing to her now. He creeps her out. She creeps herself out. *What was I thinking?*

The horror of Birth

Aside from the paedophilia (never a good way to begin a sentence), one of the factors that made *Birth* so difficult to receive was its refusal to conform to genre. What was it, exactly? A horror film? It initially presents itself as such, or at least as a supernatural thriller. Children have long been used in horror as interlopers, demons, or eerie figures whose not-quite-us-ness marks them as uncanny: from *Village of the Damned* (1960) to *The Omen* (1976) to *The Sixth Sense* (1999). Nicole Kidman herself had recently starred in the successful ghost story *The Others* (2001). Her haircut in *Birth*, as noted, echoes Mia Farrow's in *Rosemary's Baby*, as does the Manhattan setting. Even Central Park had previously featured in the horror comedy *Ghostbusters* (1984).

The supernatural element in *Birth*—reincarnation—isn't one that has had much traction in cinema. That's partly why Jean-Claude Carrière, when consulted at the start of the project, came up blank after checking the film encyclopaedia. In terms of tone, the most relevant antecedent is Hitchcock's *Vertigo* (1958), a film that, like *Birth*, uses a fraudulent supernatural conceit—a kind of fake McGuffin—as a vehicle for exploring trauma and obsession. There will be an explanation, eventually, but it won't justify everything that has happened. It will be thin. The film itself is broader and more elusive than any resolution can account for.

It's a bit like an episode of *Scooby-Doo* (1969–1986). The supernatural element turns out not to be real (the amusement park isn't haunted), but the real revelation is somehow worse: it was a nasty adult all along. The janitor, inevitably. And so we're left in a world where terrible things are done not by demons but by ordinary people, driven by greed or petty malice or motives we don't fully understand.

All horror posits a universe in which that horror is possible. Edgar Allan Poe's universe is one of thundering, poetic justice—a moral cosmos in which individuals are hideously punished for their own misdeeds or those of their ancestors. H. P. Lovecraft, by contrast, imagines a cold, indifferent universe: amoral, impenetrable, and actively hostile to human understanding. Probe too deeply and you may go mad, or you may go mad anyway, without probing at all.

The Exorcist (1973) remains one of the most terrifying films I've ever seen, not because of the vomit or the grotesque scenes of self-harm, but because it ultimately endorses a worldview in which the universe is not just governed by evil, but thoroughly and enthusiastically validated by the Catholic Church. *The Exorcist* tells you that the Catholics are right. For Poe, evil deeds bring about their own supernatural retribution. For Lovecraft, it's enough to lead a scientific expedition or take the wrong turn. Madness and cosmic horror await. For *The Exorcist*, a child can be possessed by the devil for no reason at all and must be tied down and brutalised by priests to be saved.

Some horror films carry moral imperatives: don't trust strangers, don't mock the locals, don't have sex before marriage. Ohers depict a universe where we are simply prey: fragile, insignificant, and subject to forces far beyond our comprehension or concern.

Birth begins in a world that dismisses supernaturalism as "mumbo jumbo." But it then shows how easily a yearning—for love, for meaning—can be shaped into belief. An idea with no rational foundation becomes more powerful as its explanation recedes. You would think someone like Dr. Bob or Eleanor—cultured, urbane—might introduce Occam's razor and dispel the magical thinking that would be scoffed at in the intellectual world of Joan Didion. Or so we would hope.

It is, after all, far easier to believe that Sean has accessed the information through some ordinary means than to invent an entire metaphysical mechanism—reincarnation—that explains not only how he knows what he knows, but also why this phenomenon has occurred only once, in this boy, here and now.

The appeal of the supernatural—whether in ghost stories or organised religion—is that it repairs a structural failing in life as it is. Christianity gained enormous traction by offering the afterlife not only as a cure for death, but as an elsewhere where the visible injustices of life could be rectified. We don't need heaven so much as we need the gates of heaven. The bouncer is more important than the club. St. Peter stands there with the velvet rope, letting the just pass through while sending rapists, murderers, dictators, and billionaires to the pit.

Resurrection promises the chance to reunite with the dead, but it respects a key boundary: the dead remain with the dead, the living with the living. Reincarnation offers a similar balm—easing grief, filling the absence of a loved one—but it does so by blurring that line. Its supposed moral logic (karma) is irrelevant to *Birth*, though it's worth noting that in Sean's early explanation of reincarnation, Anna comes back as a bird. What did she do to deserve that? Is that how he sees her? Flighty? Twittering? Birdbrained? There is something birdlike about Kidman, with her crop haircut and wide, alert eyes—like the last robin clinging to a winter branch.

For Anna, reincarnation becomes plausible not through philosophy but through need. The Sean-shaped hole in her life has remained unfilled for ten years. What she loses in Sean's confession is not just the illusion of his return, but the foundation of her grief. The child Sean may be "a liar," as she bitterly accuses him—but her Sean was a liar too. The person she loved, and the love itself, are cast into doubt. Her capacity for love has been poured into the wrong vessel.

Does Anna ever learn about Clara and the letters? Does she ever get a full explanation of what really happened?

She tries to repair her life, to reconcile with Joseph— making a supplicant of herseof, defiantly half-apologising with a "sorry-not sorry" as she kisses his hand, like he's Pope Joseph of the Corner Office.

But there's no forgiving, and no forgetting, for Anna herself. What she has revealed to herself is her own fragility, the hollowness not just of her present and future, but of her past as well. The universe is indifferent. Her love meant nothing. The act of marrying in thirty churches over thirty days—what once looked like romantic excess—now looks like what it always was: a massive, manic overcompensation. An empty gesture.

For Sean, this has been an episode of mental illness, something he hopes to recover from. He writes Anna a letter, which we hear him read in voiceover during the film's final scenes. It's mature for 10-year-old. It recalls the suicide note Kidman reads in *The Hours*, an apology written from inside a fog of unwellness. Sean becomes a kind of precocious Holden Caulfield, post-breakdown, at the end of *The Catcher in the Rye* (1951).

The school photo session is telling: children quickly shift identities on cue. At the photographer's direction, they move from guarded, neutral expressions to beaming, photogenic smiles. They know how to perform. "A big smile, there you go. Wonderful." A child like Sean is pliable. He might grow up to be schizophrenic—or this might simply be a strange episode in a difficult childhood. Time will tell.

Anna has no such elasticity. She has lost herself. She returns to Joseph not out of love, but with an even deeper sense of resignation—of settling.* Just as Eleanor advised. This return is also framed as an act of family restoration: the wedding will take place at the beach house Eleanor

---

* In Frank Oz's 2004 remake of *The Stepford Wives*, Kidman plays a TV executive whose most famous show is "I Can Do Better," essentially a reality TV show like *Temptation Island* where spouses are tempted away from their partners by porn stars.

suggested, continuing a family tradition—or, more eerily, re-enacting her parents' marriage.

Though *Sexy Beast* and *Birth* are generically and stylistically worlds apart, they share the same narrative arc: an ostensibly happy family is disrupted by the arrival of an interloper. With great effort, he is expelled, and life returns to its superficial calm—but the interloper lingers, whether under the swimming pool or in the psyche. The consequences persist. (*The Zone of Interest* follows a similar arc, though here it is the father who must remove himself, displaced not by a visitor but by the pressures of work.)

As Sean is photographed as a "normal" child, Anna is posed as a "normal" bride. But for her, the imposture is a step too far. She cannot maintain the facade. Or rather, in the very act of pretending, she becomes fully aware of the distance between what she's supposed to feel and what she actually does—the gap between the self she performs and the self she inhabits. She begins to unravel.

This spring is no season of renewal. It looks bitterly cold. The Atlantic pounds the beach, and Anna stands distraught, paralysed by uncertainty. This could be a suicide, if only the water weren't so cold. And we might find ourselves thinking once more of Kidman's performance in *The Hours* or the protagonist in Kate Chopin's *The Awakening* (1899). As Stevie Smith wrote in 1957: "I was much too far out all my life/And not waving but drowning."* Joseph will lead her away—but whether back to the wedding or to a hospital remains unclear.

The final song is "Tonight You Belong to Me," performed by sisters Patience and Prudence. The lyrics describe a lover who, though now with someone else, will spend one last night with the singer: "My honey I know (I know)/With the dawn that you will be gone/

---

* Stevie Smith, 'Not Waving but Drowning' in *Not Waving but Drowning* (Deutsch, 1957).

But tonight you belong to me."* Maybe it's prurient to assume that "one more night" implies sex, but I honestly can't think of any other interpretation. And it adds yet another layer of irony. We can—and should—get our knickers in a twist about the sexualisation of children in *Birth*, but this single, which reached number 4 on the Billboard chart in 1956, was performed by girls aged 11 and 14.

Birth was a commercial failure and widely ridiculed by critics, with a few notable exceptions—Will Self in the *Evening Standard*, Roger Ebert in the *Chicago Sun-Times*. The film had been troubled in production, particularly with its script, which led to extensive post-production work to assemble a releasable version. For Glazer, *Birth* marked an ambitious step into the big league, utilising the star power of Kidman, an Oscar-winner and arguably the most luminous movie star of the moment. It was a deliberate move away from the stylish pulp of *Sexy Beast*. This was his second album syndrome, and the project bore the weight of his own uncertainty. If "director's jail" is real—and apparently it is—Glazer was sent straight to solitary. His next feature wouldn't appear for another nine years.

Rewatching the film now, all that noise has receded. What remains is a poised, controlled, and quietly astonishing piece of cinema. Just like its star. The film's absurdity is still intact, but it no longer feels silly. It's the absurdity of Buñuel or Lynch—or even Kubrick, for that matter. (A luxury hotel in the Rockies that closes for ski season? The premise is as stable as late-stage Jenga.)

Desire is absurd. It makes us absurd. Part of the sorrow of tragedy is how ridiculous it renders us, how humiliating it is to feel so much. We cry ugly. Ophelia

---

* "Tonight You Belong to Me," written by Billy Rose and Lee David in 1926, was covered several times before the popular version by Prudence and Patience was released.

with her flowers. Humbert Humbert hunting for Quilty. Anna, in her wedding dress, walking into the sea. And the sense that lingers is this: the kindest ending for her may be simply to let her go.

FIVE

THE DISCOMFORT ZONE
Commercials, 2000-2024

Dreamer

After *Sexy Beast*, Glazer returned to his work in advertising. His final contribution to the Guinness campaign—which had begun with "Swim Black" and "Surfer"—culminated in "Dreamer," which premiered in April 2001. The 60-second spot is dense with visual invention, surreal gags, and ambitious imagery. The ad centers on a man known as the Champion of the Dream Club, played by Lajos Kovàcs (the fleeing man from Glazer's "Karma Police" video), who goes to sleep pondering the question, "What are you drinking?" and wakes to find the answer before him: a perfect pint of Guinness. Shot in the same luxurious black and white as "Surfer," the film continues Glazer's animal motif. After the Champion dozes off, a squirrel in a squirrel-filled pub bolts awake and exclaims, "I just had the weirdest dream."

The execution—complete with photorealistic talking squirrels—is witty and precise. It could have carried an ad on its own, but here, it's just the beginning. Next, we find the Champion sleepwalking in the street, swept up in a running crowd. Glazer breaks the

180-degree rule, disorienting the viewer as the crowd moves back and forth. The Champion begins stripping off layers as he runs, finally joining a frenzied heap of men scrambling over one another to peer through a peephole high in a wall. Their bodies stack into the shape of a Christmas tree. The Champion climbs, hurling others aside. In the background, a horse rolls on its back (possibly a nod to Tarkovsky's *Andrei Rublev*) while little dogs bounce in excitement. The setting evokes a fevered Mittel Europa between the wars: Kafka after a few too many, or early Bergman on MDMA.

"Tonight's dream, the big question: what's the meaning of life?" intones the voiceover. At last, the Champion reaches the top, gazes into the disturbingly sphincter-like hole, and snaps awake back at the pub — laughing so violently it startles the other patrons of the Dream Club.

Outside the pub, a silent horde stands motionless — a slightly nightmarish vision. They appear to be waiting to enter, yet their expressionless patience suggests they know they never will. "Welcome to dreamland," say the voice with deadpan irony.

The advert failed to match the success of "Surfer," either commercially or critically, and it marked the end of Guinness' "Good Things" campaign, which the company soon abandoned in favor of a strategy more adaptable to international markets. Glazer and copywriter Walter Campbell had grown increasingly ambitious with each new entry, and "Dreamer," like Glazer's later music videos, feels like an effort to stretch the advertising brief to its absolute limit. The technology required to bring the photorealistic squirrels to life necessitated custom-built software. Years later, *Under the Skin* would similarly demand new micro-cameras, discreetly embedded in the van Scarlett Johansson drove through Glasgow. Glazer's commitment to experimentation remained constant.

But perhaps more striking than the technical innovation is the tone. The darkness isn't just visual. Where "Surfer" offered feel-good aspiration—with its rhythmic grandeur and life-affirming bravado—"Dreamer" is disorienting, bleak, and vaguely hungover. It's a beautifully crafted shaggy dog story that feels like it was conceived one drink too many into the night.

Odyssey

If "Dreamer" had suffered from trying to cram too much into sixty seconds, Glazer's 2002 spot "Odyssey"—an ad for Levi's Engineered Jeans—took the opposite approach. Conceptually, it was stripped down to its essence. The brief was clear: counteract the so-called "Clarkson effect," the creeping association of jeans with paunchy, middle-aged men like the ever-present British TV presenter Jeremy Clarkson. Levi's wanted an advert that radiated youth and dynamism.

A young man with the kind of heroin chic of Ewan MacGregor in *Trainspotting* (1997) sprints full-tilt through the walls of an apartment building, crashing through brick and plaster. He's soon joined by a young woman, and together they tear forward in a breathless race. The use of Handel's Sarabande—famously featured in *Barry Lyndon*, with Kubrick never far from Glazer's mind—lends the sequence both a rhythmic propulsion and a sense of timeless grandeur.

In the final moments, they break through the last wall and sprint across the tops of tree trunks—echoing Chow Yun-fat and Michelle Yeoh in *Crouching Tiger, Hidden Dragon* (2000)—before making a final, weightless leap toward the distant stars.

The production took six months and cost around $3 million, blending digital effects with practical stunts. The two actors ran through sixteen walls—each one rigged with hidden openings that allowed them to pass, while debris and dust were blasted outward by air cannons to heighten the impact. There's no narrative in the traditional sense, just a visceral rush of excitement and liberation. One of the key visual inspirations was Roy Batty (Rutger Hauer) crashing through a wall in Ridley Scott's *Blade Runner* (1982). At its core, the ad is pure attitude—cool, youthful, and blasting away the cobwebs.

Chicken

Figures in motion were rendered even more simply in Glazer's 2003 series of adverts for Barclays Bank. Each features Samuel L. Jackson delivering a monologue while walking toward a retreating camera. In one, he strides through the rain reciting a passage from *The Comedy of Errors*; in another, he compares money to a chicken: "If a dollar was a chicken, would a chicken be evil?" he muses. The tagline: "Money speaks in many languages. We understand all of them." The animals appear in brief codas—chickens, naturally, but also a centaur and a bull. It's fitting for the cock-and-bull story Jackson is telling.

The ads carry a kind of stark oddness but ultimately fail to land. Back in the late '80s, Rutger Hauer's Guinness commercials—where the *Blade Runner* star famously claimed, "It's not easy being a dolphin"—struck the right surreal note. They were strange, quotable, and somehow worked with a pint of stout. Barclays, by contrast, is a bank, and banks rarely do irony well. There's something too calculated, too arch in these spots, especially when trying to sell the idea that banks are not, in fact, evil. (At the time Hauer was empathising with aquatic mammals, many were boycotting Barclays for its investment in apartheid South Africa.)

It's the corporate equivalent of a bank manager trying to crack an edgy joke through the borrowed cool of Samuel L. Jackson, and even he doesn't look entirely convinced.

The Return of Don

In 2004, another countercultural icon resurfaced: Don Logan from *Sexy Beast*. He returned in a series of sixty-second ads produced by Walter Campbell, scripted by Louis Mellis and David Scinto, and performed once again by Sir Ben Kingsley. Directed by Glazer and shot over a weekend, the ads aired in slots donated by Mercedes to support Band Aid 20, the charity campaign for poverty relief in the developing world. The premise is simple: Don Logan is baffled to find himself doing good. He's donated to charity and feels disoriented by the unfamiliar sensation of having done something worthwhile. "It might be addictive," he mutters, half in awe, half in fear. He urges viewers to buy the Band Aid record, reassuring them they don't even have to listen to it.

The direction is stripped back, with only a touch of surreal blocking (a comically tall barman) to offset the otherwise straightforward staging. But none of that matters. We're here for Don Logan. He's crawled out from under Gal's swimming pool to pitch Bob Geldof's charity single.

There's always a risk in repurposing a character like this. It nudges them toward caricature, toward being a national treasure. Alex from *A Clockwork Orange* ends up on Camden market t-shirts. Horror icons follow the same trajectory: Leatherface in *The Texas Chain Saw Massacre* (1974), Michael Myers in *Halloween* (1978), Freddy Krueger in *A Nightmare on Elm Street* (1984)— each one slowly morphing from genuine menace into comic-book villainy through endless sequels and reboots. Don Logan was always funny, but not release-a-charity-record funny.

Paint

"Colour like no other" was the tagline for "Paint," the commercial Glazer was commissioned to direct for Sony Bravia TVs. The concept is simplicity itself; the execution, decidedly less so. A deserted Glasgow housing estate was rigged with explosives, each detonation sending paint bombs splattering across walls, windows, and stairwells. According to Naresh Ramchandani in *The Guardian*, the production cost £2 million, required relocating 60 residents, five days of clean-up, and a hefty fee for Glazer himself.[*]

The result is breathtaking. The rhythm and composition are precise, even balletic. The lifeless seems to pulse with new energy, all of it choreographed to Rossini's Thieving Magpie overture—famously used in *A Clockwork Orange.* There are other film echoes too: a long interior corridor conjures *The Shining*, while a fleeing clown brings with him spooky *It* (1986) vibes from Stephen King's novel.

Despite its "like no other" claim, "Paint" is actually a sequel to 2005's "Balls," in which a quarter of a million coloured spheres tumbled down the hills of San Francisco, the city's most kinetic spectacle since Steve McQueen tore through the city in a blue polo neck. Both adverts share a vivid, physical commitment to in-camera effects, proudly eschewing CGI. Both were also supported by full-blown behind-the-scenes documentaries, showcasing the technical audacity and logistical headaches that went into making them. The ads invite a very modern sort of awe: *how did they do that?*

But as Ramchandani points out, there is a tonal difference. Balls is playful and full of childlike wonder. "Paint," by contrast, feels colder, more alien—spectacular, yes, but disquieting. "I don't find it easy to warm to a

---

show-off,"* he admits, even as he praises the advert's beauty, surrealism and intelligence. His distinction is valuable. Glazer's work—whether commercials, music videos or films—thrives on estrangement. In "Paint," aside from the clown, there are no people at all. The star of the show is absence.

There's beauty in Glazer's images, but also a lingering otherworldliness. An uncanny presence always seems to lurk, like a centaur just out of frame, or the inexplicable blood leaking from beneath the sofa in Jamiroquai's "Virtual Insanity." Darkness seeps through the cracks. And when people do appear, they're often glimpsed from an alien's perspective or living next door to a concentration camp.

Several commercials directed by Glazer were completed but never aired—haunting, self-contained visions that ended up shelved, too strange, too dark, or simply too uncompromising for the brands that commissioned them.

Clay
This uncanny quality—the discomfort zone at the heart of Glazer's vision—led to one of the most remarkable episodes in his career: the rejection of his advert "Clay" by the client, Motorola Red. Made the same year as "Paint," the commercial features a spinning form accompanied by distorted electronic sounds. Gradually, the shape resolves into the naked body of a black man, then a black woman. The two figures spin faster, as if on a demented potter's wheel, until they begin to fuse— melting into one another even as they embrace.

The tagline that follows is jarringly earnest in both tone and phrasing: "There's a phone designed to help

---

* Naresh Ramchandani.

eliminate AIDS in Africa—Please buy it." Is this capitalism at its most compassionate or the commodification of suffering to move product? The spinning black bodies, stripped of agency or identity, become "clay" in the hands of a white European director and the American telecom giant backing the campaign. One doesn't need to reach for a semiotics textbook to understand why objections were raised—nudity aside, the optics speak for themselves.

Flake

Another Glazer commercial would be rejected—again, not without reason—but in this case, it's hard not to feel the clients were being spoilsports. Cadbury's Flake, long marketed with the tagline "only the crumbliest, flakiest chocolate tastes like chocolate never tasted before," had a history of sensual ads: women eating chocolate in bathtubs, sun-drenched fields, or summer rain, all with a strong undercurrent of soft-focus eroticism. The aesthetics always hinted at soft porn and oral sex. But for a planned revamp, Glazer pushed that subtext to the surface—and the resulting spot was deemed far too provocative for broadcast.

Denis Lavant plays the devil in a regency wig and black leather trousers, somewhere between a fop from Peter Greenaway's *The Draughtsman's Contract* (1982) and Tim Curry's Lucifer in *Legend* (1985). He dances down the Spanish Steps in Rome before summoning a group of women in gauzy *Hammer House of Horror* nightdresses, who crawl toward him, scrabbling at the chocolate he flings at them. The devil spins around a fiery fountain in orgasmic glee. The new tagline? "Succumb to the Crumb."

It's glorious camp, deliciously risqué, but unsurprisingly, a brand dependent on family sales was never going to welcome headlines about satanic orgies and chocolate. The original Flake ads had mastered a kind of Pixar-effect marketing: the sensuality was there for the adults, but kids just saw a bar of chocolate. The new version replaced innuendo with full-blown metaphor, and Cadbury flinched.

The ad has since resurfaced online, earning cult admiration and adding a kind of forbidden luster to Glazer's résumé. But having a finished commercial pulled is never great for business. Presumably, in both the Motorola and Flake cases, the clients had signed off on the pitch meetings, the storyboards, the scripts. Then, somewhere along the line—likely after seeing the final cut—they balked. Those reversals would have been not just embarrassing but ruinously expensive. Soon after "Succumb to the Crumb" was shelved, Cadbury dropped Saatchi as their agency.

Cars and cameras
In 2010, Glazer directed "The Last Tango in Compton" for the Volkswagen Polo, a beautifully shot ad featuring a tango performed by two dancers in casual streetwear, suggesting a blend of street credibility and elegance. The tagline—"Tough. Beautiful. Polo."—lands with a thud. I've driven a Volkswagen Polo, and at no point did the words tough, beautiful or tango enter my mind. This is, of course, one of the fundamental problems with advertising: no matter how striking the execution, you're still selling a product.

Some products lend themselves to poetic interpretation—Sony Bravia, for instance, where the concept of "amazing colour" invites aesthetic freedom. Glazer would later make another spot for Sony, promoting its new line of 3D televisions. But other clients—Cadbury's, say—are less accommodating of untamed imagination. Some, however, are simply grateful to bask in the glow of borrowed artistry.

Another car commercial offered a sports-themed opportunity: "The Ring," a tribute of sorts to Stanley Kubrick, whose early short *Day of the Fight* (1951) chronicled a boxing match. But here Glazer subverts expectations by focusing not on the fighters, but the referee—a thankless, unglamorous figure who exists solely to keep chaos in check.

For Glazer, commercials were laboratories, places to experiment with form and technique without the weight of a traditional narrative. In 2014, he made two striking ads for Canon that offered total freedom from story or slogan. As Marshall McLuhan might have said, the medium was the message—and the message was pure image.

One, titled "Come and See," depicts Calcio Storico, a medieval Florentine game of football in which 27 bare-chested men per team compete with almost no rules—punching, grappling, and brawling in a blur of muscle and dust. The hypermasculine spectacle, at first brutal and tribal, gradually softens into camaraderie, a kind of wounded brotherhood. The second spot, "Urban Deer," used 21 cameras to capture deer as they wandered into a housing estate at night, lured by the scent of rotting apples. Filmed over eight nights, it's eerie and hypnotic, a quiet intrusion of the wild into the man-made.

Under the Skin, shot the previous year, had begun to explore this blend of observational cinema and covert surveillance. With "Urban Deer," that interest deepened, and would be developed even further in *The Zone of Interest*, where watching—cold, mechanical, sustained— becomes the central aesthetic and moral position.

Motion and emotion

As Glazer's career in commercial directing has progressed, two core preoccupations have become increasingly apparent: first, an ongoing fascination with the technical possibilities of filmmaking—experimenting with equipment, blending practical, special, and digital effects, and pushing the limits of cinematic form; second, a persistent interest in the human body in motion.

That latter focus reaches new heights in his 2018 Super Bowl spot for Squarespace, featuring Keanu Reeves surfing a motorcycle down a highway. The image gestures back to *Point Break* (1991), as well as Glazer's own much-celebrated Guinness ad. A long aerial swoop establishes Reeves riding his bike as though it were a surfboard. He gains confidence, gradually straightening his posture until he stands tall, knees unbent, while a flock of birds soars behind him and cars whip past in the opposite direction. There's a tension between the ordinary and the superhuman—the everyday road and the impossible act. When Reeves finally sits astride the bike, it lifts into the air. Why wouldn't it?

The following year, Glazer returned to flight with a commercial for the Apple Watch. A young woman breaks into an athletic sprint, only to be caught in a gust of wind that lifts her above the clouds. What follows is a stunning airborne dance, choreographed and performed by Inka Tiitto, a world champion at air dance—a form of indoor skydiving—digitally enhanced to heighten its dreamlike quality. She plummets back to Earth, landing with a splash in a mountain lake.

Taken together—"Odyssey," "Tango," "Keanu" and "Flight"—these commercials channel a shared exhilaration: the liberation of motion, the transcendence of physical boundaries, the joy of flying. It's a through-line in Glazer's work, this striving for a kind of spiritual elevation. The perfect wave, the airborne motorcycle, the sprint through walls, or Denis Lavant in "Rabbit in Your Headlights," crawling from the wreckage only to rise—becoming something like an urban angel.

First Light: Alexander McQueen
Spring/Summer Collection 2021

This short film occupies a liminal space between commercial and cinema. Clocking in at just under five minutes, it showcases an haute couture fashion line—though the line itself straddles art and commerce so thoroughly that the label "product" feels almost beside the point. Shot during a Covid lockdown, the film makes haunting use of London's emptiness, an atmosphere reminiscent of the post-apocalyptic quiet Danny Boyle captured in *28 Days Later* (2002). Filmed from the banks of the Thames, two women walk upriver, half-submerged, as impervious to the cold as the alien in *Under the Skin*.

The soundscape is unsettling: birdsong, electronic bleeps, drips and sloshes—but no engines, no sirens, no human noise. It's the absence that feels uncanny. Why isn't the city louder? Glazer has long found meaning in voids, and here, again, emptiness is a texture: white skies, blank faces, the stillness of lockdown as aesthetic.

A woman and man lean against a wall beside the river. On the bridge above, a gang of young men (Droogs, perhaps) prowl, looking for trouble: the kind of stylised hoodlums the fashion world creates, sharp enough to cut you with their cheekbones, light enough to be knocked over with a breath. The woman at the wall steals the man's wallet as he kisses her neck. Elsewhere, a young woman with a shaved suede-textured head sits in the mud in a ballerina's tutu and what look like Doc Martens. A cluster of models, if that's the correct collective noun, share a picnic, while one of them sobs silently, channeling Maria Falconetti in *The Passion of Joan of Arc* (1928).

The whole thing has the solemnity—and joylessness—of a late Antonioni film. At times it verges on parody, an *SNL* spoof of a fashion film. You half expect Derek Zoolander to wander into frame and unleash

Magnum. The palette is nearly monochrome: everything tinted with river fog. The suede-headed woman lies back in the mud and flaps her limbs to create a sewage angel. As with the soundtrack, what's most notable is what's missing: smell. This is the Thames, after all, the river that gave London The Great Stink in 1858. Thankfully, it remains off-camera.

Only at the end, when the brand name appears, does time return. A time-lapse shot shows the river rising and falling with the tide beneath the bridge. And here, at last, comes colour.

Gallerie — Prada
At the time of writing, Glazer's most recent commercial is "The Gallerie," a 2024 spot for luxury fashion house Prada, shot in New York and starring *Under the Skin* lead Scarlett Johansson. The ad opens with Johansson struggling to deliver lines from Shakespeare — Cleopatra, Macbeth, and others — while a cacophony of sound swells around her: pages rustling, voices murmuring, ambient clatter. The audio disorients both viewer and performer. In stage parlance, it's all noises-off.

Shot in stark black and white, the piece partly pays homage to Ingmar Bergman's *Persona* (1966), a portrait of an actress unraveling. The mechanics of filmmaking are exposed via a direct shot of the camera, shown from Johansson's point of view, which resembles HAL 9000 from *2001: A Space Odyssey*, but rotated on its side. Johansson cycles through a rapid-fire sequence of emotions: grief, rage, seduction, laughter, vulnerability. Then the artifice collapses. The black and white bleeds away, and makeup artists and hair stylists swarm the frame.

At the film's end, Johansson slips out the studio's back door with her capacious Prada handbag and climbs into a waiting yellow cab. "53rd and 1st," she tells the driver. She could be headed to the Madison Restaurant, the Irish pub, the QQ Nail Spa, the Heavenly Market Deli—or any one of a thousand Manhattan destinations.

The brand is self-congratulatory luxury. As another campaign once put it: Because you're worth it. Prada doesn't need something as downmarket as an advert. Appropriately, the credit reads simply: "A film by Jonathan Glazer." What we're watching is less a commercial than a meditation on performance—specifically, on Johansson's range, which Glazer had already tapped to extraordinary effect in one of her finest roles.

Johansson will, of course, take centre stage in the next chapter. But before we move on, it's worth noting that even as he was making commercials, Glazer remained deeply committed to what he called his "day job": cinematic filmmaking. "Commercials interest me," he told Anne Thompson in 2014. "Some were used as sketches for the film, we were testing out gear. I did a couple of music videos and set projects. It was isolating, writing for that length of time, even with a friend of mine. At times I wanted to get out of the room and point the camera at something. It's a headfuck working on that kind of material for that length of time."[*]

That headfuck was *Under the Skin*.

SIX
UNDER THE SKIN

An important but underappreciated way in which Glazer has mimicked his primary cinematic hero, Stanley Kubrick, is in allowing such long gaps between his releases: four years between *Sexy Beast* and *Birth*, ten between *Under the Skin* and *The Zone of Interest*. Nine years passed between the critical drubbing and commercial failure of *Birth* in 2004 and the premiere of *Under the Skin* at the Venice Film Festival in 2013.

The delay could have been due as much to a stint in director's jail as to a desire to emulate his directorial daddy, Kubrick, but the project actually predated *Birth*, and so, in an alternate universe where *Birth* was a smash, we might have seen *Under the Skin* as early as 2006, starring Brad Pitt and Gemma Arterton. Glazer said: "Ten years? It was very easy for me to spend that much time on the film. That's what it took, from an immense amount of time thinking about it to completing it."[*]

The film tells the story of an Alien (Scarlett Johansson) who drives around Glasgow, Scotland, in a white van, preying on young men. The storyline has the absurdity of *Birth*, the generic triteness of *Sexy Beast*. It will risk silliness, but as with his previous films, Glazer's

---

[*] Anne Thompson.

seriousness of purpose—his deadpan celebration of the dark—will lead to an utterly compelling work of art.

But first, bats…

Batgirl

In his 1973 paper "What Is It Like to Be a Bat?" Thomas Nagel argues that consciousness is not exclusively human. "Conscious experience is a widespread phenomenon. It occurs at many levels of animal life, though we cannot be sure of its presence in the simpler organisms […] No doubt it occurs in countless forms totally unimaginable to us, on other planets in other solar systems throughout the universe."[*] He argues that if there is something like it to be the organism (or alien), something for the organism (or alien), then they possess consciousness.

In attempting to answer the title question of his paper, Nagel challenges reductionism, which seeks to explain consciousness through physical processes, and behaviourism, which defines beings by what they do. A bat is inarguably conscious, he argues, but knowing what it feels like to be a bat escapes us, because bats experience the world in ways fundamentally different from humans: "anyone who has spent some time in an enclosed space with an excited bat knows what it is to encounter a fundamentally alien form of life."[†] If we were to attempt an experiment in which we gradually became bats—in a slow-motion version of Jeff Goldblum's transformation in *The Fly* (1986)—we could only report back while still partly human and partly bat, and therefore never fully cognisant of either state.

Similarly, if we tried to imagine what it feels like to be a bat by drawing analogies between their attributes

---

[*] Thomas Nagel, "What Is It Like to Be a Bat?," *The Philosophical Review*, October 1974.
[†] Ibid.

and our own—flying is a bit like running; echoloca-tion is a kind of hearing and seeing at once—we would quickly recognise the unsatisfactory gaps between these similes and any convincing sense of their lived reality.

Nor is this a uniquely human-to-bat problem. How can we know what life feels like for a deaf person, or for someone both blind and deaf, or colour-blind? What is their subjective reality? One difference, perhaps, is that they might not have written that last sentence, which so automatically consigns them to a "they" to be studied.

Or for that matter, what would it be like to be Younghoon Kim? The South Korean polymath holds the record for the highest IQ ever registered—276, compared to the average score of 90–110—a result confirmed when he competed in a world championship of the mind.* What would it be like to eat breakfast as Younghoon? How does he experience the world? Is it the cognitive equivalent of being three metres tall? We might be tempted to say, "He puts his trousers on one leg at a time like we all do," as Jake Gittes says of John Huston's villainous patriarch in *Chinatown* (1974). But that's not really going to cut it.

And how would someone experience our life? For all his genius, how could Younghoon access my decidedly average-IQ reality? What about someone with aphantasia—the inability to visualise mentally? Someone reading this book with aphantasia would see the words "green apple" and nothing more, while the rest of you are "seeing" a green apple in your minds.

---

* I've never tested my own IQ, or I would give it here in the interests of full disclosure. My reluctance is partly inspired by the feeling it will be low, or at least lower than I'd like. And partly because then I would be inundated by IQ tests by the algorithm which doesn't seem to understand there are somethings you only want/need to do once.

A strange phenomenon, perhaps, but it's estimated that almost 4% of the population are aphantasics.*

Nagel flips his question, too: "In contemplating the bats we are in much the same position that intelligent bats or Martians would occupy if they tried to form a conception of what it was like to be us."†

The idea that different consciousnesses have different subjective experiences of reality can be taken further: different consciousnesses might live in different realities altogether. The world of dogs is dominated by smells; the world of birds by altitude and the shifting pressure of air; whales live in a reality made of depth, pressure again, song, and epic journeys. And yet, in trying to understand—or even describe—what those experiences might be like, we inevitably anthropomorphise them. Note my passing reference to "whale song."

There are even arguments that plants and fungi—even cells and atomic particles—have a form of consciousness. In *Ways of Being*, James Bridle gathers examples of non-human intelligence, including slime mould that can organise public transportation systems, and plants that can "remember" having been dropped.‡

When discussing *Under the Skin*, Jonathan Glazer insists that it is about an alien. An ALIEN. Not how alienated it feels to live in society, but about being an actual alien. Interviewing Glazer, David Poland interprets the film as a coming-of-age story about a young woman. While acknowledging he can't control how others read his work, Glazer responds: "I really hoped that we would protect the idea of the Alien from beginning to end so that you were really none the wiser

---

* C. J. Dance, A. Ipser and J. Simner "The prevalence of aphantasia (imagery weakness) in the general population," *Consciousness and Cognition*, January 2022.
† Ibid..
‡ James Bridle, *Ways of Being* (London, 2022).

of whom you were looking at at the end of the film as you were at the beginning. To be alien, it needed to remain alien and inscrutable in some sense."*

Nagel uses the idea that if we accept it must be like something to be a bat, this defines consciousness—I can't imagine what it's like to be a brick, for instance—but we're also confronted with an unknowability that similes and metaphors cannot bridge. We are all dying, in a way, but some of us have terminal diseases. There's an important gap there.

Not to mention, this isn't a one-way street. Bats perceive us. We are looking at an alien who, in turn, is looking at us. We know nothing about this alien. We might try to interpret its experience according to how we imagine it might go—how it would go if it were human. "A coming-of-age story about how it is to be a 20-year-old girl," for instance—but we have no reason to believe that's the case.

And a 20-year-old girl might well take umbrage. That's not what it's like at all. I might feel alienated, she might say, but I'm not an actual alien.

Loving the Alien
In much of science fiction, the Alien—the Other—can usually be read as a human being in an alien suit. In H. G. Wells' 1897 novel *The War of the Worlds*, the Martians are essentially colonists, doing to Europe what Europe had done to the rest of the world: mercilessly killing thousands of natives, empowered by vast technological superiority, bleeding the place dry of its resources, and polluting its natural beauty. (It's a red weed they bring from Mars.) Eventually, they fall foul of tropical diseases. The Martian imperialist does to England what England did to India, to large parts of Africa, and beyond. Wells' novel is a book to read

---

* D/P30 The Oral History of Hollywood, 28 September 2013.

alongside Joseph Conrad's *Heart of Darkness* (1899), published just two years later.

Wells' darkly funny joke is that the tropical disease fatal to the Martians is the common English cold. Your ordinary is someone else's exotic. In 1950s science fiction films like *The Day the Earth Stood Still* (1951) and *Invasion of the Body Snatchers* (1956), the Alien could be a communist infiltrator or a McCarthyite snitch, depending on the viewer's own paranoia and political leanings.

The "serious" science fiction films of Stanley Kubrick (*2001: A Space Odyssey*) and Andrei Tarkovsky (*Solaris* and *Stalker* [1979]) did away entirely with any direct representation of the Alien. The Aliens are a shaping absence, hinted at by offscreen sounds or the artefacts they leave behind.

In *Roadside Picnic*, the 1972 novel by brothers Arkady and Boris Strugatsky on which *Stalker* was based, it is suggested that the objects left behind might seem portentous to us but are, for the Aliens themselves, nothing more than the kind of rubbish discarded after an actual picnic—a sweet wrapper, an empty can of pop. Exposing the latent narcissism in most alien-encounter stories, the Strugatskys and Tarkovsky contemplate a consciousness that has no interest in humanity at all, one that makes no attempt to communicate with us, just as we make no attempt to communicate with the gnats that bother our summer evenings. They don't even notice we exist.

In Ridley Scott's *Alien* (1979), the Xenomorph is understood partly as an animal and partly as a kind of organic machine. Its greatest admirer is the onboard synthetic Ash, played by Ian Holm, who says: "It's the perfect organism. Its structural perfection is only matched by its hostility." It is revealed that the mission has always been to bring the Xenomorph back to Earth, where it can be studied and weaponised as a form of biological warfare. The Alien may have an interiority or subjective experience, but we are given no access to it. Though it appears humanoid, Swiss artist H. R. Giger's design is so original that it avoids the usual creature-feature clichés.

Despite this originality, the Alien remains psychosexually human. Its retractable penis/vagina dentata is its most formidable and "alien" attribute, and yet it is recognisable as a composite of human anatomy—like much of Giger's work, which is littered with penises and vaginas scattered willy-nilly throughout.

As the franchise goes on, the alienness is diluted. The Xenomorph settles down and has kids (*Aliens*, 1986), impregnates Sigourney Weaver's Ripley (*Alien³*, 1992), and finally makes its way to Earth (*Alien Resurrection*, 1997). With *Prometheus* (2012), the Xenomorphs are revealed to be the creations of Engineers—basically hairless tech-bros—and all sense of Alien's alienness is lost in a mishmash of Erich von Däniken and expositional prequalitis.

Denis Villeneuve's *Arrival* (2016) does a good job of suggesting alienness, but only by taking a leaf out of H. P. Lovecraft's Necronomicon and using squids and ideograms as the template for his pebble-driving aliens.

And lest this seem overly harsh, let me emphasise: this is not about the poverty of our imagination—science fiction has offered incredible insights and variations on the human experience. But it is almost impossible to conceptualise something truly alien, something that in no way resembles anything we have ever seen or experienced on Earth. Take, for example, the *Star Wars* franchise, where we get desert planets, forest planets, and ice planets—all of which look like places on Earth but with, you know, different weather.

There's no argument here that Glazer fully escapes this conundrum, but *Under the Skin* at least attempts to take it seriously. Its narrative arc presents a problem: narrative may be an inherently human way of perceiving the world. Do bats have narrative arcs? Do they perceive them in other bats?

And that's the important thing. Our understanding of the film—my understanding of the film—could be completely wrong, because the lead character is a bat.

The Woman Who Fell to Earth
When I saw the film at the Venice Film Festival—where it was both applauded and booed (because festivals)— I spoke with a colleague who didn't like it and saw in it a deeply misogynistic story. "Take away the science fiction stuff," he told me, "and imagine this is a story of Eastern European gangsters using a honeypot trap to trap, rob and kill men. The woman who acts as the bait grows a conscience and runs away and, without the protection of her criminal associates, she is raped and murdered brutally by a stranger. Her rape is the punishment for using her sexuality to kill those men earlier in the film."*

This is a simplification, but it was, more or less, his argument. For me, the phrase "take away the science fiction stuff" was doing far too much lifting. I wanted to shout: Wait! There's a baby in that bath water.

The film is not (merely) a stand-in for something else. The story can certainly be interpreted as a symbol of x or a metaphor for y, but why not read it as the thing itself? It's like saying: take away the religious stuff and the Bible can be read like this—which, of course, it can—but then you're doing something else. You're no longer accepting the integrity of what you're looking at; you've fundamentally changed the text you're working

---

* Neil Young was that critic. No relation to the Canadian free world rocker.

with. (In reality, the Bible is probably the worst example I could have chosen, as it's a collection of disparate texts, many of which weren't originally religious in nature, nor were they ever intended for the book they eventually found themselves in. *The Song of Songs* is, after all, a set of sexy love lyrics.)*

The tendency with science fiction is to treat it immediately as an extended analogy (often because it is). But it is never only that. I reduced *The War of the Worlds* to a political critique in the last section, but it is obviously also a beautifully written adventure novel, rich with much more than a commentary on imperialism.

Published in 2000, Michel Faber's debut novel *Under the Skin* belongs to the tradition of the what-if thought experiment, in the lineage of Wells' book. Rather than imperialism, it targets the industrialised production of meat. The narrator, Isserley, is an alien who has undergone surgical modification to walk upright and appear sexually attractive to human males. Ironically, her altered form is considered grotesque by her own kind. She drives through remote parts of Scotland, picking up hitchhikers, drugging them via a weaponised passenger seat (a James Bond-style gadget), and delivering them to a farm where they are castrated, have their tongues removed, and are then fattened and slaughtered to produce vodsel—human meat, which resembles veal.

---

* Neil and I are both right and wrong. There is no "thing itself" (see criticism of Kant) that can't also be interpreted. The conceptualisation of something is an interpretation, even as I interpret it as the "thing itself." But the postmodern idea of a thing that only exists via interpretation of what it is similar to but crucially not leads us to a *Lady of Shanghai*-style hall of mirrors where all is confusion (itself a meta-comment on Orson Welles' earlier film *Citizen Kane*) and where, epistemologically speaking, there's a good chance we'll end up shooting the wrong person.

The Wikipedia entry for the novel reports—under the subheading "Themes"—that "its themes include sexism, big business, factory farming, animal cruelty and experimentation, environmental decay, class politics, rape, and treatment of and attitudes toward immigrants. It reflects on more personal questions of sexual identity, humanity, snobbery, and mercy."

"Wouldn't it be terrible if aliens treated us the way we treat other animals?" That, in essence, is the provocation posed by the book. Except, of course, in *Under the Skin*, we aren't treated exactly the same way we treat animals, which is where the analogy begins to fray. We don't lure our meat by picking up hitchhiking cows from a planet ruled by cows. But that doesn't necessarily matter. An analogy doesn't need to hold at every point. Faber himself has stated that his novel was never meant to be confined to a single moral claim. "For me, *Under the Skin* is not about the evils of eating meat but about the evils of evading moral responsibility for the decisions we make. The novel is strong enough, however, to adapt to the needs of each reader."[*]

The act of picking up male hitchhikers is where questions of gender enter the frame. Sex and power are explored as Faber plays on misogynistic stereotypes of the femme fatale, while also unsettling our assumptions about female beauty—Isserley's surgically altered appearance may appeal to human men, but her own species finds it grotesque. This inversion is recognisably human in its resemblance to body dysmorphia.

Our feelings toward Isserley shift as the novel progresses and we learn more about her place in her own alien society—how deeply stratified it is, and how powerless she truly is within it. A female worker in an abattoir may rank above the animals but still below

---

[*] Michel Faber, "*Under the Skin* changed my life for good," *The Guardian*, 5 December 2020.

her male co-workers, who themselves are beneath management. So, class enters the picture too.

Each of these thematic layers depends on a movement away from the alien and towards the human. Isserley becomes increasingly like us—she "discovers" humanity (as though that were an a priori good, a universal quality all civilisations should strive for)—and the alien system around her also starts to resemble our own. The aliens operate under an exploitative economic regime that looks a lot like capitalism. There's even a familial element to the power structure, made evident when the boss' son arrives. He's a vegetarian, a recognisable example of the privileged having the luxury to be critical of the structures that sustain their privilege, in contrast to those working at the coalface—or, in this case, on the abattoir floor.

What if Isserley somehow managed to become completely human and found that all she could get was a job at an abattoir? A *human* one, where we kill cows and calves and make veal instead of vodsel. Would she be back to square one? An eternal regression?

This de-othering of the Other erases the alien. She's just like us—*under the skin*. At the end of the book, Isserley triggers the self-destruct on her vehicle and imagines herself dissolving into the universe. It's as if Faber has concluded that identity and difference must ultimately be eradicated, dissolved into the ether. We are everything and nothing. Which makes writing books about films both completely redundant, and vitally important.

Analysis, too, has a way of de-othering. In *The Tempest*, Caliban can be read as many things, but is often interpreted as a figure for the colonised, an unfortunate and unhappy subject of European imperialism. But in the play itself, he is also a supernatural creature. The tendency to make everything "just like us" is a narcissistic move, masquerading as liberal tolerance, but in fact it passively—or actively—absorbs the Other into ourselves. It erases the essential difference that gives identity its shape. Caliban would likely give us an earful if we told him he was just a symbol—a projection of our anxieties—instead of recognising him as a consciousness, a being, a universe of perceptions entirely his own.

Life is wider than argument; being is broader than the symbol for being.

When Jonathan Glazer was first handed the book by his producer James Wilson, his initial intention was to make a relatively faithful adaptation. Working with his friend and mentor from the advertising world, Walter Campbell, a couple of drafts were completed and financing was secured, with tentative casting in place, including, at one point, Brad Pitt. The film was very close to being made. There would have been two aliens—a couple—living a kind of back-to-nature, organic farm-style existence, producing human meat in the process. But the project encountered obstacles, and Glazer turned his attention to *Birth*.

Following the completion of *Birth*, and with Pitt now out of the picture, Campbell and Glazer began to reduce the script to a more skeletal structure. The project's long gestation is detailed in Maureen Foster's invaluable *Alien in the Mirror.** Glazer compared the process to taking a massive rock band and stripping it down to P. J. Harvey.† The version that became the film's blueprint moved away from the novel's thematic overload toward something narratively simpler yet thematically richer. Pared to its essentials—backstory and exposition removed—mystery crept in and the Other reasserted itself.

Something genuinely Alien emerged.

---

* Maureen Foster, *Alien in the Mirror: Scarlett Johansson, Jonathan Glazer and Under the Skin* (McFarland, 2019).
† Anne Thompson.

Glazer explains: "Seeing the world through an alien lens was our North Star."* Yet he immediately faced a variation on Nagel's question: what is it like to be an alien? "You can't show an alien entity. It's impossible. But you can allude to it—the feeling of it, the dread of it. She's not really a 'she.' She's an 'it.' It's a force, a dispassionate entity. Like the sea." This insistence on preserving otherness is key to the film's uncanny power. Echoing Kubrick, Glazer avoided science-fiction clichés of spaceships and hardware: "The spaceship was her. The body as craft is very much the central idea of our film. The paradox of body and soul. That was our science fiction. She was our science fiction."†

Exchange *soul* for *consciousness* and you have Nagel's point: the irreducible, unknowable core of experience. What is it like to be an alien as an alien? The film gives only thin, mostly negative clues: she doesn't like cake, can't have sex, and so on. But the story isn't about our discovering what an alien is; it's about an alien discovering what we are. If *Under the Skin* were Nagel's essay, it would be titled "What Is It Like to Be a Human?" not "What Is It Like to Be an Alien?"

This is the response I would offer my fellow critic, post-Venice. In the crime-movie "honey-pot" version, I am empathetically close to the protagonist: I know what it's like to see and hear the world as a human, to dream, eat cake, feel temperature, endure "the thousand natural shocks that flesh is heir to." I have visited Glasgow as an outsider; I can imagine driving a large white van, even sex work, through art and culture. *Under the Skin* asks us to take its premise literally and thereby resists easy empathy.

It is a story told in an untranslatable language: painting by echolocation, the lyrics of whale song.

---

* Jonathan Glazer, Film4 Interview Special, March 2014, YouTube.
† Ibid.

A Star is Made

Scarlett Johansson was involved with *Under the Skin* from early in its development, remaining attached to the project for several years before cameras began rolling. Though Glazer had initially preferred to cast an unknown—no recognisable stars—he realised that raising finance for the film would be impossible without at least one bankable actor.

Johansson had already established herself as a child actor with films like *North* (1994), made when she was just 10 years old. By her teens, she was being directed by Robert Redford and Sofia Coppola, starring opposite Redford, Bill Murray and John Travolta in as *The Horse Whisperer* (1998), *Lost in Translation* (2003) and *A Song for Bobby Long* (2004). Collaborations with the Coen Brothers and Woody Allen followed, as Johansson combined mainstream appeal—*The Nanny Diaries* (2007)—with more critically admired work. It was her performance in *Vicky Cristina Barcelona* (2008), the third of her collaborations with Allen, and a specific shot from the music video for her song "Falling Down," that caught Glazer's attention. In the video, she sheds her public persona as she gets into a car—a fleeting transition from cheery celebrity to private, withdrawn self. That moment convinced Glazer she could carry the film.*

There's a meta-element to *Under the Skin* in the mere presence of an American star, amost unrecognisable in a black wig, driving a white van through Glasgow. Much was made of this during the film's publicity, particularly the unscripted interactions with members of the public, who—according to the filmmakers—were unaware they were being filmed until approached afterwards and asked

---

* It is also revived in the Prada spot, where the performances feel like a form of disintegration, until she strides out of the studio and towards a yellow cab to head into the heart of the city with an "I'm Scarlett Johansson" confidence.

to sign release forms. But this is foreignness, not alienness. Johansson speaks with an English accent—still foreign in Glasgow, but from a neighbouring country, so less jarring.

The Alien doesn't change its accent. It doesn't have one. It isn't speaking in mother-tongue English—or in any human language. In fact, the film suggests that the Alien has no verbal language at all. Everything it says is imposture: a performance with a specific goal in mind, unrelated to the words we, the audience, hear. If we listen to them, we are being taken in.

Even the *act* of talking—using a mouth to form words—is suspect. Like the wings of a butterfly that mimic staring eyes, the Alien's voice and language are decoys. Not just the content but the *medium* is alien.

We open on an approaching dot. The noise on the soundtrack is uncertain. Is this music or ambient sound? The sound of some process, perhaps? Mica Levi, the film's composer—trained at the Guildhall— approached the score in an unconventional way: "The idea was to follow Scarlett Johansson's character and to try and react in real time to what she was experiencing, not to pre-empt or reflect on things which had already happened in the film. Some parts are intended to be quite difficult."[*]

The dot resolves into a fractured, haloed beam of light. As an audience, we're challenged by the paucity of information. This is abstract, so we are tempted— forced—to interpret what we are seeing.

This kind of prelude has become a recognisable element in Glazer's films. It serves as a palate cleanser, a preparation ritual, a reset. Gal baking in the sun; the jog in *Birth*—these are transitional moments. Here, too, the film asks us to settle in. And in *The Zone of Interest*, Glazer will take this technique to another level.

---

[*] Mica Levi, "Mica Levi got *Under the Skin* of her first film soundtrack," *The Guardian*, 15 March 2014.

It creates an air gap between the non-watching viewer and the now-watching viewer, putting us immediately into a questioning frame of mind.

What is that? How long is it going to last? What are we in for?

We see what might be a conjunction of planets, immediately recalling the opening of *2001: A Space Odyssey*. But the stars are actually the component parts of an artificial eye coming into being. Our sense of scale shifts—from the astronomical to the biological. We move from *2001* to *A Clockwork Orange*, from cosmic alignment to the eye that watches the eye that watches. We also hear vocal exercises—recordings of Johansson practising her Estuary English accent in the van: "film—films—foil—fail—films—field."

When we first see Scarlett Johansson, she is naked—but lit so starkly that she appears only as a dark silhouette against a field of white. Not under the skin yet, but skin. The whiteness represents birth, a beginning—contrasted with the blackness of the tarry infinity pool where men are trapped and slowly digested or processed. As white as the other is black: uncanny in their perfection.

A motionless young woman (Lynsey Taylor Mackay) lies on the floor, stripped of her clothes by the Alien, who then puts them on. But the Alien is not, in fact, naked—it is already dressed, in its woman-suit.* It may be the case that the Aliens have no concept of nakedness at all—like Adam and Eve before the Fall.

The identity of the woman lugged from the ditch and brought to this white space in the van is also ambiguous. We might initially assume she is a human victim—that this is an abduction—but later, we may need to revisit this moment with fresh understanding.

If we think we're watching a human, it resembles a reverse striptease—an infernal, inverted version of

---

* This is Lynsey Taylor MacKay's only credit on IMDb.

Jane Fonda's zero-gravity disrobing in Roger Vadim's *Barbarella* (1968). But in contrast to the hyper-sexualised Fonda—who reportedly had to drink vodka for courage before filming, and then repeat the entire sequence the next day after a technical glitch—and despite Johansson's frequent appearance on "Hottest Celebrities" lists, this is a resolutely unsexy scene. There is no self-consciousness. Her movements are utilitarian, matter-of-fact. Dispassionate.

It is a serial killer perfunctorily stripping its victim; a guard stripping the body of a prisoner about to be executed. A Sonderkommando processing the dead. The woman on the floor is paralysed, which makes the horror worse. We know—or at least can imagine—how she feels.

A tear leaks from her eye.

The Alien pauses and leans in, but, due to another audience miscue, we realise it is not responding to human emotion, either with sympathy or sadistic glee. It is, instead, fascinated by an ant. Could the ant resemble the Alien's true form more closely than the body it has assumed? The blackness of the ant against the stark white background recalls the album artwork for Massive Attack's *Mezzanine*.

We're not watching a human. That should be obvious.

But human beings anthropomorphise everything. Pets and cartoon animals. Two dots and a curved line. In *Everything Everywhere All at Once* (2022)—and contradicting my earlier point about the uncon-sciousness of a brick—Michelle Yeoh's multiverse-hopping character is briefly rendered as a pebble with googly eyes. The pattern recognition software lodged deep in our brains compels us to see faces everywhere. Cars and boats, clocks and teacups come to life and dance because we harbour a lingering suspicion that everything is alive with a vaguely human consciousness. The Japanese have animism and Hayao Miyazaki; the West has latent paganism and Walt Disney.

Our struggle with *Under the Skin*—and the journey the film takes us on—is toward humanisation. It gives us something we can read as human: a figure learning a human lesson, going on a human journey. In this interpretation (and I concede it is the dominant one), the Alien begins by hunting human beings for some undisclosed motive—possibly to do with meat—but through a series of encounters begins to feel a connection to its former victims. It's *Dances with Wolves* (1990): Kevin Costner learning to love the Sioux. It's *Avatar* (2009): Sam Worthington switching sides to join the Na'vi. A betrayal rooted in the discovery of shared values. Except the Na'vi are aliens—and they're not. They are the de-othered Other. The marginalised turn out to be just like us. Under the skin, we're all the same. Except in *Under the Skin*. That reading is the cinematic equivalent of putting pants on Caliban.

Speaking of pants, the Alien appears dissatisfied with the clothes taken from the paralysed woman. Perhaps they smell of ditchwater and decay. So it goes shopping. We see it descend from what looks like an abandoned high-rise as strange lights—perhaps the spaceship that contained the white space—drift off into the sky. It climbs into the white van and, in the stillness of its interior, sets off: a shopping expedition.

It selects a colourful top. People move around it without reacting, which shouldn't seem odd—but this is Scarlett Johansson, and we know how films work. Surely there must be a crew somewhere. But the point of view is low, waist-height, looking up. These people don't look like extras. Their clothes aren't colour-coordinated in the way background artists are often dressed to preserve a film's palette, and they aren't engaged in those exaggerated "natural" conversations that scream acting school. They simply exist. They're not pretending.

Reality takes on an uncanny quality when projected on screen. As Alex says in *A Clockwork Orange*: "It's funny how the colours of the real world only seem really real when you viddy them on the screen."

The world appears alien and unfamiliar—partly because it is local and specific. Although shopping centres possess an enervating sameness, Glasgow and Glaswegians are still very different from Chicago and Chicagoans, or Lagos and Lagosians, Barrow and Barrovians. The products and the muzak may be variations on the same theme, but the people are particular to their places. And because we are used to seeing such a curated version of reality in our cultural outlets, it can come as a genuine surprise to see relatively ordinary people outside the framing of local news reports.*

We see them as the Alien sees them: odd, distracted, drunk, eating, on mobility scooters, hurrying back from lunch, smoking cigarettes, checking their phones, homeless, unaware of what their faces and bodies are doing while their minds are elsewhere.

What's on television this evening?

Why hasn't she texted?

Do I even like Greggs?†

If the body is the spacecraft, as Glazer says, then the clothes are its cloaking device—rendering it invisible and visible at the same time. They allow it to blend in,

---

* Reality TV threatened to ruin the idea of the ordinary person, but it quickly became clear that its casts were made up not of the ordinary, but the pre-famous—people chosen for their looks and their knack for low-stakes drama.

† For non-UK readers, Greggs is a popular pastry chain where I used to buy cheese rolls and veggie pasties, despite the fact they almost always gave me a stomach ache. And yet I kept going back. It's one of the few experiences that truly unites the United Kingdom.

even as it draws attention to itself. Its lipstick is bright and applied liberally. We see this via a hand mirror — one of several mirrors the Alien and we will look into — emphasising that when it looks in the mirror, it doesn't see what we see. We see ourselves; it sees the Other it has temporarily become.[*]

The scenes are constructed to give us only the minimum information necessary. The camera roves from side to side, tracking people as they move through the city — reminiscent of the camera in Radiohead's "Karma Police" — but these aren't just random passers-by. They are specifically men. The crowd spilling out of Ibrox Stadium after a football match isn't incidental. The Alien hasn't taken a wrong turn; it's been drawn to a massive concentration of men, perhaps scenting their testosterone, moving intently through traffic, searching for a victim. But a victim for *what*?

When it speaks, its patter sounds natural, an innocent query about the location of a motorway. There's a frisson of weirdness for a UK audience hearing words like "M8" and "Asda" next to Scarlett Johansson's face, as if a panther has been given beans on toast. Later, when we hear the same script repeated, we recognise it as a script. We begin to suspect a deeper, more sinister purpose. These are pickup lines. The Alien is trying to gain trust, to open an interaction, and ultimately, to persuade men to enter the van.

Men are specifically targeted. And there are logic gates in place — decision points to guide the Alien's attention. If a man is unaccompanied, continue. If he isn't expected anywhere, continue. Once the man is inside the van, the flirtation level increases. The Alien's blandishments are unconvincing, its vocabulary slightly

---

[*] We might be minded to think of Clara from *Birth* and her use of the mirror and the camera's use of the mirror as a form of not self-revelation but deception.

off: "I think you're charming." Charming? But who's going to look a Scarlett Johansson in the mouth or in the eyes, because it's the eyes we'll return to. The be-all and end-all. The windows to the soul. The Alien adjusts the temperature inside the van to encourage the man to partly disrobe—to remove a hat or scarf, pull back his hood—allowing a better look, a better assessment of the meat. The shots keep the Alien and its potential victim compartmentalised—separate, never sharing the frame. The Alien remains in the driver's seat, both narratively and literally. And then, for the first time, we cut to what should be a two-shot—both driver's and passenger's seats in the frame—but the man has vanished. Between one shot and the next, he has been absorbed, disposed of, disappeared.

In a word: eaten.

We are taught the process step by step. Levi's score helps us understand when the hunt is on—the rhythm of the chase. Percussion becomes a metronomic hypnotism: the lulling before the culling.

Victims are lured first into the van, then to a derelict-looking house (certainly not a home), and finally to the black room, located upstairs, or perhaps somewhere else entirely. Impossibly. The Alien strips, prompting the victim to do the same. Only when fully naked can the man slip beneath the black surface. Whatever they are being turned into cannot be contaminated by the materials their clothes contain.

A later victim we follow beneath the surface sees the remains of an earlier one, now in the final stages of disposal. The body has become inflated, then is suddenly and violently drained until only a bag of skin floats, as eerily beautiful as a supermarket carrier bag drifting under the Irish Sea among the jellyfish.

Something with the consistency of offal is extracted, then, via a red laser, transmitted elsewhere. None of this is obvious or definitive. This is simply one reasonable interpretation, drawn from multiple viewings. The film offers no explanation. No exposition. And it has already taught us that we'll be wrong—repeatedly. The initial planets-to-eye misdirection was only the beginning. *Under the Skin* refuses to clarify. Work it out; don't work it out. It's all the same to the Alien—and to Glazer.

There are variations in the process. Dangers, too. When the Alien follows a man, it is caught in a crowd of young women who sweep it into a nightclub. It clearly wants to leave but is cornered by the man it had initially targeted. When I was at Liverpool University, going out to clubs in search of casual sex was casually referred to by both men and women as "sharking." This man is like that. He too has his patter, his script. But he's surprised when the Alien takes control: "I saw you outside," it tells him. As it leads him into the black room and down into the thick viscous liquid, he continues to dance—utterly unaware—his erection comically visible as he's drawn forward and submerged.

A behaviourist might argue that we can discover what something is by observing what it *does*, but the film suggests that this only gets us so far. We can determine that the Alien is hunting and capturing men, but the nature of their disposal—and the motivation for this behaviour—remains opaque. Earlier drafts of the script were reportedly more explicit, and the source novel provides more narrative scaffolding. But by paring all that away, the film denies us the safety of a clean analogy.

People might be meat, as I've already suggested. "Soylent Green is people!" as (spoiler) Charlton Heston yells at the end of *Soylent Green* (1973). Or perhaps these men are being harvested to produce some rare medicine that cures Alien cancer, saving billions of Alien children. Maybe it's something in the Y chromosome. Or maybe—more disturbingly—the "man juice" is used for something as trivial and grotesque as elephant-foot umbrella stands or whalebone corsets. A complete set of ivory billiard balls required the death of eight elephants.[*] Maybe these men are being converted into equivalents of medicine, furniture, or clothing—but perhaps such concepts have no meaning in the alien context. Maybe it's something else entirely. Something with no analogue. Maybe it's the spice melange from Frank Herbert's *Dune* (1965), essential for space travel.

Abandoning the meat analogy—or at least reducing it to one possibility among many—reasserts the alienness of the Alien. It is an Alien. And it is doing something we do not understand. It might be analogous. It might not. The film offers no clue that allows us to do anything but guess.

We've seen it construct itself as a "she." We've seen it behave like a specifically recognisable she: middle class, probably university-educated, English (not Scottish), from the south of England. We know she is vastly more likely to be the victim of sexual violence than the perpetrator of it—ditto with violent crime more broadly. We know she has far more to fear from men than men have from her. And yet, despite overwhelming statistical evidence to the contrary, culturally women continue to be disproportionately represented as the threat: the femme fatale, the black widow, the psycho-bitch. But all of that is reading the mask—the "skin job," as Bryant (M. Emmet Walsh) calls Replicants in *Blade Runner.*

You might be getting slightly irritated by my continued use of the pronoun *it* instead of surrendering to the obvious: Scarlett Johansson is a she playing a *she.* But Glazer himself referred to the character as it in interviews, and would correct himself when he

---

[*] Sathnam Sanghera, *Empireworld* (Penguin, 2024).

slipped into *she*. Its alienness, as we've seen, was his "North Star." Some collaborators called it Laura, but this anthropomorphic impulse must be resisted if we are to properly understand the film's central idea. (We're not watching an Eastern European sex worker, Neil!) Given how the discussion around pronouns has evolved in recent years, it's worth noting that calling the Alien Laura and using *she/her* pronouns isn't just misgendering—it's *mis-genusing*.

The person we see interacting with men in the van is not the Alien's true form. We recognise that early. When it learns a man is not a suitable victim, its charm shuts off like a switch. No point wasting energy. Its face returns to a blank, Resting Alien Face—resembling Resting Bitch Face, but again, it isn't. Our instinctive discomfort at the perceived two-facedness of "the woman" reveals more about our own misogyny than it does about the creature. And this discomfort is misplaced: it isn't a woman.

Some may point out that even outside the skin suit, the Alien is clearly gendered—its body has breasts—and that its subordinate relationship to the "male" Aliens seems to reinforce a female role. But we have no idea how gender works for this species—or whether it exists at all. It remains one of the more remarkable failures of male-authored science fiction: that in imagining warp drives, hyperspace, hive minds, time loops, and fifth dimensions, it so rarely reimagines gender. In contrast, the works of Ursula K. Le Guin—particularly her 1969 novel *The Left Hand of Darkness*—place gender fluidity and ambiguity at their very core.*

We have seen the Alien pick up men, lure them, and destroy them. So its appearance on a windswept,

---

* Watch *Blade Runner 2049* (2019), and marvel at how a future can be rendered in which the technology is from the future and the gender roles from the forties. I owe this observation to a conversation with Helen O'Hara, which can be heard on our episode of the Writers on Film podcast (2021).

stony beach is immediately incongruous. It is no longer in the van, no longer in an urban setting. Its clothes, despite the short faux-fur jacket, now look inadequate. The weather, after all, is horrible—Scottish. A man is swimming nearby in a full-body wetsuit; a family— man, woman, dog, and child—will likely leave soon, giving the Alien space to pursue the swimmer (Krystof Hádek). He jokes when he first sees it: "I thought you were after my towel." He is socially awkward, resistant to its approach, and—significantly—not British. He is Czech, a foreigner. Another alien. But a familiar and far safer one.

Soon—and shockingly—the conversation is interrupted by a tragedy unfolding just over their shoulders. The family's dog has been caught in the riptide, pulled away from shore by the thundering waves. The woman, in a desperate and misguided attempt to save the animal, throws herself into the sea and is quickly dragged out. The man dives in after her. He too will soon be in danger.

The swimmer reacts without hesitation. His rescue attempt is rational, competent: he doesn't head straight for the drowning pair but runs along the shoreline, calculating the optimum entry point before diving in. He chooses the person he has the best chance of saving—the man—over the one he is less likely to reach. In this brief but charged moment, the swimmer displays qualities we might admire, even be awestruck by: courage, selflessness, compassion—the best of humanity.

And yet, even as he drags the man ashore, that man breaks free and hurls himself back into the waves, unable to abandon his wife. His decision is futile but not irrational. He is driven by love, another virtue. What we witness is a perfect vignette of altruism: altruism undone by love. Everyone is doing the right thing for the right reasons—with terrible results.

Finally, the Alien resolves to act. But it doesn't understand its environment as the swimmer does. Where he calculates, the Alien simply walks—a straight line across the beach and into the water—apparently immune to the freezing temperature soaking its jeans. Unfeeling in every sense. It picks up a rock, brains the exhausted swimmer, and drags his unconscious body to the van.

The man and woman are presumably dead or drowning. The Alien does not look back. Nor does it acknowledge the screaming baby—who, along with the pounding surf, has become part of the scene's unbearable soundtrack.

The Alien isn't wired the way we are. It is not disturbed by a crying baby. But our instinct is to judge it on human—and, pointedly, misogynistic—terms. "Laura" has no maternal instinct. "She" is cold, indifferent, inhuman. But that's precisely the point. It is not a woman. It is not a human. This is what it means to be alien: not understanding, not connecting, not decoding our world or our values.

The Alien sees that humans are horny and lonely. It can work with that. It can use it. But screaming babies? They don't compute. They're irrelevant.

Inside the van, there's a guilty sense of relief: finally, silence. No more crying baby. It's exhausting to care. The van is both trap and spacecraft. Its ambience is one of quiet control: the B-flat hum of the engine (the same frequency we hear in the womb), the soft tick of the indicator. The swimmer is buckled into the passenger seat.

In the scene that follows, the Alien hears another baby crying. And—for the first time—it registers something. A flicker of awareness. It may just be coincidence, a glitch in the matrix. Two unconnected events occurring close together. Déjà-vu.

We return to the beach. The motorcycle Alien arrives to clean up the scene, to erase the swimmer's existence. The toddler struggles to her feet—presumably a girl, since otherwise the Alien might have had some "use" for her. It is a devastating moment of helplessness, of yearning, of fragile life about to be extinguished.

This is Beckett-bleak. To be "born astride the grave," left alone on a stony shore, screaming into the gathering darkness, until death from exposure comes— unwitnessed, unremarked.

And then, in one of the film's darkest, most obsidian moments of humour, the Alien picks up the child's blanket. Not the child. The blanket. The child doesn't register. The blanket is evidence; the baby is not. The baby lies outside its purview. Outside its *umwelt*.

This is a scene we witness, but the van Alien does not—unless, of course, the Aliens are in constant telepathic communication. It's possible.

But when the Alien glances toward a baby in another car (its cries muffled behind panes of glass) a shift begins. A curiosity is born.

What is it like to be a human being?

"This isn't Tesco's"
The body is a spacecraft. The van is a larger version. The derelict house is the space station. Inside, there is a bright white space where an Alien can don its body suit and human clothing—and a black space, a blacker-than-black visible darkness.

The science fiction of *Under the Skin* exists between the lines. Lights move in the sky above a Glasgow housing estate, but no spaceship is ever shown escaping Earth's gravitational pull or hitting lightspeed. The Alien's true form appears briefly, midway through the film, though it's not clear whether we are seeing another Alien or the Scarlett Johansson one, stripped of its skin.

The moment is so fleeting it's easily missed, or not linked to the character we've been following.

The absence of traditional sci-fi markers is not new. Jean-Luc Godard's *Alphaville* (1965) is an obvious precursor. Tarkovsky used the existing landscape of Tokyo to suggest a future Earth in *Solaris*. Nicolas Roeg's *The Man Who Fell to Earth* offers glimpses of alienness and futuristic tech, but as in *Under the Skin*, what is truly alien is Earth—or, in Roeg's case, America. David Bowie's Thomas Jerome Newton is alien because Bowie himself, at that stage in his life, was drifting through the world in limousines and an amphetamine haze, never quite touching the edges.

Under the Skin frequently disguises its own visual effects. The pursuit of realism led the filmmakers to rig the white van with up to ten hidden cameras, specially designed to film Johansson's interactions with unsuspecting non-professionals. A glance at IMDb reveals that even those with speaking roles—Lynsey Taylor Mackay, the woman/old Alien who provides the clothes; Jeremy McWilliams, the motorcyclist; and the early victims—have no other acting credits. This adds to the uncanniness.

As mentioned earlier (and as Glazer's Prada short will later toy with), Johansson's movie-starness stands out. Like Bowie, she carries her celebrity into the role. She can switch her charisma on and off, just as the Alien can. She too goes through makeup and costume. She too wears prosthetics. She too has her performance space— the van—where she recites a script designed to provide a thin human motivation: "I'm moving some furniture for my family."

What if the Aliens had been monitoring our media for some time and chose Johansson precisely because she features on "Hottest Celebs" listicles? The "halo effect" is a well-documented cognitive bias: we tend to assign positive traits (kindness, trustworthiness, intelligence) to people who are attractive or successful in other domains. If the Aliens understand human psychology, they know we're far more likely to trust a beautiful woman than an ugly man.

If this were a rom-com (Scarlett Johansson trying to live a normal life in Glasgow), we would expect epiphanies. She would learn simple but profound life lessons, à la Audrey Hepburn in *Roman Holiday* (1953) or Julia Roberts in *Notting Hill* (1999). But Johansson is playing an it.

Does that arc still hold?

We see curiosity emerge. An openness—perhaps even a need—to understand what's happening around it. The baby is the first crack. Then, later, a flower vendor at a traffic light cuts his hand and bleeds on the rose he hands to the Alien (paid for, unsettlingly, by another man in the traffic jam).* The Alien looks at the blood—not with empathy, but with curiosity. Puzzlement.

Later, it will become clear that the Alien doesn't bleed. It doesn't eat. Presumably, it doesn't defecate. It likely doesn't possess the orifices required for sex—beyond oral sex. So this isn't a "Cut me, do I not bleed?" moment of human recognition. It's more: What is this red stuff? This is a world of physical existence the Alien doesn't understand, and we don't understand *its* physicality.

The Alien Motorcyclist confronts the Alien Van Driver. It inspects it. Their communication, if that's what it is, is entirely non-verbal and utterly opaque to us. It feels intimidating, like a drill sergeant dressing down a recruit. But that's only what it seems to be. We

---

* Traffic jams in films (*Otto e Mezzo* by Federico Fellini being the most famous) and in life always make me think of Leonard Cohen's lyric from "Boogie Street": "I'm wanted at the traffic jam. They're saving me a seat."

can't know. It's not even a gesture-based language. It's positioning. One moves. One remains still. Curiosity, it seems, is a problem. A distraction from the job.

This inspection takes place in a space as black as the black room, but with a cobbled floor. It focuses on the Alien's eyes. Something is wrong. A man—one of its victims—will later notice this too. We've already seen the eye being constructed at the beginning of the film. We understand it can fall apart. Break down. Malfunction.

How long can an Alien stay in a skin suit? What's the turnover rate? The churn? Why else have routine inspections unless breakdown is anticipated?

Let's return to the woman in the van at the beginning of the film. It wasn't a woman at all, it was another Alien, one who had reached the end of her shelf life. Paralysed. Useless. Her tears meant nothing to the newcomer, who was more interested in the ant, because under the skin, it looks more like an ant. That moment also explains why the clothes fit. Why "the woman" looked vaguely like Scarlett Johansson. It was an off-the-rack *skin* job. We aren't watching a heartwarming tale of an Alien learning "what it means to be human." We're watching the attrition rate of a worker in an unpleasant job.

"An unimportant clerk/Writes I DO NOT LIKE MY WORK/On a pink official form," as W.H. Auden wrote in "The Fall of Rome," a poem composed on a bet with Cyril Connolly to write something that would make him cry. (It didn't.)

The Alien continues its work. But now it begins to look differently. Its gaze has widened. It doesn't just see men. It sees women too. Children. It observes how humans treat their children, especially how women treat them. It sees female bodies that have aged, failed in some way. Does it see their mobility scooters as equivalents of its van? Is it recognising a kind of solidarity? Or perhaps imagining a transcendence? The Alien exits the van and walks down a city street. It has left the van before—at the shopping centre, on the beach, in the nightclub—but this time there is no clear destination. It simply walks. And then it falls.

In the novel, Isserley's surgical modifications—necessary to allow her to walk upright among humans—are imperfect. Painful. Movement is difficult. The disguise, like the job, is unsustainable.

The Alien's fall draws people toward it—random strangers, passers-by who happen to be nearby. They help it to its feet, anxious for its wellbeing. It becomes the recipient of the very kind of solidarity the swimmer had shown to the drowning family earlier in the film. The altruism of the crowd.

But the Alien cannot react. It's off-script. Its ability to communicate beyond its memorised patter is severely limited—non-existent, perhaps. After the fall, we see it get up and continue walking, the people around it falling into step beside her. As Glazer says: "She's part of the throng now."*

And what is that throng?

As mentioned earlier, one of the most remarkable things about *Under the Skin* is its highly specific, localised setting. Scotland—specifically the city of Glasgow—gives the film a texture and atmosphere almost never seen on the big screen. *Gregory's Girl* (1981), *Local Hero* (1983) and *Trainspotting* (1996) stand out as important cinematic representations of Scotland, but British audiences likely see more of Texas than they do of Glasgow.

The Scottishness of the film is most evident in the voices of the people the Alien encounters. The accents, cadences, and dialect phrases mark them as local and

---

* "Anatomy of a Scene," *The New York Times*, 4 April 2014.

particular. As a result, we, the audience, often find ourselves more aligned with the Alien than with the humans onscreen. After all, we can understand what *it* is saying.

At the Venice screening, non-English-speaking journalists were surprised—some even annoyed—that there were no English subtitles. I told them I hadn't understood much more than they had. The irony is glaring: we understand the well-spoken Alien better than we understand the working class of a Scottish city.

The men the Alien lures, the bus driver, and the quiet man who later befriends and shelters it, all speak with strong regional accents, often peppered with redundancy, diversions, pauses, and half-heard, half-formed thoughts. Their speech is deeply *human*.

When the Alien approaches a man with a facial deformity (Adam Pearson), the familiar pattern breaks. He does not have a Scottish accent. And the usual script—"Can you help me find the M8?"—feels suddenly inadequate. The Alien doesn't react to his face with any visible emotion—no revulsion, no empathy—less than the audience might, in fact. But it adjusts. The patter changes.

Instead of flirtation, it appeals directly to loneliness. The man has never had a girlfriend. He has no friends. He shops at night because, in his words, "people wind me up."

There is a profound irony here: this man, whose condition—neurofibromatosis—has made him more "other" in the eyes of society than almost anyone, is still more recognisably *human* than the attractive woman beside him, who isn't human at all.

But the Alien isn't repulsed. It simply recognises that its standard tools won't work. It improvises. It praises his hands. And for the first time in the film, we get a two-shot: the Alien and a conscious human, side by side in the van. In close-up, the man touches the spot where the Alien's fingers brushed his skin. The moment is—literally—touching. It's tender. This man, by his own admission, has very little physical contact with others. The tragedy—the black joke—is that the one who touched him wasn't a person at all.

He resists the Alien's approach. "This isn't Tesco's," he says when it stops the van. For UK viewers, this is another moment of cognitive dissonance—Scarlett Johansson, Hollywood royalty, doesn't belong in the world of supermarket chains. It's like watching Brad Pitt sell Japanese toothpaste. The line also undercuts the grandiosity that science fiction tends to imply. This is space opera by Ken Loach. After all, this is a "we-are-not-alone" film, a story of interstellar travel, of other intelligences, potentially vastly superior, given the technology on display. And yet, where are we? Not Tesco's. If we lean into the meat metaphor, maybe the man is heading for the shelves of some alien supermarket. But there I go again: de-othering the Other.

It's so tempting. And so easy.

The stripping of the Alien has been progressive throughout the film. Each return to the black room reveals a little more. Now, fully naked, standing before the man, the Alien starkly confronts us with our assumptions about physical beauty. This body—the voluptuous body—is the current ideal of female desirability. *GQ*'s Babe of the Year in 2010. *Esquire*'s Sexiest Woman Alive in 2006 and again in 2013.

Johansson's hyper-sexualised public image fits squarely into a science fiction tradition: the nude female alien as a figure of simultaneous fantasy and threat. Think Mathilda May in Tobe Hooper's *Lifeforce* (1985) or Natasha Henstridge in Roger Donaldson's *Species* (1995). These women are eroticised aliens who seduce and destroy, femme fatales from outer space turning men into the cucks of Planet Earth. Yes, we would die, the heterosexual men and lesbian women might think—but what a way to go. When the same trope is briefly reversed in *The Terminator* (1985)—with Arnold Schwarzenegger striding naked into a biker bar—it immediately becomes camp.

Johansson, notably, doesn't typically do nude scenes. I haven't seen *We Bought a Zoo* (2011), so I can't claim to be a completist, but this alone makes *Under the Skin* unique in her filmography. Are these scenes sexy? I'm not sure. What is sexy? Or its middle-class cousin, erotic—the word we use when we don't know if something is sexy or not.

Adam Pearson is also naked in this scene. And what is our reaction to that? Are we being dared to shudder? To stare? To be turned on? Is this a kink? Is he being punished for being horny? Because deep in the reptilian prudishness of our brains, we assume all the victims are. They've all been led here by their little heads—not their big ones. Their penises pointing them to doom. And just as *Birth* hinged on a single fulcrum moment of transformation—a shift we can only observe externally, during the opera scene—so too does *Under the Skin*. As the Alien walks down the stairs, it stops in front of a mirror and stares. Maureen Foster intriguingly suggests that this may not be a mirror at all. It could be a portal into the black room. Or a form of interstellar communication. It could be anything. And perhaps the phrase "it stares into the mirror" is already inadequate. How do we know how it sees? Its perception may extend beyond the visible spectrum. We have seen its eye being constructed: a marble-like iris sitting on what looks like a fried egg white. The drama of the moment is conventional—introspection via mirror study—but Glazer undercuts this immediately. In the next shot, a trapped fly buzzes against a windowpane. The Alien is more moved by this than by its own reflection. As it was, earlier, by the ant. Insects, it seems, are more kin to the Alien than we are.

Douglas Adams, in *The Hitchhiker's Guide to the Galaxy* (1979), undercuts anthropocentric science fiction with the joke that Earth was a giant supercomputer run by mice, and humans were only the third most intelligent species on the planet—after mice and dolphins. When the dolphins abandon Earth prior to its destruction, they perform one last trick at a water park, which translates as: "So long and thanks for all the fish."

The Alien frees its final victim as casually as you might let a gerbil out of its cage. It has no interest in the man's safety, only in getting him out of the way. Back to the wild—let nature take its course. Anyone hoping to glimpse empathy at this point will likely be disappointed. This isn't about compassion for others. It's about quitting a job it no longer wants to do.

Without a backward glance, the Alien walks away as the man stumbles naked into the morning. Another slow-motion stripping begins here and continues through to the end of the film—but this is as far from the eroticism of *Barbarella* as one can get. The fur coat is gone. The van will soon be gone. Eventually, the skin suit will be torn away—bloodlessly—and burned.

Earlier in the film, cruising Glasgow, the Alien resembled a spaced-out Travis Bickle. Now it's Marion Crane, fleeing the old order, driving towards a new life, except without a lover or even a plan. It knows it's in danger. It knows it's being pursued. It leaves the city, no longer with a script, a persona, or even a purpose beyond escape.

The van runs out of petrol and into a whiteout, a thick, obliterating fog that mirrors the sterile white space we saw at the film's beginning. This phase of its journey feels like a rebirth. But instead of gliding through the world as an agent—dominating, manipulating—now it's just a speck in the landscape, an insect marching down a road to nowhere.

The Alien drifts into a village that feels like an eternal Thursday afternoon of imminent drizzle. Scriptless, purposeless, it can't start a conversation. Why cast bait if you're no longer fishing?

Earlier, its persona served a specific function: seduction, entrapment. Now, as the recipient of "the kindness of strangers"—the bus driver calling it a "wee lassie" and treating it with care—the Alien has no way to respond. It can't process kindness. Computer says "no."

The pebble-dashed mundanity of the Alien's setting—the banality of a hotel restaurant, a logging lorry—contrasts sharply with the grandeur of the landscape, the sublime terror of the weather, and the unshared cosmic perspective it must carry. Unshared, except in a few moments when we glimpse something approximating its constant viewpoint.

As the Alien cruises through Glasgow near the end of its mission, at the apotheosis of its attempted empathy, it absorbs overlapping impressions of street life, all superimposed one upon another, until its face is suffused with a golden light that suggests something transcendent, a transhuman understanding. If its sensory capabilities surpass ours, this may not be a sudden epiphany, but simply the way it always perceives the world—granted to us, briefly, through the medium of cinema.

Later, we'll see the Alien's body hovering above the Earth (a brush of Tarkovsky) and elsewhere merging into a forest-scape, hinting again at its capacity to interface with its environment on a scale we cannot grasp. So vast and profound that we cannot enter it, any more than we can navigate by echolocation. These are also the moments where the film aligns its cinematic language with the Alien's perception. Cinema, after all, can make us see the world like bats. Or like Aliens.*

We've seen that the Aliens are physically powerful—dragging the swimmer back to the van—and impervious to pain and hunger. They don't appear to feel panic or fear. They also seem to perceive reality in ways that transcend our normal senses. Beyond the Alien's own moment of transcendence, the Motorcyclist Alien displays foresight and precision that suggest further, unsuspected powers. It locates and dispatches the final freed victim with unerring efficiency—breaking into the car, opening the boot, all before the capture in the garden has even occurred, as if the outcome is already known. Its stare at the watching neighbour is both menacing and dismissive. Does it perceive time differently? Is that another advantage it holds over us?

Given all this, its inability to eat a slice of cake hardly seems tragic. But that moment depends entirely on us mistaking the Alien for human, and the Alien mistaking a human activity for something that should matter. There's a faint echo of *Marie Antoinette* (2006), where, in Sofia Coppola's vision, the doomed queen is surrounded by sweets and delicate confections until she herself begins to resemble one. The Alien can't eat cake. Is it a food intolerance? Like dogs and chocolate? Or is all our food repellent to it, like pouring sand in our ears, biting into wax fruit, or licking an image of an apple? We don't know. Because ultimately, the Alien is unknowable.

We empathise with it, alongside the bus driver and the kind stranger, imagining how cold it must feel, though we've no real evidence that it experiences temperature as we do. Earlier on the beach, it walked straight into

---

* It's also reminiscent of the moment in *Birth* with a series of dissolves of Sean looking in various directions. A moment of self-conscious camera-trickery.

the freezing surf without hesitation, unaffected. It sheds the fur coat and the van with no sign of discomfort. It accepts another coat later, but not out of need. The kind man who takes it in gallantly carries it over a puddle (now it's Queen Elizabeth and he is Walter Raleigh) and prepares food for it, but we already know: it doesn't feel the cold, and it can't eat the food.

Nor can it have sex.

How can something so obviously sexual—tabloid "hottest celeb" lists and "sexiest woman alive" titles notwithstanding—not be capable of sex? But this is based on a narrow, penetrative definition. This is about hardware. Where would the food go? How is internal temperature regulated? Where does the penis fit into any of this? Is it Barbie before *Barbie* (2023), a film that ends with the pursuit of the right biological orifice? Is the Motorcyclist Alien a penis-less Ken?

On a literal level, the film plays as a comedy of errors. The Alien is simply wrong about a series of things. The scene in which it uses a table lamp to inspect between its legs—apparently to check whether it has a vagina—is particularly absurd. How could it be so confused? Has it forgotten what it's wearing? What is it even hoping to see? A latch? A mechanism? This is a moment when we might reasonably wonder if the Alien is, in fact, stupid. We're so focused on the idea of alien intelligence, we overlook the necessary corollary: alien stupidity. As Rick Deckard asks Tyrell in *Blade Runner*: "How can it not know what it is?" As in *Birth*, there is an absurdity at the core of the film. Tilt the perspective slightly and *Under the Skin* becomes a "fish out of water" story: *The Brother from Another Planet* (1984) meets *Crocodile Dundee* (1986).

An Alien Planet

The one aspect of Michel Faber's book that remained constant through the film's many permutations was its setting in Scotland. Glazer recognised in Scotland a sense of the mythic—"legendary," as he put it in one interview—that would be lost elsewhere. Scotland has a particularity, a deep locality. The urban lowlands of Glasgow, with their derelict housing estates, red brick, rain-drenched high streets, discos, and football stadiums, give way to an ancient landscape of drizzle and cold: rain, wind, snow, and that frost line where not-snow becomes snow. The beauty here is always of the cold, "I wouldn't want to live there" kind. Waves crash against the shore with shuddering drama, but the riptide will carry you off and drown you.* It is a landscape immediately full of danger: fogs will confuse you; the wind will shove you; forests will swallow you whole; snow will bring oblivion. There's a sense that the universe—and the landscape itself—is utterly indifferent.

When we first see Scotland, it is night. A motorcycle winds along a road that cuts through the hills like a stream. It is a dark, unknowable landscape. When the Motorcyclist Alien retrieves the body of the first Alien, the composition places it between the scrabble of weeds along the roadside verge at the bottom of the screen and the glittering lights of the distant city at the top; in the middle is darkness.

A key image in David Lynch's cinema is the emergence of a figure—a beautiful woman across the hall in *Eraserhead* (1977) or Laura Dern's Sandy in *Blue Velvet* (1986)—out of a profound shadow, so that the figure

---

* I note in passing that Glazer does not like to go to the seaside. *Birth* and *Under the Skin* show the beach to be inhospitable and the sea to be freezing and potentially fatal. In *Sexy Beast*, Gal is taken to the beach at night so Don can bully him and punch him in the stomach.

seems not just to come from the darkness, but to be made of it.

The Alien does much of its hunting at night. The nocturnal drives are lit by sodium street lamps, their glow caught realistically by digital cinematography, in keeping with the lighting philosophy of *Birth*. This street lighting—the light version of pebble-dashing—is part of a broader aesthetic of the local and the mundane. The street lamps, the corner shop, the pebble-dashed houses, the Tommy Cooper sketch it watches on TV, the Deacon Blue track playing on the kitchen radio—all of it points to something I personally bring to the film: an ordinariness, a banality that, somehow, reaches the sublime.

I grew up in a pebble-dashed house in a hamlet just south of the Lake District. Cumbria is a border county, sharing Hadrian's Wall with Scotland, and it shares many of the same characteristics: a vast geography, a sparse population, and that same sense of desolate remove. "If there's a bright centre to the universe, you're on the planet it's farthest from," Luke Skywalker says of Tatooine, with his awkward intergalactic syntax. When people ask where I come from nowadays, I have a line: I didn't come from the middle of nowhere. We had to get a bus to the middle of nowhere.

This remoteness is what fuelled my love of science fiction growing up. From Frank Herbert's *Dune* (1965) and Arthur C. Clarke to Philip K. Dick and Michael Moorcock, science fiction offered me a way to escape planet Earth—and, more specifically, the soil-coloured, cow-shit-scented planet of Cumbria.

Then along comes Jonathan Glazer to show us that the alien planet is the one we're already on. That even when we're on Earth, we're still in space. The shot of the Alien walking down the lane past the bus stop looks exactly like the village near where I grew up, near the pub where I had my first pint. It was that strange hybrid of urban-rural where our next-door neighbour would race his motorbike up and down the lane every Sunday morning, and everything stank of silage and motor oil. The kind of place where you'd find black bin bags full of porn mags dumped in the corners of fields, and a row of dead crows strung up on a barbed wire fence as a warning to others—a murder of crows indeed. Green fields, black roads, and slate walls that went darker when it rained—and it rained all the time. The streetlights from the town across the estuary looked like something out of science fiction, but it was just another sad town called Millom.

For years, cinema couldn't quite capture street lighting. Night scenes were shot on sound stages, artfully lit but nothing like the lived experience of the night. They lacked the fizz of real light. Or they were rendered in the unnatural blue of a day-for-night filter that turned everything a pale imitation of darkness.

As technology improved and filmmakers began to experiment with digital cinematography, a photo-realistic experience of night became possible. Michael Mann achieved it in *The Insider* (1999) and especially in *Collateral* (2004) and *Miami Vice* (2006). David Fincher, too, in the opening of *The Social Network* (2010), captured something startlingly real—the diffuse, rust-coloured ambience of contemporary light pollution.

In *Under the Skin*, the night can glow with that same copper hue. But it also moves toward extremes: a whiteness without a source, and a blackness so absolute it becomes a vacuum. These binaries—pure white and total black—are fundamental spaces in the film. But in between, in a domestic, lived-in setting, the Alien sits before an electric bar fire, orange-red and ordinary, examining its body in the warm domestic glow. When it investigates the absence of a vagina, it does so using a bedside lamp awkwardly thrust between its legs.

By the time the Alien meets the Kind Man (so named in the script), we have been lulled into sensing romantic potential. We are dupes, just as he is. He believes the Alien to be human: a stray, traumatised, in need of care. A knight in shining armour, he lifts the Alien over puddles, lends it a coat, cooks a meal it can't eat, and takes it to visit a castle—a gesture freighted with the afterimage of chivalry.

We, as an audience, know it's an alien but assume it longs to become human. Neither we nor the Kind Man has a clue. When he performs his small, kind rituals, we are in on the irony, but such is the force of narrative expectation that we still reach for meaning: surely this is the turning point. Surely it's learning something. But maybe it isn't. Maybe none of it is there. Maybe that lesson—the one about humanity—is a human fantasy, not an alien one.

The Alien might be more Gal than *E.T.*, done with the job, hoping to disappear. Or maybe it's Don Logan: chaotic, intractable, entirely opaque. Why do we assume it would want to be human? Why is that the upgrade? Maybe it would prefer to be an ant. Or a fly. Its retreat into the forest is as much a move away from humanity as it is from its own kind. Out there with the mulch and the birds and the insects, it is undisturbed.

And what if it's a machine? We've seen the eye constructed. Perhaps there is no biological Alien at all— just hardware. Maybe we never see anything alive. But then again, maybe that question is itself meaningless. Would we even know how to tell the difference between alien intelligence and alien artificial intelligence?

The Forest
The move to the forest takes us into a realm of enchant-ment and childhood fears: the fairytale, the lost child, the wanderer, the wolf. We've already been to the castle, so why not the woods? But here the classical reversal takes hold, and with it comes punishment. Hunt or be hunted. In this Manichean world, cruelty is a rule of order.

The man it encounters brings with him the same Micah Levi soundtrack we haven't heard since the van. We know what it means: the hunting music. His friend-liness is a script. He dispenses advice, performs benevo-lence, but it's all part of the mechanism of extraction—information, vulnerability, trust. He's not the wolf; he's the woodcutter—a logger by trade, and traditionally Little Red Riding Hood's father, the killer of the wolf. But here he gives the Alien paternal attention—protec-tive, interested, solicitous.

The film is screaming reversal: comeuppance.

And despite everything the Alien has done, we're screaming: Run.

The Alien becomes Sleeping Beauty, and its sleep feels enchanted. Its first act that resembles anything human. Who knew it slept? But this sleep folds it into the forest floor, into the mulch and leaf litter, into the consciousness of the Earth itself. The suggestion is that its awareness is broader, more diffuse, and more encom-passing than we can guess.

Then comes the rude awakening. We already suspect what the soundtrack confirms: the woodcutter is the hunter. Little Red Riding Hood, Sleeping Beauty—all just precursors to the "final girl" of horror. The Alien wakes to the monster. Not a wolf but something worse: a man. A rapist, a killer. Like the Alien in the van, he hides in plain sight, in a high-viz jacket, driving a work vehicle. But unlike the Alien, his method is force, not seduction.

He does not lure or mesmerise. He grabs, rips, rends. The Alien's victims were stripped by desire—submerged willingly, vanishing whole. This man's victim is torn, piece by piece.

One emotion is legible, unmistakable—and not unique to humans: fear. The Alien is in its grip. We haven't seen this before. Not even when the van was attacked did it feel fear—only confusion, calculation. But now, in the panicked flight through the woods, there is no mistaking it. We feel for it. We can't help but read the attack as a sexual assault, and we recoil as we would watching a woman brutalised. But it isn't a woman. And if we don't know what sex is to it—or even if it has a concept of sex—can we even speak of sexual assault? Or are we once again projecting ourselves where we don't belong?

The man is a rapist, but he realises he is trying to rape something that isn't human and immediately stops. Disgusted and horrified, he swings to another misogynistic extreme: the witch-burner. In the brief pause—when we might assume he has fled—the Alien experiences a moment of self-reflection. It regards the face it has peeled off, which remains alive in its hands. The human face—Scarlett Johansson's—looks up at the Alien's, its eyes flickering, trying to comprehend this doubling. Is it like Charlotte Corday, whose severed head, after being guillotined, was said to blush in rage at the indignity of being slapped by the executioner—as if decapitation weren't enough?

Except for one brief earlier glimpse, this is the first real moment we get to see the Alien as it truly is. It resembles an Alberto Giacometti sculpture: charcoal black, mineral-textured, more stone than flesh, or perhaps something insectile, an exoskeleton. Is this why it showed more curiosity towards insects than humans throughout the film?

The burning of the Alien is shocking. The man's motivation is never explained. It's an impulse—*burn the witch!*—more than a plan. The camera now chases the Alien through the woods, its movement suddenly chaotic and ragged—for the first time, not cool or composed. It's a shot that merges the violence of the rapist with the desperate POV of the victim. And the fire itself—uncontained, bright, real—is something we haven't seen before. Just as we left the city for something more primal, we've arrived at the elemental. We've witnessed death by water, death by dark gloop. Now we have death by fire.

Although the Alien's end is shocking, it's not surprising. The pursuit was relentless. In a final shot, we see the Alien Motorcyclist giving up the chase—though it's possible it simply sensed the death of its quarry, just as it had located the Alien's predecessor and the final male victim. But the Alien's death is also a resolution to an unresolvable problem. Would it—something we've never seen sleep—have simply remained in the hut, unconscious, until disturbed? It could have stayed there for weeks before anyone happened by. And what then? Where was it going? What place did it have in the world? We were never going to get inside it—not truly—because its otherness had slipped beyond identity. It was an Alien that had forgotten how to be alien without becoming human.

We might deplore the irrational cruelty of the woodsman, but his violence cleanses the film of its own impasse. It ends a story that refused closure, transforming a potential farce into a tragedy. The Alien is punished for its misdeeds.

What remains is our ability to empathise with non-humans that look human—just as we can, to a lesser extent, empathise with non-humans that don't. We may not know what it feels like to be a bat, but most of us would recoil at the sight of bats being burned alive. We instinctively feel—rightly—that fear and pain are not exclusive to humans, and that inflicting them needlessly on another being is wrong.

In *Do Androids Dream of Electric Sheep?*, Philip K. Dick makes acute empathy with non-humans—specifically animals—the defining test of humanity. In the aftermath of nuclear war, with most animals extinct, empathy has become both precious and fragile. Banquets of meat, clothes made of animal skins—these are meant to provoke instant disgust in anyone truly human. Androids, by contrast, can only simulate that disgust, and not convincingly. The irony, of course, is that we—readers in 2025—would likely fail the Voigt-Kampff Test. We would barely flinch at leather wallets or beef stew. In this sense, we are closer to the sociopathic androids than we'd care to admit.

As the Alien dies, violently, beneath the gentle fall of snow, we're left disturbed—haunted by the uncanny. We've seen something like us, yet not like us, and the gap between is unbridgeable. With a bat, it's relatively simple. We've studied them. There are aspects of their lives we can understand—others we can only imagine—but we at least know which parts we're imagining. What would echolocation *feel* like?

With the Alien, we don't know any of that. It might very well be a "she," or something utterly different—like the ambisexual inhabitants of Gethen in Le Guin's *The Left Hand of Darkness*. The very notion of sex might be incomprehensible. Hence my resistance to the "sex worker" interpretation.

But if we admit the Other as the protagonist, as I believe we must, then an obvious question arises: why are we watching this? What is it? It's not the first time we've felt that creeping doubt—that no matter how cleverly the film has been made, how stylish it looks and sounds, we wonder: is there really a *there* actually *there*?

Sexy Beast defies our expectations of the "one last job" film, in which the reluctant protagonist typically dies. And yet it still functions perfectly as a crime thriller. *Birth* appears to be about reincarnation, but then (importantly, and somewhat deflatingly) isn't. It might have worked as a film about delusion, psychology, emotional trauma—but it's not wholly that either.

Under the Skin is science fiction that refuses science fiction's tropes. "You can't fall back on convention, on things you've seen," Glazer says. "You have to make your own language."*

It refuses to humanise the Alien. Even Bowie's Newton in *The Man Who Fell to Earth* becomes recognisably human—an alcoholic with fake eyes who can't go home. Even early on, he has familiar drives: sex, hunger, thirst, ambition. He wants to return to his family. He says the trains are different on his home planet—but they still have trains.

Under the Skin, by contrast, gives us nothing of the Alien's world beyond the job it's doing here, and even that is unexplained. For all we know, it's harvesting a life-saving drug that is vital to its planet, and its desertion is a catastrophic dereliction of duty. Maybe the Alien is impervious to fire the way it's impervious to cold. Maybe it only runs around burning because it's confused, just as it failed to register the mob attacking its van in Glasgow. Maybe once the snow puts out the flames, it will simply lie there and wait for Spring.

All we have are our own reactions.

The film is not a thought experiment. It doesn't engage us intellectually so much as viscerally. Like the Alien, we sample taste, sex, violence, extreme cold and heat. The question is not what the Alien is, but how we

---

* Anne Thompson.

respond. How much do we feel for the unfeeling? How humane can we be toward the inhumane?

It is a Voigt-Kampff test, except this time the Alien is the one in the scenario, replacing the tortured animals.

Did you pass?

Are you human?

SEVEN

SHORT FILMS

Glazer made two short films in 1993 — *Pool* and *Mad* — both calling-card works, full of technical prowess and a flair for witty originality. *Pool* is the more clearly aligned with his future in commercials and music videos: a series of visual jokes culminates in a man regurgitating a black inflatable float, which then explodes into a swimming pool. There's a grotesqueness reminiscent of Francis Bacon, combined with the setting of David Hockney — an anticipation of *Sexy Beast*'s opening.

Mad, by contrast, leans into high-minded artiness. Franz Kafka is the obvious touchstone, recently revisited in Steven Soderbergh's *Kafka* (1991). Once again, Glazer crafts an atmosphere of visually striking and witty sequences. Manic in its cutting, visually disorienting, and relentlessly eager to surprise and impress, it is a showy showcase of talent: a look-at-me extravagance designed to inspire confidence and attract clients.

The two films did their job. The adverts and music videos that followed paved the way — as we have seen — for a film career that unfolded gradually over the next two decades.

The Fall

Some twenty-two years and three films later, Jonathan Glazer directed another short film. *The Fall* appeared one Sunday evening in October 2019 on BBC Two, the second channel of Britain's public broadcaster.

The first thing we hear is the sound of several people shouting hoarsely and aggressively. No words are discernible, though the cadence sounds English, like the gangsters' garbled shouting in *Sexy Beast*. Masked figures stalk through a wood, stomping on the undergrowth and breaking branches. It is dark — folk horror darkness — but there is light pollution, and modern textiles are worn. A lynch mob via Urban Outfitter.

In a long shot, we see the trees and the lighting behind them, as if from streetlamps. One of the trees begins to shake violently. A pounding is heard, then another — an alien musical instrument. A non-diegetic sound.

Several figures stand around a tree which they are vigorously shaking. The camera looks up at a man clinging to the trunk high above, also wearing a mask. The music becomes recognisably music and joins in the violence, with percussion and tambourines merging into the sound of the shaking tree — until the man drops to the ground. The group move towards him, the bystanders joining in. A bright light shines, and the group is caught for a moment in the white glare as a photograph is taken. The man is held around the throat. Others grip his arms. All try to be in the picture. The victim and the mob wear similar black clothes: outdoor gear, shiny in parts; casual, perhaps uniforms, perhaps workwear. Indeterminate, but clearly modern.

The victim's mask shows a scared expression. The others show expressions of anger, bared teeth. Mouth-breathing perhaps. But they are masks all the same, with no attempt at verisimilitude. The elastic bands holding them are clearly visible. Japanese Noh theatre. Or the masks from *Eyes Wide Shut*. The full photograph is then presented to the viewer the way it might be shown in the end credits of a rom-com. A trophy picture. A triumphant prelude to an atrocity.

A noose is placed around the man's neck and, as his tormentors move away, he suddenly drops, without ceremony. As unexpected as a pratfall.

The title of the film comes up like a dark joke: *The Fall*. We return to the forest and hear the sound of the rope running out as the man apparently continues to fall off camera. The camera moves in and up to where the rope is beginning to smoke from the friction. The gallows are concrete, and there are tall walls. This is not the deep dark woods of folklore: the street lighting and the concrete suggest an urban copse. We now see from above as the rope continues unspooling into a dark, square pit. The reverse shot, looking up at the rope, reveals a geometry: squares within squares, abstract shapes—until we are drawn back to the situation as the masked faces appear at the edge of the pit, peering down. Have the frozen faces changed, or are we projecting fear onto their expressions instead of anger? Is that on us, the way we read humanity onto the skin of the Alien in *Under the Skin*?

The rope has run out; it does not appear to have burned out or broken, it simply seems as if there was only so much of it, and the end was not attached to anything. Is this part of the ritual? After such a fall, the man would be dead anyway—from the drop rather than from strangulation or a broken neck caused by the useless noose. The mob moves away: a mix of defeat and triumph. An angry little dance from one of them is at once pompous and ridiculous. Like Martin Sheen in *Badlands* (1973) or Jack Nicholson in *The Shining* having a little psychotic tantrum.

The rope is now the centre of the screen—the protagonist—as it continues to fall through space. It is a long shot—almost a minute—as it falls under its own weight, bisecting the screen, and again we are looking at something abstract and inhuman. A line moving against a dark background. It appears the camera is also travelling downwards at speed, but always maintaining the rope in the centre of the frame, until it pulls up with a jerk. But not the noose-tightening, neck-breaking jerk of execution. The man has braced himself against the walls of the shaft—the pit, the well, the chimney. Whatever it is. This hole that leads endlessly down. To the underworld? To Hell?

How did he stop himself? It is the sort of thing that happens in films, or cartoons. The man is loosening the noose around his neck and, timing it to perfection, drops it just as the end of the rope passes him, so that it continues its journey, spiralling into the depths without dragging him with it. He breaks the fourth wall for a second, glancing at the camera like Oliver Hardy realising he is in another fine mess. He looks up at his predicament and then, with the patience of Sisyphus, starts the difficult climb back to the surface.

The credits take up almost half the running time of the short.

What to make of this short film that ambushed viewers of BBC Two one Sunday evening, between the usually affable shows? Catherine Shoard wrote in *The Guardian*: "Abruptly, BBC Two dropped us into Hell." According to Peter Bradshaw, *The Fall* was "a Haiku of horror."*

The Guardian interview was the only press Glazer did to promote the short film, and even then, he confined himself to replying to questions via email. He noted

---

* Catherine Shoard, "Nazism Took Hold Like a Fever: It Looks Like It's Happening Again," *The Guardian*, 27 October 2019.

several influences, although his primary influence—the spark—was a snapshot of Donald Trump Jr and Eric Trump holding the corpse of a dead leopard in a trophy photograph taken in Zimbabwe. Night surrounds them, but it is the flashbulb whiteness of the teeth that shows the darkness of their souls. "The day I saw a picture of the Trump sons grinning with a dead leopard," he says, was the moment the film came to him. In comparison, the expressions of the masks look benign.

There are other influences. Many, considering the film is just over five minutes long—seven with credits. First, there is Francisco de Goya's etching *The Sleep of Reason Produces Monsters*, which shows the artist sleeping at his desk while wild animals—owls and bats— gather around him with chaotic intensity. It suggests the film is a dream, or more obviously a nightmare. It is also what happens when reason sleeps or is relinquished.

"Also, his *Disasters of War* etchings, urgently titled *I Saw It or This Is Worse*. Hell on earth, witnessed like a photojournalist such as Robert Capa or Don McCullin. Ferocious, factual, unflinching," Glazer says. In this sense, the film is supposed to have something of the documentary to it. As fantastical as the masks are, the scene is found rather than set up. A moment of urban anthropology. Like sneaking up to a place popular for dogging, or some other manifestation of postmodern folk horror. This sense of horror at the resistible rise of Donald J. Trump is giving way to a sense that we are preparing for a time of potential atrocity.

"I think fear is ever-present. And that drives people to irrational behaviour. A mob encourages an abdication of personal responsibility. The rise of National Socialism in Germany, for instance, was like a fever that took hold of people. We can see that happening again."*

---

* Catherine Shoard.

Another reference point was a Bertolt Brecht poem written in the 1930s, when the dramatist was exiled from Germany: "In the dark times/Will there also be singing? Yes, there will also be singing/About the dark times."*

The Fall, like many short films, smacks of experiment. Something that would not work as a feature is worked out. It is a sentence, both in terms of language and punishment. The darkness has fallen; the night feels endless, and the climb back to the surface is not guaranteed. The groove worn in the concrete of the gallows suggests that this failed hanging is repeated frequently. Perhaps that is the ritual all along. Maybe there will be an exchange of masks. Ultimately, we are all just the mask-wearers of more profound historical forces. As Percy Shelley wrote: "I met Murder on the way, He wore a mask like Castlereagh."†

Someone else will be hunted and hanged, and then have to climb out of the hole—or die. Or it will be the same person again. An endless cycle of cruelty and repetition.

What are we to do with how neat it looks? The symmetry, the coolness, the music, the atmosphere. The aesthetics. It is a refined look at barbarity: a subtle evocation of brutality. Light is artfully shed on darkness. Is there a price to rendering darkness visible in this way? Does it make it less dark? Should we see their faces, or are we just going to watch their masks? These questions are not Glazer's alone. You could just as readily ask them of Goya. But we shall need to revisit them.

---

* Bertolt Brecht, *Motto to the Svendborg Poems*, translated by John Willett (1939).
† Viscount Castlereagh was the foreign secretary at the time, in the reactionary government of Lord Liverpool. He had already gained infamy for his violent repressive measures in Ireland, and later cut his own throat.

Strasbourg 1518

On 14 July 1518, Frau Troffea came out of her house and began to dance in the streets. There was no music, and no occasion for it. She was soon joined by others who imitated her. Over the next few days, dozens of other choreomaniacs joined in the non-stop dancing, several dying from exhaustion and an apparent inability to stop. Their movements were spasmodic and convulsive. Some died of strokes and heart attacks; their feet were rendered into a pulpy mass of bruised flesh, and puddles of blood formed in which they continued to dance.

The illegal rave scene exploded in the late 1980s. Fuelled by ecstasy and speed, ravers would dance for hours on end, usually in warehouses with few amenities. Danger came from dodgy drugs, the general unsafety of the environment, and dehydration. In Liverpool, I attended a number of all-nighters in the 1990s at the club Cream. There was a purity to the experience of dancing. You would go with friends, but much of the night was spent in a haze of dry ice, strobe lights, endless crescendos reaching rapturous heights, and strangers with whom you suddenly connected on what felt like an intimate and incredibly loving level. This could go on continuously for five or six hours. The house lights would come on to reveal a strange, hard, ugly room: lined faces, sweat-stained hair, bloodshot eyes — a world that had existed all that time beneath the real world, sustained by sensational music. The matte black walls, the scaffolding, the scuffed floor, the glass collectors and bouncers ushering everyone to the exits and outside, where the day was breaking. If it was not already broken.

As with the events in Strasbourg in 1518, there was something compulsive in the new drug-fuelled dance plague. The electronic music — videos for which Glazer would later direct — could trigger an automatic response, setting ravers dancing long after the drugs had worn off. In the TV show *Spaced*, Michael Smiley's raver/cycle courier would be set off gurning and dancing by any repetitive electronic sound, from a microwave beep to a pedestrian crossing.[*]

In 2020, as the pandemic interrupted preparations for his next feature film, Glazer decided to return to this "Dancing Plague" from the Middle Ages for a ten-minute short film entitled *Strasbourg 1518*. "What caught my attention was the people of Strasbourg, 500 years ago, dancing in despair," Glazer told *The Guardian*, "and the connection between them and Pina Bausch saying, centuries later, 'dance, dance, or we are lost.'"[†]

Working with Artangel—the organisation responsible for art projects such as Rachel Whiteread's *House* and Steve McQueen's *Year 3*—Glazer developed a project that would reach back in time to speak to the isolation and madness of the lockdown created by the medical emergency.

In Strasbourg, the authorities had been at a loss as to how to handle the mass psychosis. One solution was simply to let the dancers get on with it, hoping they would wear themselves—and the disease—out. A stage was even built to give them a place to dance and so keep the streets clear. Then a religious solution was proposed, viewing the outbreak as a God-inspired punishment, and leading to a crackdown on sinners (prostitutes, gamblers, the usual suspects) in the town, which had no effect. Finally, the victims were rounded up, bound, and taken to a shrine dedicated to St Vitus, the patron saint of dance, where they were treated with prayer and holy oil, and had red shoes placed on their feet (which would

---

[*] Directed by Edgar Wright and written by Simon Pegg and Jessica Stevenson, *Spaced* ran on Channel 4 between 1999 and 2001.
[†] Sarah Crompton, "*Strasbourg 1518*: Reliving a 16th Century 'Dancing Plague' in Lockdown," *The Guardian*, 19 July 2020.

inspire Hans Christian Andersen's tale and then Michael Powell and Emeric Pressburger's film *The Red Shoes* [1948]). This seemed to work.

Glazer's film uses Mica Levi's insistent score. The dancers mostly hail from Tanztheater Wuppertal Pina Bausch. Botis Seva, the British choreographer, and Germaine Acogny, the Senegalese dancemaker, were also recruited as collaborators.

Using Zoom, Glazer gave his instructions. "All I really did was talk through the idea with them, then send Mica's music," Glazer says. "And [said] if they liked the combination, to think about what they wanted to express, from their rooms basically. A few days later they showed us a run-through and we went from there. I felt privileged to see what they were producing. Each dance was like a monologue." At three different times of the day and night, filming employed iPhones to create the footage, with cinematographer Darius Khondji.

"When I watch it now," Khondji says, "it is one piece, one dancer."[*]

"How are you? From ten to one? From ten to zero?" a voice asks, as a dancer in a nondescript room stretches sleepily and laughs, a little unhinged. The title appears on screen in large fuchsia capitals. Then we cut to a dancer in a room. She has long, wet hair like the ghost girl from the Ringu films. The music is contemporary dance music, and her movements are a mixture of dance and obsessively compulsive gestures of washing in a large wooden bucket of water, into which she also drops her hair. The scene cuts to later— first twilight, then night—and she is still dancing. The diegetic sound of her laboured breathing and her hands slapping the walls, as if they are confining her, and her feet slapping the floor, can be heard throughout. These are sounds that are not painful now, but might become

---

[*] Sarah Crompton.

so through sheer repetition. Her exhaustion begins to take over, but her return to the bucket and the scrubbing of her hands replenishes her and sets the whole cycle in motion once more.

Another dancer takes off her cardigan and puts it on again over her head, over and over. Dance is no longer exuberant, no longer a celebration of the human body in motion; rather, it is compulsive, contorted, a punitive force possessing and damaging the dancer. It no longer depicts the dancer's control of the body or defiance of gravity, but rather the way they must succumb to it and to a greater power. The darkness may represent the time passing in which they dance—or they may themselves embody darkness, silhouetted figures moving against the light. The initial sense of isolation—solo dancers in minimalist rooms, with hard floors and continental power sockets—is bound together (rather than unified) by the music and the increasingly frenzied editing. A woman in a red dress becomes a beat marker, a punctuation point, repeated over and over as a man in another room continues his dance: a series of gestures somewhere between frivolous abandon and collapsing exhaustion.

Beckett comes to mind. In *Waiting for Godot*, Estragon suggests that Lucky could "dance first and think afterwards, if it isn't too much to ask him."

As with many pieces of art produced during lockdown, the constraints are written into it. The isolation of artists doing things from confined spaces, improvising. And at the same time, there is an unevenness. The sense of boredom is there, as well as claustrophobia: the idea is too close to its inspiration. Strasbourg occurred in the open air and was communal. This is a madness taking place indoors, and separately. The rooms all have a stifling roominess to them—not roomy in the sense of spacious, but unmistakably, almost oppressively, rooms. The dancers could be estate agents showing us around—flamboyantly, madly. This is life on Zoom. Suddenly, journalists and experts, politicians and late-night hosts, colleagues and bosses were speaking to us from their spare rooms, with bookshelves or laundry in the background.

The dancers have cleared their rooms for the dance—and dance they must. The lack of clutter renders the space lifeless and surreal. Who keeps a huge bucket of water in a bedroom?

Something distinctly unhuman is happening to human beings. We are being experimented on—by global viruses and new ideologies of hate. The dark is rising, but it will not extinguish art. And our response to it—the dancing, the filmmaking, the music—will be to try and make that darkness visible. To repeat Brecht: "Yes, in the dark time there will be singing, singing about the dark times."

EIGHT
THE ZONE OF INTEREST

The Barbarism of Cinema after Auschwitz
I first saw *The Zone of Interest* at its premiere in Cannes in 2023. Afterwards, I didn't want to talk about it, let alone write about it. I wanted to go home and go to bed. I wanted to think about it. To worry about it. To mull, to ponder.

I felt guilty for admiring it. At one point during the screening, I even became angry with it. The film encapsulated why I've never wanted to visit Auschwitz. It stirred a feeling I didn't trust.

There was a priest from the village where I now live in Italy who used to boast about how many years he had been taking groups to Auschwitz, how many coach trips he had organised. I never joined him, but I could imagine him knowing just the right place to stop for lunch—somewhere away from the tourists. I could imagine him greeting the guards at the entrance with a practiced familiarity: "Hello there, me again! Look who I've brought this time." That may be an unfair projection, but his breezy rapport with the site of atrocity felt like a diabolical inversion of the Church's denial of that very history during—and in the immediate aftermath of—the Holocaust. Too much, too late.

I didn't want to be on a coach. I didn't want to have the feelings I knew I'd have. I didn't want to place that site on the map of my life. I didn't want to tick it off a list and then reconvene in the parking lot. I didn't want to wait for the right moment to eat my packed lunch.

It wasn't because I didn't care. I want to say: I cared too much—but that sounds self-important.

Rather, it was because I felt that whether I cared or not was beside the point—irrelevant, even. Inadequate.

The enormity of the Holocaust defies response, depiction, containment. We must both talk about it and remain silent. As Kurt Vonnegut once wrote: "There is nothing intelligent to say about a massacre."* Except, of course, for that line. Leave it to Uncle Kurt—and respectfully retreat. (Though I've always been bothered by the fact that in the same book—*Slaughterhouse-Five, or The Children's Crusade*—Vonnegut quotes David Irving in his description of the bombing of Dresden.† How can the chronicler of one massacre become the denier of another, far greater one?)

There's something about conversation that cheapens things. Even the most sensitive dinner-table discussion risks reducing what I felt after watching *The Zone of Interest* to something like idle chatter about mass murder.

And that "experience," that response—what even was it? What is the viewer's reaction supposed to do? Mean? What is cinema supposed to do with Auschwitz, except turn it into a genre—a test of a director's mettle?

---

* Kurt Vonnegut, *Slaughterhouse 5, or the Children's Crusade* (Delacorte, 1969).
† Vonnegut quotes David Irving's 1963 book *The Destruction of Dresden*. At this stage, Irving was a reputable historian, but was later revealed to be an antisemite and Holocaust denier. However, even his history of the bombing of Dresden relied on uninterrogated and shaky evidence which multiplied the number of deaths by a factor of ten.

Claude Lanzmann's *Shoah* (1985) remains a grueling act of witness, offering no concessions to the viewer's attention span or comfort. Testimony is delivered in the original languages—Polish, Hebrew, German—then translated on camera into French, subtitled in English. People speak in their living rooms, surrounded by knick-knacks, bad curtains, and houseplants. They walk the ground where the death camp once stood. A village crowds around as a witness speaks to Lanzmann, only to begin repeating the very prejudices that fed the Holocaust in the first place.

You sit through the nine hours—probably over several nights—as an act of self-imposed duty. "Look at me," one thinks. "Not watching Schwarzenegger. Not watching Stranger Things. Watching a nine-hour Holocaust documentary."

You may even see yourself in Woody Allen's Alvy Singer in *Annie Hall* (1977), taking each girlfriend to *The Sorrow and the Pity* (1969)—part test, part attempt to impress. The Holocaust as date movie.

It would later become a television miniseries called simply *Holocaust* (1978), with Meryl Streep famously losing weight to portray her Auschwitz-bound character. The series has faded somewhat from memory, but at the time, shown across consecutive nights, it was a television event. Despite—or rather because of—its soap-opera elements, the series played a major role in introducing the concept of the Holocaust (and the term itself) into global consciousness. In West Germany in particular, it was watched by tens of millions, triggering a vast public reckoning with a national shame long suppressed.

Schindler's List (1993) became the first—though not the last—Holocaust "feel-good" movie. That year, Spielberg seemed split in two: his entertainment instincts channeled into *Jurassic Park*, while *Schindler's List*, an adaptation of Thomas Keneally's 1982 novel, was heralded as proof of his final maturation—after a few false starts—into a serious filmmaker.* Or perhaps "bifurcation" is the more accurate term, given that he was shooting Schindler's List by day and returning to his hotel at night to review the digital effects shots for *Jurassic Park*.

Spielberg's DNA is popular American entertainment, and even when he turns to darkness—and there are moments of genuine, horrifying darkness in *Schindler's List*—he can't help but offset the genocide with humour, suspense, and a touch of cinematic flourish. Liam Neeson, Ben Kingsley and Ralph Fiennes all look suitably grave in black and white, even as the train pulls into a death camp. The little girl in the red coat is a moment of magical cuteness and also deeply moving, but you can feel the fingers curled around your heartstrings as they are expertly pulled. To then see her decomposing body thrown onto a pile of burning corpses is a moment of radical dissonance for Spielberg—as if he's casting his own sentimentality into the abyss.

Yet in the end, for these characters, the showers contain water, not Zyklon B; the Nazi party member is a saviour, not a killer; good prevails; and the future offers hope, regeneration and Israel.

The Holocaust becomes a backdrop for a lesson in the resilience of the human spirit—a triumph of one great man's courage and his legacy. As Terry Gilliam noted in a 2005 TCM interview, *Schindler's List* turns the Holocaust into a success story. "Schindler's Jews" become a group whose lives are owed to him. The language is uncomfortably proprietary, reinforcing the idea of people as possessions.

---

* If Stanley Kubrick makes no appearance in this chapter, it is perhaps because his Holocaust film *The Aryan Papers* was abandoned as a result of the success of *Schindler's List*. Billy Wilder had once been attached to the novel as director, but publicly supported Spielberg's version, claiming he could not have done a better job.

Roberto Benigni's *Life Is Beautiful* (1997) goes even further, transforming the Holocaust into a comedy, in which denial becomes the central conceit. Benigni plays a clownish father who turns the death camp into an elaborate game to preserve his son's innocence. The film's final line is the child's joyful exclamation: "We won!" The game is over.*

The Boy in the Striped Pyjamas (2008) likewise attempts to address the Holocaust in a way that won't be too traumatic for children, while still offering a moral lesson. Of all the films discussed here, it is geographically the closest to *The Zone of Interest*, centring on the child of an SS officer who lives in the immediate vicinity of a death camp and befriends a Jewish inmate of the same age. The ending is surprisingly—though fittingly— downbeat for a children's film. A hard lesson is learned. But whether that lesson is actually "the Holocaust is a bad thing," rather than something more banal like "keep a closer eye on your children," remains unclear. It risks reading more like a cautionary tale about work/life balance than a reckoning with human cruelty.

This is the problem. The Shoah resists becoming a "learning moment." The historical events that make up the Holocaust cannot be reduced to a single lesson. The accumulated weight of millions of murders cannot be distilled into a tidy moral takeaway, a single sentence, a visual motif, or a teachable theme. To seek such a lesson is, in fact, anathema.

Even the iconography of the Holocaust—even the name itself—is fraught.† In his two-volume history, Saul

---

* As tasteless as Benigni's film might appear, it was actually following through on an idea by Jerry Lewis whose incomplete film *The Day the Clown Cried* (1972) was recently revisited in the 2024 documentary *From Darkness into Light*, directed by Michael Lurie and Eric Friedler.

† The word "holocaust" literally means burnt offering, a sacrifice to be made on the alter. This creates a universe in which the murder

Friedländer points out that the majority of Jews killed in the Holocaust had already been murdered before the first brick of Auschwitz was laid. The ditch and the bullet to the back of the head lack the terrible theatricality of the gas chamber, but they formed the essential apparatus of mass murder.

In Tim Blake Nelson's *The Grey Zone* (2001), there's a scene in which the Jewish doctor Miklós Nyiszli—played by Allan Corduner—who assists Mengele in his grotesque experiments, argues that his collaboration might eventually serve some greater good, and in doing so, ease his guilt. But, as another prisoner points out, he is guilty precisely for trying to salvage a meaning from the horror surrounding them. Because meaning—any meaning—is perilously close to mitigation, even justification.

To assign meaning to the Holocaust is a dangerous act. Perhaps even an evil one. Theodore Adorno wrote: "Cultural criticism finds itself today faced with the final state of the dialectic of culture and barbarism. To write poetry after Auschwitz is barbaric. And this corrodes even the knowledge of why it has become impossible to write poetry today. Absolute reification, which presupposed intellectual progress as one of its elements, is now preparing to absorb the mind entirely. Critical intelligence cannot be equal to this challenge as long as it confines itself to self-satisfied contemplation."[*]

It should be noted that Adorno did not call poetry "impossible"—as the line is so often reduced in paraphrase—but rather "barbaric," and opposed to culture. The word barbaric itself is rooted in a xenophobic linguistic distinction. To the ancient Greeks, barbarians

---

of six million people makes some sense in a wider metaphysical universe.

[*] Theodor W. Adorno, "Cultural Criticism and Society" in *The Holocaust: Theoretical Readings, Edinburgh* (Edinburgh, 2003).

were those who didn't speak Greek, whose language sounded like meaningless babble—"babababababa." A gabble. Not refined, not articulate, not coherent. At least not to those in power. Poetry, then, becomes a language one can no longer understand—a foreign tongue.

Adorno would later adjust his opinion: "Perennial suffering has as much right to expression as a tortured man has to scream; hence it may have been wrong to say that after Auschwitz you could no longer write poems. But it is not wrong to raise the less cultural question whether after Auschwitz you can go on living—especially whether one who escaped by accident, one who by rights should have been killed, may go on living. His mere survival calls for the coldness, the basic principle of bourgeois subjectivity, without which there could have been no Auschwitz; this is the drastic guilt put on him who was spared."*

In Vassily Grossman's novel *Life and Fate*, a Jewish prisoner is forced to lead new arrivals from the train to the gas chambers, a role mirrored by the protagonist of *Son of Saul* (2015). He rehearses his motivation, trying to justify his actions to himself, comparing his behavior favorably to that of a colleague. But then he reaches a horrifying insight: "What did it matter what the two of them felt? If the job they did was the same, what did it matter if one felt happy and the other felt sad?" His conclusion is stunning: "And he was dimly aware that if you wish to remain a human being under fascism, there is an easier option than survival—death."†

Adorno, himself a survivor, expressed his guilt in haunting terms: "By way of atonement he will be plagued by dreams such as that he is no longer living at

---

* Theodor W. Adorno, *Negative Dialectics* (1966), translated by E. B. Ashton (Routledge, 1990).
† Vassily Grossman, *Life and Fate* (1960).

all, that he was sent to the ovens in 1944 and his whole existence since has been imaginary, an emanation of the insane wish of a man killed twenty years earlier."

If it is barbaric to write poetry after Auschwitz, how much more barbaric is it to make films? Comedies like Taika Waititi's *Jojo Rabbit* (2019)? Horror films? Children's films? Or, in the case of *The Reader* (2008), a coming-of-age romance?

The Zone of Interest offers evidence that poetry can exist—if not after, then during Auschwitz. A voice in Yiddish tells us: "Text by Joseph Wulf, written in 1943. Oświęcim, Auschwitz 3." But the poem itself, "Sunbeams," is not spoken. It is rendered silently, via piano music, while subtitles deliver the words visually— voiceless, but not absent.

Wulf smuggled poems out of Auschwitz. Having survived, he devoted the rest of his life to documenting and exposing Nazi crimes. He wrote several books, but eventually took his own life. In a final letter to his son, he wrote: "The mass murderers walk around free, live in their little houses, and grow flowers."*

It's a moment that stands in stark counterpoint to the main action of *The Zone of Interest*, which documents the domestic routines of the Höss family, who live in a villa with expansive gardens and vibrant flowers, directly beside the death camp. Rudolf Höss (Christian Friedel) is the commandant of Auschwitz. His wife, Hedwig (Sandra Hüller), lives there with their children: Klaus, Hans-Jürgen, Heidetraut, Inge-Brigitt, and their newborn, Annegret.

All this information is offered by the film only incidentally.

In fact, we begin in darkness, with Mica Levi's distorted score. This is perhaps the most necessary of

---

* Quoted by Lillian Crawford in "The birds still sing at Auschwitz: On Jonathan Glazer's *The Zone of Interest*," Rabbit Foot, 2024.

Glazer's airgaps. The pause acts as both preparation and prelude. We are entering a different zone and, as in Tarkovsky's *Stalker*, there must be a transitional journey—a passage from the state we were in when we entered the cinema, found our seats, and settled beside one another, to a state of unease: apprehensive, uncertain, expectant. How long is this going to go on for?

The first images we see are unexpectedly concerting after such a disconcerting introduction. Birds sing. The screen fills with a sunlit meadow overlooking a lake. A family is having a picnic. Swimmers strike out purposefully across the water.

The framing is precise, composed, painterly—recalling Kubrick's *Barry Lyndon*. But here it is sharpened by digital resolution. There is no patina of brushstrokes, no grain of film. This is a paradise rendered in 6K UltraHD, a world where the only dangers are nettle stings or sunburn.

The family return to their cars. If we look closely, we might glimpse the "SS" on the registration plates as they pull out onto a country road. In the car, the children bicker as they drive through pitch-black countryside. Even this darkness, untouched by modern light pollution, holds a strange kind of comfort. "Not a cell phone in sight," as the meme goes. At home, the children are put to bed. The man of the house locks the doors and switches off the lights. This is his task: to bring the darkness—domestic, historical. It is his leitmotif.

A smash cut returns us to daylight and another beautiful summer morning. For this family, there is no true boundary between light and darkness. Or at least, not a thick one.

The scenes we witness are familiar. It's Höss' birthday. His family blindfolds him to surprise him with a boat. The children imagine future excursions. They go off to school with merry *Sieg Heils*, as automatic and unthinking as "Have a nice day." Höss heads to work. Hedwig stays behind with the baby. She takes a quiet moment among the flowers, an intimate and timeless gesture of maternal serenity.

A prisoner delivers bags from the camp: food, clothing, small luxuries. The gardener tends the grounds. Hedwig distributes undergarments to her servants and, upstairs, tries on a fur coat. In the pocket, she finds a lipstick and applies it. When her friends arrive for coffee and gossip, they laugh about someone who misunderstood the term Canada, believing it referred to the country rather than the warehouses where plundered belongings are sorted and redistributed. There is no innocence here. No wife or child is shielded by the separation of domestic life and labor. The household is integrated into the machinery. There is no excuse. What we see are the house, the garden, the picnic. What we hear are gunshots, shouts, the occasional scream. A train whistle. A deep industrial churn. We hear what happens behind the wall—the invisible remains audible. The camp is partially visible: the wall, the watchtower, the rising steam from a passing locomotive. But that is all.

"The foreground film, the one we see, is largely uneventful, largely undramatic," explains Glazer. "But it is imbued by everything you hear. And what you hear bears down on every frame. The atrocities committed in the camps are perpetual, so there's no quiet moment. There are certain scenes which are all about the sound. In other scenes the sound is ambient. A writer used the term 'ambient genocide', which I thought was very appropriate to this and what we protect ourselves from, what we disassociate from, to have our comfortable lives. The sound was a huge part, the sound is the other film, and, arguably, *the* film, for me."*

---

* Mark Salisbury, "Jonathan Glazer on *The Zone of Interest*," *Screen Daily*, 27 November 2023.

There are several ways to describe Glazer's approach to his subject—a film that took nine years from conception to release. Mindful of the enormity of his task and determined not to repeat what has come before, he sought to create something singular: a Holocaust film unlike any other.

I would sum it up in three terms: perspective, reality, and banality.

Perspective
The first significant choice is that of perspective.

This comes primarily from the original Martin Amis novel, published in 2014. Glazer had read the novel prior to publication, and the rights were secured early by him and his producer Jim Wilson, allowing them the independence to develop the project without outside interference from studios and investors. The novel tells a fictionalised version of events in the Zone of Interest, the forty square kilometers of land surrounding the Auschwitz-Birkenau camp complex, including its work sites and rivers.

These characters interact, often tangentially. Szmul has the unusual distinction of being the longest-serving of the Sonderkommando—someone living on borrowed time, a witness to atrocities, party to them, and yet also a coerced participant who knows he will inevitably be a victim. He and his team sleep above the crematorium, warmed at night by the heat emanating from the burning corpses of their victims: "We are in fact the saddest men in the history of the world."[*]

This character does not appear in the film, unless he is present unnamed—as the gardener, perhaps, or as one of the other nameless prisoners who occasionally work in the garden. Or we might hear him screaming on the soundtrack.

---

[*] Martin Amis, *The Zone of Interest* (Vintage, 2014).

Thomsen also does not appear in Glazer's film, and the entire storyline of his adulterous affair with Hannah, Paul Doll's wife, is abandoned. In fact, Amis' novel is used primarily for its title and setting. Without the fictionalisation, Paul Doll reverts to Rudolf Höss and Hannah to Hedwig. The perspective is almost entirely from the point of view of the perpetrators and functionaries of the Shoah, not the victims. As an audience, we are not allowed the moral salve of immediately identifying with the victims, because they aren't visible. They're audible. We overhear what is happening to them. But to overhear something is not to witness it—and it certainly isn't to experience it.

In Spielberg's *Schindler's List*, we are allowed—indeed encouraged—to identify with a number of Jewish victims and survivors. Would it be unfair to suggest that he picks particularly photogenic ones? The little girl with the round glasses, the handsome smuggler of black-market goods?

We are also encouraged to align ourselves with Schindler himself. We feel his humour, his scoundrel-like appeal. Incapable of being faithful, he packs his wife off on the train with a cheerful goodbye. Liam Neeson brings with him a boatload of Gallic charm, along with his movie idol looks. We even feel his frustration with Stern for his increasing demands. Given the situation, we might think, Schindler is doing the best he can.

The Jews, in contrast, are passive as they are shipped from one place to another, utterly dependent on Schindler's bravery and Stern's moxie to save them. At the end of the film, the actors accompany the real-life survivors they played—or their families and descendants—to lay stones on the grave of the real-life Oskar Schindler.

We leave the cinema exhausted from weeping, utterly spent but also renewed in our belief in the basic goodness of humanity—and, by extension, ourselves—

who, even in this darkest moment in human history, managed to save 1,200 lives. The sum might seem paltry beside the six million lives lost in the Holocaust, but as Stern tells Schindler, "He who saves a life, saves the world." And look at their descendants.

But then, killing six million people kills six million worlds—and let's look at the descendants who now didn't descend.

British philosopher Gillian Rose writes of an imagined film which—in contrast to Spielberg's—would take its point of view from the side of the perpetrators rather than the victims.* We would see the "life story of a member of the SS in all its pathos, so that we empathise with him, identify with his hopes and fears, disappointments and rage, so that when it comes to killing, we put our hands on the trigger with him, wanting him to get what he wants. We do all this with an innocent enthusiasm in films where the vicarious enjoyment of violence may presuppose that the border between fantasy and reality is secure." Instead of provoking Mamet's "emotional pornography," we would watch the film "with the dry eyes of a deep grief."†

In Amis' novel, Hannah is granted plausible deniability, and the playboy Thomsen breezes through the camps as if he's amoral, when, in such a situation, being amoral is obviously deeply immoral. This is a mistake he only comes to realise at the novel's conclusion, when Hannah makes clear that nothing good can come of the Zone of Interest: neither a belief in humanity nor a love affair. Nihilistic despair is as good as it gets. Or suicide.

Glazer's film follows Rose's suggestion. The perspective is firmly (though not exclusively) on the Höss family. We see their day-to-day life as an idyll: the birthday party, the coffee morning, the business meeting,

---

* Gillian Rose, *Mourning Becomes the Law: Philosophy and Representation* (Cambridge University Press, 1996).
† Ibid.

the gardening, the visit of Hedwig's mother, and the party to celebrate her arrival. A series of festivities and treats. Sometimes a bit boring, the way summer tends to be, but pleasantly so. There are excursions: the picnic; Rudolf's horse rides with his eldest son; the trip up the river with his younger son and daughter, which ends when human remains from the camp float downstream and a rainstorm—like something out of a Victorian novel— breaks over them, making the moment unbearably miserable, tempting us to feel sorry for them.

As the young boy is washed in the bathtub, the nanny admonishes him: "It won't kill you." The residue of human ash remains in the tub to be scrubbed by the maid, who pauses, knowing full well she is looking at dead people. She might also be looking at her own imminent future.

Reality
There is another element to this perspective that is more generic: reality—or, more accurately, the film's hyper-reality. As already noted, the images are pristine, with a clarity made possible only by current lenses and technology. Not 4K resolution, but 6K. Cinematographer Łukasz Żal says: "We wanted to see every pixel." This is not black and white, not handheld, distorted, or aged. The film stock hasn't deteriorated. Everything in the house is in sharp focus, from the far wall to the nearest chair. Everything is lit with natural light—streaming through the windows by day, or coming from electric lamps at night.

We are seeing with crystal-clear 21st-century eyes, not the eyes of 1943–44. The clothes everyone wears are not vintage—they are brand new. This temporal concertina-ing was one of Glazer's very first concepts: "The first time I went to Auschwitz was with a view of making a film there. I hadn't been as a boy. I often go to the place that I think I'm going to be making something in, and I start with the space; that can begin to inform me; to make sense to me just by being there. I remember coming out of those camps and stopping. For anybody who's been there, it's obviously a grim experience. But I remember writing in my book at the time that I needed to weave the here and now with the there and then."*

The film looks with new eyes, but the world also feels brand new. The house has been freshly renovated and painted. Hedwig tells her mother what work they have done: the roof, the central heating, and the garden—the flowers and vegetables.

Glazer and his team renovated a nearby house because the original Höss residence was too dilapidated to use. (The only scene filmed in the actual Höss house is the one in which Rudolf descends into the tunnel—yet another tunnel—that connects the house to the camp.) The cars are spotless, polished to a shine. All that slave labour must come in handy. The new boat gleams with a fresh walnut sheen. Boots are left at the door to be cleaned by a prisoner.

As when filming the white van scenes with Scarlett Johansson in *Under the Skin*, hidden cameras are once again used. Glazer deployed up to ten cameras in the house and more in the garden, shooting simultaneously and allowing the editor to cut between locations in real time as characters move from room to room, or in and out of the house. Cameras were hidden—for instance, in a child's teepee in the garden or in holes in the house walls, out of sight of the cast and of other cameras covering alternate angles. Focus pullers were stationed in the basement, while Glazer and his team positioned themselves in a container disguised as a camp building nearby, watching everything remotely.

---

* Cinema Ritrovato, Bologna, June, 2025.

This technique meant that the actors—especially the children—could be captured behaving naturally rather than self-consciously acting, without the distraction of equipment and crew around them, and without the usual breaks needed to adjust lighting, hair, makeup, or reset camera positions. Ordinary blocking and the stop-start rhythm (or lack thereof) that usually plagues a film set were thus largely eliminated. The cast could go about the tasks they had been instructed to do and forget they were in a film, delivering naturalistic performances. Glazer referred to it as "Big Brother in a Nazi house."[*]

Although there's a risk of tastelessness in such a comment,[†] it captures an important point—one that relates back to both perspective and reality/"reality." We are watching these people the way we have become accustomed to watching people today. Our voyeurism—encouraged by reality TV—now finds us ready to watch the apparent story-less spectacle of events unfolding in the Höss household. We are media-trained to observe narrative-less events, confident that (a) this holds a fascination in and of itself and (b) a narrative will eventually emerge if we watch long enough. The children read the guest book, the teenagers neck outside, and the commandant, dressed in an impossibly white suit, leans with a cigarette on the porch fence.

Narrative usually implies the organisation of events, not just the presentation of them, but this seems to be simply one thing happening after another—alongside other things happening at the same time. A daughter walks proudly through the garden, boasting of its flowers and vegetables to her mother, while the Polish serving girls prepare the outdoor tables for the upcoming party and the family dog wanders freely, inevitably stealing

---

[*] Sean O'Hagan, "Jonathan Glazer on his Holocaust film *The Zone of Interest*," The Guardian, 10 December 2023.
[†] A *big* risk.

some food from the picnic table. The sight of that dog by the food was disturbing—which is absurd, considering what's happening on the other side of the wall.

Reality TV shows like *Big Brother* give audiences the illusion of interactivity. Most obviously, we get to vote for people to stay in the house or be expelled. But on another level, we are also interactive in choosing when and how to watch, via the 24-hour feeds available to us. Which rooms? Which people? Which strands of story to follow? Or do we attempt to recreate Jeremy Bentham's Panopticon, his design for a perfect prison, still used in prison architecture today and a prototype for our present-day surveillance societies? We can watch people sleep, brush their teeth, chat, or pass time in other seemingly aimless ways. Some TV shows now focus entirely on watching people watch television. Scratching themselves. Having sex. We can choose to build a narrative from these fragments or wait for the edited highlights, compiled by the producers for later broadcast.

In *The Zone of Interest,* this is something of an illusion. We are already watching the highlights reel. A story is emerging, even though it doesn't look like one. We feel the people aren't performing.

Hedwig, before trying on a fur coat brought from the camp, carefully closes the door, leaving the dog outside. She believes herself to be alone and tries on the lipstick she finds in the coat pocket. It's a rare moment of vanity for a woman who, in other respects, is rather gauche and—at least on the surface—careless about her appearance. She thinks no one is watching, except herself, as she looks into the mirror.

But we are watching her. We are seeing what she is really doing. It's a moment of intimacy. Does it also create a sense of shared identity? The lipstick looks good. You should keep it. When she wipes it on her hand before applying it, is she testing it or is she wiping away the traces of the previous owner's lips? That previous owner has, by now, been gassed and cremated.

Rudolf stretches out on the sofa, caught somewhere between listening to the football match on the wireless and reading a book. We soon realise that the cause of his restlessness is an anticipated telephone call, which eventually comes. We learn that he is being outmanoeuvred and kicked upstairs, removed from his post as commandant. It will mean relocating the family—something he delays telling Hedwig, knowing she won't take the news well.

When Rudolf and Hedwig argue about leaving Auschwitz, we have already overheard the letter his powerful relative has written on his behalf, and we have seen Rudolf receive confirmation that the transfer has gone through regardless. We can feel his frustration, and we sympathise with Hedwig's surprise—only to then be surprised ourselves by her solution: she will stay with the children.

Here, the disjunction between our potential empathy for Hedwig's "hopes and fears, disappointment and rage," as Gillian Rose writes, and the historical reality we know as Auschwitz reaches a perfect dissonance.

As an audience, we become guilty of caring about what happens to these people. We might side with Hedwig in her wish to preserve the family home she has built with such time and painstaking effort. Or we might feel for Rudolf, shocked to realise that she would rather be separated from him—and have him separated from the children—than leave her beloved garden and the comforts of the house. He cuts a pathetic figure, in need of consolation from his wife. Rudolf Höss, the commandant of Auschwitz.

We might even want someone to just grab hold of that dog and keep it away from the cold cuts.

With a potential solution to their problem, they return to the party, chatting about the prospects for National Socialist happiness after the war. This is classical irony: we know more than the characters. We know their postwar lives will not be National Socialist lives. We know Rudolf will be hanged within sight of the house Hedwig adores. The ideology reminds us that these aren't people we want to see happy, or victorious. And yet, even in their loss, can we help feeling a twinge of sympathy—even if it is for the devil?

An excellent moment in *Schindler's List* is the execution of Amon Göth, played by Ralph Fiennes. It lands as a jarring beat. Göth is structurally the second lead, Schindler's mirror—the antagonist. His job is to kill Jews, as Schindler tries to save them. He's given a parallel storyline and nearly equivalent screen time. Göth's misogynistic treatment of women is paralleled with Schindler's promiscuity, which, despite its carelessness, is portrayed as essentially kind and loving. Schindler even tries to reform Göth through their friendship, to lessen his violence, to appeal to what Abraham Lincoln called "the better angels of our nature." He sees good in his friend—something Stern tries to counter with accounts of Göth's psychopathic and sadistic violence.

Despite Stern's efforts, the film presents these two men as alternate ways of being. It's the old cliché: *We're not so different, you and I.* Villain and hero, confronting each other throughout the film.

So when, in the final act, Göth's storyline is dropped—his killings now irrelevant as Schindler's Jews must be saved—he becomes insignificant.

The last time we see him is at the moment of his execution. He stands on a stool beneath makeshift gallows, like Höss in sight of his villa. He adjusts his hair, gives a "Heil Hitler," and the stool is kicked away. It takes several attempts. His hanging is botched. The soldiers don't take his death seriously.

The moment is chastening because we have taken him seriously. We have pondered his character, his complexity, his interiority. We have asked the Thomas Nagel question: *What is it like to be Amon Göth?*

The freeze-frame of him dangling seems to say: *We've wasted enough time on this man. We're not going to wait for him to die. He was hanged for crimes against humanity. Don't give him a second thought. He's dead now. It would have been better if he had never existed.*

A lot for a freeze-frame to say, I know.

But it also says: this man is banal.

Banality

In 1963, Hannah Arendt published a series of articles in *The New Yorker*, which were later compiled and expanded into the book *Eichmann in Jerusalem: A Report on the Banality of Evil.*

An Austrian functionary of the German state and a Nazi Party member, Adolf Eichmann was the man who made the trains run on time—specifically, those to the death camps. His genius for organisation, skill with bureaucracy, and much-vaunted expertise in the "Jewish Question" placed him—despite his relatively low rank—at the core of the Final Solution, including the infamous Wannsee Conference, where the extermination of European Jewry was ultimately decided upon… in the morning. Then there was lunch and an informal conversation. An opportunity for networking, as we'd call it today.

Following the war, Eichmann escaped from Poland and Germany and managed to make his way to Argentina, where he was kidnapped by the Israelis and transported to Jerusalem to stand trial for his role in the genocide of the Jews.

For Alissa Wilkinson, *The Zone of Interest* is "a sidelong horror film adaptation of Hannah Arendt's *Eichmann in Jerusalem*."* The reason lies mainly in the book's subtitle, which introduced the world to the concept of the "banality of evil" and linked it inextricably to the Holocaust. In describing Eichmann, Arendt was not depicting the monster of popular folklore—a gremlin, an inhuman beast, visibly different from the spectators in the courtroom or the respected judge and lawyers who presided over the proceedings. She writes: "Despite all the efforts of the prosecution, everybody could see that this man was not a 'monster,' but it was difficult indeed not to suspect that he was a clown." The idea of his status as a clown posed a direct threat to the seriousness of the trial, Arendt writes: "and was also rather hard to sustain in view of the sufferings he and his like had caused to millions of people." Because of this, "his worst clowneries were hardly noticed and almost never reported." Eichmann claimed he would never take an oath and then chose to testify under oath when offered the opportunity to do so without one. He repeatedly assured the court he would not plead for mercy, then submitted a plea for mercy.

Eichmann, in Arendt's view, was a man who spoke in clichés and stock phrases—one of T. S. Eliot's "Hollow Men." He wasn't a fanatic or a true believer, according to Arendt's reporting, but a shallow, egoless cipher.

Eichmann's personality (he was examined by a series of psychologists, all of whom found him boringly normal) is supposed to hold some kind of meaning. We are looking for the psychological roots of the Holocaust, as Schindler will ponder Amon Göth. But to search for meaning in conventional terms in the Holocaust is like looking for palm trees in Antarctica.

---

* Alissa Wilkinson, 'This Year's Scariest Horror is *The Zone of Interest*,' *Vox*, December 2023.

In his 1947 book *If This Is a Man*, Holocaust survivor Primo Levi writes about arriving at Auschwitz and breaking off an icicle from a window frame, only to have it torn from his hand by a guard and thrown to the ground. When, in his naïveté, he asked the soldier "Why?" he was told an important truth: "Hier ist kein warum." ("There is no why here.") When answering readers' questions about the hatred the Nazis had for the Jews, Levi wrote: "Perhaps one cannot—what is more, one must not—understand what happened, because to understand is almost to justify."*

As we saw earlier with *The Grey Zone*, understanding is too close to justifying because it places the Holocaust within a rational order. But Levi's point continues: "Let me explain. Understanding a proposal or a form of human behaviour means containing it, containing its author, putting oneself in his place, identifying with him. No normal human being will ever be able to identify with Hitler, Himmler, Goebbels, Eichmann, and the endless others. This dismays us, but at the same time it provides a sense of relief, because perhaps it is desirable that their words and their deeds cannot be comprehensible to us. They are nonhuman words and deeds, really counter-human, without historic precedents, difficult to compare even with the cruellest events of the biological struggle for existence."†

Levi is identifying the perpetrators of the Final Solution as similar to the Alien in *Under the Skin*: "nonhuman... counter-human." The agents and their actions are placed outside the moral compass of humanity. Not understanding isn't a failure—it's a fundamental insight into what happened.

---

* Primo Levi, trans. Ruth Feldman in *The New Republic*, 17 February 1986.
† *The New Republic*.

"There is no why" is quoted by Martin Amis in the afterword to his novel *The Zone of Interest*. The novel is rich in banality. The boozing Paul Doll is gross and vulgar, much like John Self in Amis' earlier novel *Money* (1984). Despite his repeated "Nicht?" we can hear his voice as that of a bullying Englishman. The libertine Angelus Thomsen, with his carelessly unaffected ways, might stand in for Amis himself—an intellectual too wrapped up in his own libido and gratification to care about what is going on around him, beyond his own survival and amorous adventures.

The plot line is recognisable and, if not banal, certainly and consciously shopworn and clichéd: the cuckolded husband, the unappreciated wife, the roué who begins to have serious feelings for his lover— for the first time in his life, to fall in love. All of this while the war is clearly being lost, and the worst mass murder in the history of the world is being committed all around the main characters. Thomsen's final declaration of love—after the war has ended—is met with baffled dismay: "Imagine how disgusting it would be if anything good came out of that place," says Hannah.

Anything good? Does that include the novel? Does that include Jonathan Glazer's film *The Zone of Interest*?

And was Eichmann really "banal"? And of what does the banal consist? Isn't it knocking down a straw man?

In a sense, yes. Arendt was witnessing at the trial what she believed to be the construction of a straw man. The insistence on Eichmann's monstrousness—and the ignoring of his banality and, indeed, clownishness— meant (for Arendt) that questions of Israeli selfhood could be more easily constructed, and more uncomfortable questions (such as what to do with all those Palestinians) put to one side. The trial was used to display the suffering of the victims of the Holocaust in a public and legal context, despite the fact that it was being conducted in breach of the Genocide Convention to which Israel was a signatory.

It meant ignoring the many Germans who had managed to survive denazification processes and were, in fact, flourishing—having once more risen to positions of power despite being as culpable as Eichmann. According to Arendt, it also meant ignoring the victim-blaming narratives that persisted and gnawed at the psyche of the Israeli state. Why didn't more Jews resist? Why did people march passively into the gas chambers? Why did the Jewish bureaucracy aid the early stages of the Holocaust, and the Jewish Sonderkommando facilitate the final moments of the Final Solution?*

But the idea of banality has since become a cliché— one repeated so trippingly off the tongue that it has begun to lose meaning. What does it mean to be banal? Does it just mean having bodily functions? Sitting on the toilet? Wearing socks? Having a job? Filling out paperwork? Does any of this make the other things you do more or less despicable? Peter Sutcliffe spent more time driving his truck than murdering women, but he will always be the Yorkshire Ripper, not the Yorkshire Truck Driver. It only takes a little bit of shit in your salad to make it the defining attribute.

Adolf Hitler himself suffered from terrible wind, farting constantly. What are we supposed to do with that? The monster farts. The monster—even in folklore—has the banal already written into it: the wolf that can look like Grandma, for instance. Banality is

---

* Primo Levi answered these questions definitively, citing practical reasons, including physical debilitation, having no knowledge of Polish, wearing easily identifiable prison garb and loud wooden clogs, etc.

not really a counterpoint to monstrosity so much as a feature of it.

It's Hitler's stupid moustache. His flatulence. His monadism.

The Höss family brush their teeth; the children go to school, heil Hitler-ing as they leave; Herr and Frau Höss bicker about the future—and the darkness of the evil around them creeps in at the cracks. It can be seen in Hedwig's lipstick and fur coat, stolen from murdered Jews. Or in the human teeth one of the boys has acquired; the human remains that flow down the river. None of this is banal as such. There's the stench in the air that causes people not used to it—like Hedwig's mother—to flee. Not all the flowers in the new garden; not all the flowers in the world can cover that stench.

Stench, incidentally, is something cinema is incapable of truly depicting. Maybe a true Holocaust film would make its audience physically ill. That would be the natural reaction to the scene in *Schindler's List* where the children, hiding from a roundup, are neck-deep in human excrement in the camp latrines.

Maybe we need to retch like Höss himself at the end of the film.

No one is innocent in *The Zone of Interest*. Höss obviously isn't. We see him enthusiastically approving blueprints for a new facility that will incinerate more "pieces" more efficiently. His wife Hedwig is not innocent either. She knows all about "Canada," as do her friends. Not knowing about it is something to be scoffed at—a naïveté that is almost a faux pas in its stupidity among the women. Hedwig is not merely a knowing witness. She threatens one of her maids, a local girl: "My husband will scatter your ashes on the fields." She has none of the immunity Martin Amis affords Frau Doll in the novel, as if Amis, like his narrator Thomsen, can't quite bring himself to believe that a pretty woman can be truly irredeemable. We've already seen ashes scattered on her flower beds. Hedwig knows of what she speaks. The roses in her idyll grow from the ashes of the murdered. When she lowers the baby to smell them, she knows this—even if she might be forgetful.

The children are not innocent either. The eldest brother, Klaus (Johann Karthaus), shoves his younger brother Hans (Luis Noah Witte) into the greenhouse and stands back with his arms folded while making hissing noises. He is playing at gassing his brother—playing at murder, just as his father does at work. The young boy himself will—on overhearing a prisoner being executed—mutter to himself: "You must obey" and "Don't do it again." All is well with the world. People on that side of the wall get killed, and it's quite right that they do. He is not playing a game like Roberto Benigni with little Giosuè (Giorgio Cantarini) in *Life is Beautiful*. Or more accurately, he is playing a game—he is setting up toy soldiers when he overhears the execution—and hears the real world happening outside his window as well.

The baby screams at night, cared for by the alcoholic nanny, and one of the young daughters sleepwalks. Is she the disturbed conscience of the family? Or is she just a little girl who sleepwalks?

Her behaviour mirrors that of the young Polish girl Aleksandra Bystron-Koloziejczyk (Julia Polaczek), who secretly leaves food for the prisoners at night. Her bicycle and dress, as well as the house she visits, all belonged to the historical person. She is filmed with a thermographic camera developed by the Polish Army, which picks up heat rather than light. In this way, we are seeing through darkness when we watch her. We are watching not light, but temperature. The glow comes from the warmth of her body and her humanity. The fruits she carries glow like magical fruit in a fairy tale. The film looks like a negative: a visual topsy-turvy of the universe that renders the humane criminal and the criminal legal.

She also receives a message from within the camp and brings it outside. It is a message written in music and played in the daylight by her on the piano. It is a moment where goodness and reality come together. The film is dedicated to her, as well as to Martin Amis, who died on the day of its premiere at Cannes.

She is not innocent. She knows what is happening, and she is—at great risk to herself and her family—intervening. If she were to be caught, the consequences could easily be fatal. She is also not innocent in another sense. The prisoner whom the Höss boy overhears being drowned is killed because "he was arguing over an apple." In other words, the good deed Aleksandra has committed has had an evil consequence, because in *The Zone of Interest*—as in Tarkovsky's Zone—events do not necessarily align with intentions. The short arc of the moral universe bends toward injustice and random violent death, to paraphrase Martin Luther King Jr.

And Rudolf Höss, we should understand, was not a banal man in the way that Adolf Eichmann could arguably be said to be. Unlike Eichmann, he was a convicted murderer before the war even began. His role as commandant of Auschwitz was not that of the clean-handed bureaucrat. In fact, the functionaries of the camps lived in a culture of performative cruelty, where a reputation for sadism and ruthless violence was absolutely necessary for anyone who harbored hopes of promotion. As Nikolaus Wachsmann writes: "To maintain their status, Camp SS men had to reaffirm their brutality over and over again ... committed SS men were eager to stand out with theatrical displays of cruelty; the ensuing competition ratcheted up the spiral of terror."* Höss might have been a stickler for rules about picking flowers—as shown in the film—but he was not beyond personally killing Jews in the camp. He was a bureaucrat who literally had blood on his hands, on his boots, everywhere.

This is not something the film shows.

There are other ellipses.

Following Rudolf's argument with Hedwig, we are presented with a scene in his office. A woman enters while he is on the phone. She takes off her shoes and undoes her hair. She is Eleonore Hodys, a prisoner being used by Höss for sex. On her Wikipedia page, she is described as "having an affair" and being a "sex slave." This terminology belongs to a bygone, tabloid approach to the brutalisation of women during the Holocaust. It smacks of kink and Nazisploitation. *Rape victim* and *sexual abuse victim* are more accurate descriptions of Eleonore—a prisoner with no power of consent, who was raped and violently assaulted, subjected to forced abortions, constantly threatened with summary execution, and kept in a punishment standing cell whenever she became pregnant. None of this context is provided in the film. She is seen by the audience as evidence of Höss' unfaithfulness to Hedwig. This is obviously not the first time she has been called to his office—in fact, it looks and feels routine—but given the context, we might interpret it as retribution for Hedwig's cold-heartedness in separating him from his family. Her status is ambiguous. It is not immediately clear whether she is a prisoner or a local sex worker.

The film, like Hannah Arendt's reportage from Jerusalem, is determined to show the Nazi functionaries—

---

* *KL: A History of the Nazi Concentration Camps* (Little, Brown, 2015).

even at the highest level—as banal. But there is a real risk in both cases of distorting the historical record to make that argument. To understand them—as Primo Levi rightly pointed out—is a move toward justifying them.

What is always evident throughout the film, however, is how porous the world of the Höss family is. Everything is connected, and there is no way of effectively keeping the pollution of one place away from another. Rudolf's office in the camp—where he rapes Eleonore—is connected to the family home via a tunnel. The river carries the bones; the air carries the ashes and the stench of burning bodies; the tunnel literally undermines the family, providing an entry point for lust and violence. Höss will once again lock doors and turn out lights. Darkness will fall inside the house to match the darkness outside—and the darkness within the characters themselves.

In another startling cut, this time from summer to winter, we find Höss in a bureaucratic post in freezing Oranienburg, back in Germany and away from his beloved family. He takes solace in appreciating a stranger's dog, recalling W. H. Auden's line from "Musée des Beaux Arts," praising the Old Masters and their understanding of suffering:

> That even the dreadful martyrdom must run its
> course
> Anyhow in a corner, some untidy spot
> Where the dogs go on with their doggy life and the
> torturer's horse
> Scratches its innocent behind on a tree.*

In a scene echoing the infamous Wannsee Conference of 1942, which set the direction of the Final Solution, Höss is seen fitting into a structure bent on making killing

---

* W. H. Auden, *Another Time* (Random House, 1940).

more efficient — one also riddled with internal politics. No matter how horrific the ideology, there is always internal jockeying for position, always opportunistic ambition. No matter the carnage, there is always paperwork to be done.

The importation of hundreds of thousands of Hungarian Jews is both a logistical nightmare and a huge career opportunity — a chance to return Höss to Auschwitz, to Hedwig and the children. The war is patently being lost around him. Wounded men sit listening to concerts in deserted bandstands, and over the PA in the hospital where Höss receives a checkup, announcements are dominated by memorial services for the recently killed.

Höss later attends a party, fresh from the triumphant news that his sojourn in Germany is over and he can return to Auschwitz to lead the campaign to kill nearly a million Jews. The operation has been named after him, in recognition of his reputation for "turning theory into practice," as one of his superiors has already remarked. Amid the polite murmur of conversation and soft string music, a large ice sculpture of a swastika is kept central in the frame. No one seems aware of its obvious symbolism: a temporary ideology already doomed to melt away into nothing.

Höss' thoughts are full of murder once more. He tells Hedwig that all he could think about during the party was the logistics of gassing everyone in the room.

"The high ceilings would make it difficult," he observes.

Is this man banal? Or is he a monster? Or is he both? His haircut suggests banality, but his murdering, his rape, and his cruelty are there as well.

The Darkness

The Zone of Interest is the film that gave this book its title and its core concept. It seems to be the film Jonathan Glazer has been preparing to make his whole career—though of course, that is the twenty-twenty vision of hindsight. The darkness the film renders visible is complicated and profound. It is the banality of sunlit picnics, of occasional kindnesses, of moments of tenderness from murderers. It is also the historical darkness of a past that is touchable and yet irretrievable, unjustifiable but unforgettable.

In a film full of formal experiments, the most radical comes in its final act. Having celebrated his return with too much to drink at a party and a late-night phone call to a none-too-delighted Hedwig, Rudolf Höss leaves his deserted office in Oranienburg and walks down the stairs. He pauses to retch. Is it the alcohol? A bad hors d'oeuvre? Or is it a sudden pang of metaphysical dread? Perhaps it's an intimation of his fate—the feel of the hangman's noose tightening? After all, he is returning to a place where, eventually, he will be hanged—within sight of his garden wall, though now on the wrong side of it.

He pauses once more on his way down. His descent is a move toward hell. It is how Humphrey Bogart and Mary Astor end *The Maltese Falcon* (1941), and how Harry Angel (Mickey Rourke) finishes *Angel Heart* (1987). This moment carries a similar film noir feel: the geometric designs on the floor, the desaturated black, grey, and white palette. A man trapped in his own delusions, in a hell of his own making. He is becoming history.

Rudolf looks into the heart of darkness—and so do we. The darkness is complete and fills the screen. Then, noises off. A crack of light breaks the black. We have been looking into another darkness. Light begins to come in. A heavy door opens. We are now in present-day Poland, in the Auschwitz-Birkenau State Museum. A team of cleaners, armed with vacuum cleaners, mops, and cleaning products, tend to the artifacts: the gas chamber, the oven, the displays of children's shoes, crutches, and eyeglasses piled high behind glass.

Here is another banality: the banality of kindness. The banality of the good.

Daily, boring work—putting the world back to rights, once the terrible things have happened—all to a soundtrack of industrial-strength vacuum cleaners.

But there is a limit. Nothing can be undone. Nor should it be. We cannot compensate in any way that erases what has been done. Consolation must not minimise. All we are left with is this act of preservation and witnessing. This is the highest ambition the film can hope for: to protect a continuing sense of what was done here. The film is at once reduced and elevated to this level. It is as ordinary—and as vital—as cleaning.

The screen fills with the colour of a flower. After we return to 1944 and Oranienburg, Höss will continue his descent, and darkness will consume the screen. The noise of that darkness begins—discordant, jangling, damned. A chorus of voices cries out as we sit in the cinema, in the darkness. We cannot leave. The credits will not come up. Not yet.

There needs to be a buffer between the film and the world—a moment in which we are forced to pause, to take it in, and only then to finally leave.

The darkness will always remain—buried in the murder pits of the past, or under the swimming pool of a criminal's getaway, or locked inside a loveless marriage, or a derelict house in Glasgow. The darkness is the fear of obliterating death, a pointless future. It is as large as the space between stars, as small as the soil-dark of the grave. Glazer forces us to confront it—and also to see ourselves seeing it.

Returning to Adorno's point, let me repeat a short-ened version of the quote: "Cultural criticism finds itself today faced with the final state of the dialectic of culture and barbarism. To write poetry after Auschwitz is barbaric. [...] Critical intelligence cannot be equal to this challenge as long as it confines itself to self-satisfied contemplation." The line about poetry is often cited, misquoted, or paraphrased by critics. But let's be clear: Adorno is talking about cultural criticism.

Critics, as much as poets, are implicated in his conclusion.

I feel it myself. How can you write poetry after the Holocaust? How can you criticise anyone for expressing anything? I don't want to admire Glazer's film as an example of Holocaust cinema that... blah blah blah. I'm not Jewish. I'm a straight, cis, white man. I would be in danger from fascism as an anti-fascist—but that presumes I would continue to be vocally anti-fascist once it became dangerous to be so. I very much doubt I would.

As critics, Adorno insists, we cannot "confine ourselves to self-satisfied contemplation." We have to get off the couch of our own opinions. We have to be disturbed—forcefully, if necessary—but we must also disturb ourselves. We have to move, and as critics, we must be encouraged to move.

The Zone of Interest does that. We are forced to consider the Holocaust—not only through the lenses of banality and reality, and not only through the filter of yesterday and filmmaking. We are made to look at it anew—and to be aware of our looking. To ask what it means, morally, that we live in a world which coexists with so much killing and suffering. A point Glazer made forcibly in his Oscars acceptance speech.

When critic Lillian Crawford visited Auschwitz, she was appalled to find that it was sunny and she needed sunglasses: "There was a gentle breeze, and the birds were singing. How dare the birds sing at Auschwitz."

Glazer begins with the birds singing—in the midst of darkness.

AN INCONCLUSIVE CONCLUSION

It's foolhardy to come to any conclusions about a film-maker who is a mere 59 years of age at the time of writing and has a mere four films under his belt. There's literally no telling what will happen next.

Jonathan Glazer could suddenly decide to make a film a year and within the decade would have more than doubled his filmography. And yet that seems unlikely.

There's a similarly unlikely possibility that *The Zone of Interest* is Glazer's last film, and this quartet will be looked on as a uniquely fascinating series of films by an artist who said everything he wanted to say. And then retired.

We could all get hit by buses tomorrow, as I constantly remind my students, paraphrasing Marcus Aurelius, or, like Sean in *Birth*, collapse while jogging in the park.

It occurred to me at a late stage of writing this that Glazer could be our last great film noir director and that was where the fascination with darkness came from. *Sexy Beast* is the broad daylight noir in the tradition of Billy Wilder's *Ace in the Hole* (1951), coupled to the one last job crime thriller. *Birth* is the female gothic noir of Alfred Hitchcock's *Rebecca* (1940) or George Cukor's *Gaslight* (1944), a central female protagonist who suffers under a delusion that is being perpetrated on her by a man (or pair of men in Kidman's case as both Seans have deluded her). *Under the Skin* features a twist on the femme fatale in its most extreme embodiment. Even Johansson's black hair makes her the brunette of sexual entrapment like Gene Tierney in *Leave Her to Heaven* (1945) or Ava Gardner in *The Killers* (1946), or later Isabella Rossellini's tortured nightclub singer in David Lynch's *Blue Velvet* (1986). *The Zone of Interest* is a family-in-peril film, as *Sexy Beast* and *Birth* are, and could be compared to *Cape Fear* (1962, 1991), with history itself arriving around the corner smoking its poisonous cigar.

But even writing this paragraph, I can feel the idea squeaking as it stretches. There is darkness in the work, noirish or otherwise, and I think it's best left at that.

Unlike my previous book on Terrence Malick, I had very little contact with the filmmakers, cinematographers, composers etc., and Jonathan Glazer himself was fenced around with people who didn't reply to my emails or politely declined to be involved. There have been some exceptions, but this was never supposed to be a behind-the-scenes book or a biography. If anything, it's a series of meditations, responses to the films and the videos, the commercials and the shorts, an attempt to see where the darkness came from and what it tells us, what comes leaking through the cracks, as Glazer himself once put it.

These films are remarkable in their quality, their consistency of quality, and their variety. Glazer as a filmmaker has evolved both in his feature filmmaking and in the adverts, music videos and shorts which are the bulk of his output. His whole corpus argues (I think convincingly) for him to be considered as the preeminent British filmmaker of his generation. Hopefully, this book will contribute in some way to that conversation.

I promised at the beginning that I would probably not provide a consistent argument and I'm happy to see it is a promise I seem to have kept.

ACKNOWLEDGEMENTS

My thanks go to Lidia Garbin, to whom this book is also dedicated. She is the reader and proof-reader. She is not patient or forbearing nor should she be. She gives me merry hell in fact, but she is always there. Paul Cronin has as ever been a huge influence, and our conversations have been important. All the guests on my podcast Writers on Film have served as inspirations and models, as well as allowing me to have weekly conversations about how you should write about film. Maureen Foster, Helen O'Hara and Lillian Crawford have each made comments which have given me fundamental food for thought. Matthew Page also read and commented on the manuscript at a late stage in a way that was incredibly heartening.

My friends on the film festival circuit offer nothing but encouragement and humour — Nick Barber, Wendy Ide, David Calhoun, Jason Solomons, Lee Marshall, Raphael Abrams, Stephanie Bunbury, Damon Wise, Jo-Ann Titmarsh, Patrick Heideman, Ed Potton, Kaleem Aftab, Neil Young, Leigh Singer and Marta Bałaga. My friends, Stephen Coombe, Joanne Body, Katy Parry and Elliot Atkins.

Also, Alice and Rosaleen. Always.

INDEX

www.ingramcontent.com/pod-product-compliance
Lightning Source LLC
Chambersburg PA
CBHW060128130626
46556CB00006B/2277